A HISTORY OF THE MALLORY FAMILY

A history of the
MALLORY FAMILY

S.V. Mallory Smith

Phillimore

1985

Published by
PHILLIMORE & CO LTD
Shopwyke Hall, Chichester, Sussex

© Sheila Mallory Smith

ISBN 0 85033 576 0

Printed and bound in Great Britain by
REDWOOD BURN, LTD.
Trowbridge, Wiltshire

CONTENTS

LIST OF PLATES

(between pages 74 and 75)

Plate 13 by courtesy of L. Peters; plate 17 by courtesy of the owner, a descendant of Daniel Mallory; all other plates by K. A. C. Smith, including plate 11 which has been reproduced by kind permission of Sir Thomas Ingilby, Bt.

LIST OF TEXT ILLUSTRATIONS

ACKNOWLEDGEMENTS

This history would never have been undertaken at all without the inspiration and encouragement of Professor Richard Griffith of Long Island University and Peter Field of Bangor University, and the kindness of St John H. Sperling, lord of the manor of Papworth St Agnes, at the outset.

The enthusiasm, generosity and continuing interest in the research, evinced by my good friends Lester Mallory and Don Mallory, and the support in finding a means of publishing the book given by my cousin Ian Mallory, Eugene Mallory, and my brother, are all gratefully acknowledged. I thank all the subscribers for their confidence.

I am indebted to the Keepers of Public Records in many institutions and in many counties, especially to M. Frankel for invaluable instruction in the mysteries of Inquisitions; to may librarians for patient assistance; to the incumbents of many parish churches; and to N. Rogers and K. Knell for good advice. I am particularly grateful for the privilege of being allowed to use the Cambridge University Library. Other acknowledgements are made in the appropriate places in the text.

Mrs. Eagle and Mrs. Venn battled with unfailing cheerfulness to convert the manuscript into typescript, and the financial assistance so thoughtfully provided by my uncle, Alan Mallory, Lester Mallory and Clifford D. Mallory, greatly eased the burden of bringing the work to completion.

My son was a staunch ally in checking references and records and my husband's lovely photographs, processed and printed with great care by Les Peters, give reality to the people I have tried to bring to life in the true stories which follow. Care, which has been matched in every particular, by the publishers, whom I have to thank for this splendid presentation of my work.

The support of my nearest and dearest, through all the years it has taken to complete this book, is a tribute to family affection and the resilience of the Mallorys (not forgetting the Smiths).

I am sad that my kind correspondents, Dr. Longridge and Edward Cope, did not live to read the results of their contributions to the research.

The book is dedicated with love, to the memory of Tidd.

Cambridge, 1984   SHEILA MALLORY SMITH

PREFACE

There has been no complete history of the Mallory family written, and in response to suggestions that it would be useful to have the reference material (some of which is not always readily available to the researcher) brought together, this compilation has been made. It has proved to be impracticable to include every anecdote and every Deed reference, but the pedigrees have been extended and the history of the more important manor houses has been continued to the present time. Their approximate positions 'as the crow flies' have been indicated relative to easily recognisable modern towns.

Records of the several branches of the Mallory family have been scrutinised for decades by scholars wishing to establish the identity of the Sir Thomas Malory who was the author of *Le Morte d'Arthur,* first printed by Caxton in 1485. A conventional assessment of the Thomases available was given in 1936, in *History of Parliament 1439-1509: Biographies* (H.M.S.O.), but there are other theories to explore.

The fact that more than half-a-dozen Thomases have been produced to be considered for the honour of authorship of the King Arthur stories is a tantalising coincidence, one of many that occur to confuse the Mallory researcher. Indeed, from time to time there is such a duplication of contemporary Mallorys with identical Christian names that this account might well have been entitled 'A Little Genealogist's Puzzle Book'.

There is confusion also between some of the manors: Drayton and Draughton, Welton and Walton, Thorpe and Thorpe Malsor, for instance.

There are many ways of spelling the name 'Mallory'. When it came to be written down, the word varied with the practice of each scribe and the fashion of the day, so that in modern times kinship is often obscured. In this book and in the pedigrees, the modern convention of writing the name 'Mallory' is observed unless a specific point is being made.

Looking for the origins of a later Mallory has resulted in the discovery that today there are (only) about one hundred families in Britain who bear the name Mallory or Malory, and a few who still spell it Mallorie or Mallery. There is an instance of Malori, in the C.F.R. for 1488, n.155, and a modern spelling of Mallari, in the Philippines (noted by Mrs. Sally Smith).

There are several thousand families named Mallory, etc., across the Atlantic, some of whom have been seeking the provenance of an ancestor called Peter, since 1637. Part of their history was written by Major Henry Reed Mallory in 1955. There are Mallorys, too, in the Antipodes in some numbers, and in South Africa.

Researchers investigating in greater depth for a particular enquiry are urged to read original documents, although these (pedigrees, wills, visitations, etc.) should be viewed with a little scepticism, for there will be omissions and errors even there. Difficulty may also be experienced in understanding the handwriting and legal terms used in documents prior to the mid-15th century. It may be useful to point out that medieval parents frequently bestowed the same Christian name on more than one of their living children. When assigning individuals to a particular father, it is sometimes only possible to be accurate in placing the heir. The size of these families occasioned considerable overlap between the generations which may not always be separated distinctly in the records.

In the past, incorrect dates of death have been deduced by some writers who have assumed that every inquisition was an inquisition post mortem.

Deeds frequently give the age of individuals as being 'X years and more'. When using this information to calculate a date of birth for the pedigrees in this book, the phrase 'and more' has been taken to mean less than a further 12 months and not some indeterminate number of additional years.

It is to Thomas Cromwell in 1538 that we owe our church records and ironic that many parish registers are incomplete for several years around 1625, some destroyed by Oliver Cromwell's zealous oafs, others hidden to preserve them and never recovered. The Commonwealth forces, the Victorians, who assiduously 'tidied' church interiors by removing memorials or even by completely rebuilding some churches, and Henry VIII's vindictive campaign of destruction, have much to answer for. Modern reorganisation of county boundaries contributes a further regrettable source of potential confusion.

Speculations about the arms of the family have not been referred to the College of Arms. In the description of arms, capital letters are used to avoid the difficulty of 'or, or', etc. However, recognised authorities were consulted for the *grants* of these arms and their *designs*.

The historians of old spent their entire lives gathering material. Reading their books, one develops a great admiration and affection for them all: for Dugdale, following the rivers of Warwickshire, investigating each house as it appeared round the next bend (later, after his appointment as Norroy Herald, we see him energetically demolishing the spurious 'Scochyns and Losenges' in the churches and mansions in his territory, to the consternation of the local gentry); for Walbran, struck dumb and unable to hold a pen in the middle of his work at Studley Royal; for Nichols, who started again after the type of his first edition caught fire on the presses.

The amateur historian is conscious of the fact that his work may be dismissed, in the words of J. Foston, as being that of a 'charlatan and a smatterer'. However, every effort has been made to gather all that may be interesting to readers connected with the family and to indicate where further information may be sought by genealogists, though that delightful Elizabethan Herald, Camden, warns us that 'fcrupulof diligence lieth open to envy'!

Writers who have been concerned with finding their own Mallory forebears have concluded their accounts with a hope that others will be inspired to go further. That hope is expressed again. The material presented in this book makes it clear that there is much fascinating research to be enjoyed in collecting Mallory history, with the certain identification of Sir Thomas and American Peter still possibly remaining as the greatest prizes. It has been said (P. J. C. Field, 1977) that the Mallorys had forgotten who they were; perhaps this book will help them to remember.

Note: The serious scholar is recommended to the following series of papers that have been published since most of this book was written. They will not, of course, assist members of the family in their private genealogical searches. The anthology is entitled, *Aspects of Malory,* Arthurian Studies, ed. by Prof. T. Takamiya and Dr. D. Brewer, 1981. Of particular relevance to this book are the chapters by Griffith, Field and Kelliher. They do not, however, alter the contents of this history, which has a wider application. Prof. Griffith presents some new thoughts about the mother of Thomas of Papworth, but the writer adheres to the Corbet identity (circumstances of the birth of Thomas; *see* text). He has further evidence to support this Thomas as a possible author of *Le Morte.* There is another speculative account of the Warwickshire man by Christine Carpenter, published in the *Bulletin of the Inst. of Hist. Res.,* vol. LIII, 1980, 52-53.

Sir Thomas Malory's own great work will be best enjoyed in the 1971 translation by Professor Eugène Vinaver, which brings the storyteller vividly to mind. (*Malory: Works,* second edition, Oxford University Press.)

INTRODUCTION

William the Conqueror came to Britain and divided the land into properties which he distributed between his relatives and aristocratic friends. They sub-let these, in smaller units, usually to the knights who followed them, and those men became the lords of the manors of England.

In *Tess of the D'Urbervilles,* Thomas Hardy wrote a novel which, although he refers to it as 'a tale' in his preface, must have been based on the progress of such a family. There are Turberville tombs in the church at Bere Regis still. The story of the Mallory family through 800 recorded years follows a strikingly similar pattern, with a rise to fame and wealth in the Middle Ages, followed by a decline and very hard times in the 19th century (especially in the branches of Northamptonshire and Yorkshire). Unlike the 'D'Urbervilles', however, in the 20th century British Mallorys see an improvement in status, if not in numbers.

The books concerned with 'looking for Thomas' contain many references to individual Mallorys, taken from the works of the great county historians; including also, Leland, Bridges, Burton, and Baker; from the Duchess of Cleveland's book *The Battle Abbey Roll,* and from the *Victoria County History* series. Some of them are repeated here, and so are extracts from the innumerable deeds they quote relating to the various properties. Many of the deeds describe inheritances, so that it is possible to use them to infer links between families and to cross-reference the pedigrees to a certain extent. Further research in the areas indicated later in the text may well produce documentary confirmation of the implied relationships.

In some instances, arguments the authors present to develop a pedigree depend upon an assumption that certain hypothetical characters actually existed. The game of discussing 'the man who wasn't there again today' will continue to be played here.

The correct order of the Mallory descent in the early period of their history is not certain. The pedigrees of the Leicestershire families do not agree in detail, neither in the accounts given by Nichols who treated each manor as an independent property, nor in those by other researchers. The alternatives are discussed below and the arguments are carried forward from one section to another, with some information being repeated, in order that the possible connections between all the branches of the Mallory family may be constantly before the reader. Although this technique is slightly tedious, its use was considered to provide the best means of developing the wide-ranging discussions in acceptably small amounts. The pedigrees, with their apparently dogmatic statements, should be tempered by studying them in conjunction with the text and bearing in mind that they may have to be altered as fresh material is discovered.

In 1700 the Herald P. Le Neve remarked that 'Mallorys sprang out at Hoton Conyers in the time of King Edward II and at Studley in the reign of King Henry VI'. We know now that they appeared suddenly in the records during the reign of King Stephen, rather earlier. There are several individuals who might have been the first Mallory ancestor in Britain: the one most frequently quoted is Fulcher de Malsour from Brittany. That he is a doubtful choice is examined later and the question of origins is considered in greater detail in appropriate chapters. The Mallorys were certainly fighting men and must have arrived with an invading force at some time. They fraternised on equal terms with leading Norman families, inter-marrying with them and holding some of their own manors 'of the King, in chief'. Although they are not included in the list of feudal barons drawn up by Sir William Dugdale, in his *Baronia Anglica Concentrata*, Sir T. C. Banks makes it clear that they were persons of worth in the Norman hierarchy. 'Lord Peter Mallory', listed in the index to the Duchess of Cleveland's *The Battle Abbey Roll*, appears to have been mythical, however. The Librarian of The House of Lords was unable to furnish any Lord Mallory.

What is not so clear is whether, under the rules of the Lords Committee of Privileges, they may have been entitled to claim their place among the lesser barons. If such a claim were valid, the interesting question arises as to the possibility of the honour extending to a modern member of the family.

After the time of King Stephen, the Mallory family is recorded as holding manors and lands in many counties, including Leicestershire, Lincolnshire, Warwickshire, Northamptonshire, Bedfordshire, Rutland, Cambridgeshire, Yorkshire and Cheshire.

They flourished, bring great devotion to their often high duties and making advantageous marriages, until the late 1600s. Then, in each house, either the male line failed or misfortune (not infrequently called Oliver Cromwell) required them to sell their properties. It was about this time that Mallorys began to emigrate to America and, continuing a well-established tradition, Peter Mallory 'sprang out' in New Haven, Connecticut.

The first Mallory may have come to England at the time of the Norman Conquest. Of the considerable properties they once owned, the last to be sold by a member of the family was Shelton in 1714. Some of their manor houses still exist, as do several of their memorials, but it is believed that only two houses retain Mallory artefacts and only the triple portrait at Studley Royal, and one other portrait, are known to be extant.

The rough estimate of the numbers of Mallorys now residing in the counties where their ancient manors are to be found, is based upon names appearing in the telephone directory. It may be salutary to note that members of just one branch of those anciently 'of Yorkshire' and using the surname spelled 'Mallory' now live in the counties of Cheshire, Northamptonshire, Kent, and London. It is misleading to assume that any Mallory living in a particular place now is necessarily a direct descendant of those who lived there in the past. In the recent past, some members of this one British branch have made their homes from time to time in a dozen countries overseas (including China and Peru). Today, with upward of fifty individuals in the immediate family, there are only two male Mallorys in the rising generation of this branch.

Stories from the past indicate that the Mallorys had diverse talents. They were useful men in tight corners with a flair for leadership and organisation, dedicating themselves and their fortunes to the causes in which they were concerned, even if their actions led to imprisonment in the Tower itself, or death. Some were what modern convention would regard as 'good', sometimes their genius manifested itself in other ways; that celebrated *enfant terrible,* Sir Thomas of Newbold Revel, being perhaps the most dazzling example.

In addition to the Thomases, other great characters emerge: Sir Robert, Prior of the Knights of St John; Sir Richard, Lord Mayor of London; the last Sir John of Studley Royal; and many others. Mallory knights were present at the battles of Crècy, Agincourt, Calais, Rhodes, the Wars of the Roses, Edgecote, Bosworth, Tournay, and in the Civil Wars. That they were daring and resourceful is self-evident; their exploits should be viewed in the context of their times.

The early members of the Leicestershire family at Kirkby Mallory appear to have been quietly uninteresting at first sight, giving no indication that the sons of the two-tailed lion were to become men of destiny, involved in the fate of the highest in the land, although they are only mentioned in local histories. When their descendants appear in Warwickshire shortly afterwards, however, the story immediately assumes a livelier aspect.

The greatest honour that may be claimed by the Mallory family is that of being direct ancestors of our dear Queen Mother, the Lady Elizabeth Bowes-Lyon, and consequently of the reigning British Royal Family. Dorothy Mallory, daughter of Sir William Mallory of Studley Royal, married Sir George Bowes of Streatlam, Durham, in 1529 (20 Henry VIII). Their line may be found in *The Lineage and Ancestry of H.R.H. Charles, Prince of Wales.* 1977, by Gerald Paget, vol. 2, Generation XV, 028579 and 028580. (*See* Studley Royal and Ped. E. below.) (The writer is indebted to G. Francis Mallory Garbutt for this reference.) There is an older connection: Robert Corbet, Q 115745 and Margaret Mallory, Q 115745, parents of Roger Corbet of Moreton Corbet, generation XVII. (*See* Cambridgeshire, Ped. G.)

Chapter One

LEICESTERSHIRE

THE WORKS of J. Bridges and J. Nichols on the history of Leicestershire provided much of the information about the manors of this county. Alternative and additional material based on all the references consulted are also included. Some Lincolnshire properties are also given. It is necessary to refer to the pedigrees to see clearly the close family relationships between the Leicestershire inheritance and the extended relationtionships in other counties. If this and subsequent chapters are to be intelligible, it is essential to begin at the beginning and read both the Preface and Introduction first. Miss Amada Highton, Mr. Faich and Miss K. Allison, M.B.E., and the Leicestershire Record Office, were very helpful in providing information about Kirkby Mallory.

The lists of the Sheriffs of Leicestershire, which office included that of Sheriff of Warwickshire from temp. King Hen. 2 until 9 Queen Eliz. I, include the following names:

King Rich. 2.15.   John Mallory of Swinford.
King Hen. 5.4.   John Mallory (he was son of the above).
King Hen. 6.3.   John Mallory (the same John).
King Hen. 7.18.   Nicholas Mallory, Esq. (of Winwick, Warwcs.).

The M.P.s for the county of Leicestershire, called to the Council at Westminster, included 'King Edw. 3.14. Ralph Mallory' (presumably Sir Ralph of the Kirkby Mallory family).

In 1979 only three families remained in the county. Two spelt their names 'Mallorie' and one 'Mallory'.

Kirkby Mallory: Mallory property before 1154 until 1377

In the Domesday Survey the township is called Cherchebi, but it was already known as Kirkby Mallory when Geoffrey Mallory was lord of the manor 'in the time of King Stephen'. He held other properties at the beginning of the reign of Henry II. Stephen reigned from 1135 to 1154; Henry from 1154 to 1189. Geoffrey may have lived before 1135 and we know he had died by 1174. A shadowy Richard Mallore is recorded in Stephen's reign, holding at Swinford (Leics.) and elsewhere. This and the inheritance of the manor of Welton (Northants.) suggest that he was very probably the father of Geoffrey Mallory.

Although Kirkby Mallory may be the cradle of the Mallorys who adopted this spelling of their name, other Mallory lords of the manor are recorded soon after Geoffrey in other counties, and variations in the spelling of their surnames were probably phonetic accidents (*see* Preface).

1

Geoffrey's other properties included Walton in Leicestershire and Botley in Warwickshire: Tachebrooke Mallory in the same county appears to have come into the possession of the family in the next generation.

There are discrepancies in the early succession furnished by other researchers and in the Visitations relating to Geoffrey and his descendants. The comprehensive Mallory pedigree which has been deduced therefrom for this book represents only a 'best option'. Alternatives are given in the text, but it was beyond the scope of the research undertaken to establish this pedigree to check every reference against its original record. There are no Mallory wills before 1383 in the Public Record Office, nor in the list of 13th-century wills to be found elsewhere (listed by Sheehan, *Genealogists' Magazine.* Surviving inquisitions post mortem do not commence until after 1216. Information required in respect of earlier times must either be accepted at its face value from recognised authorities or sought in the miles of Rolls, Escheat Records, Fines, etc., in all their various locations. Some correction was, however, possible.

The Visitations provide two reference points on which part of the pedigree for Kirby Mallory may be fixed. The confirmation of arms in the 1569 Visitation of Nottingham to a descendant of Thomas Mallory, Lord of Walton, temp. Henry II, is the first. Thomas, living before 1189, was perhaps a brother of Geoffrey, but more likely his eldest son. His arms were 'Or A lion rampant Gules Collared Argent'. (A lion without a forked tail, it seems.) The second, in the Visitation of Leicestershire in 1619, confirms the arms of Sir William Mallory of Kirkby Mallory, temp. Henry III (1216-1272), as 'Or A lion rampant Gules Double Queued'. ('Double' is assumed to be here synonymous with 'forked'.) The Visitation further states that the grant was to 'Mary, daughter of Sir Anketil Mallory obit 1393', who was the 'great grand-son' of Sir William. (That Sir William was still alive in 1293. His grandfather, also Sir William, is noted as alive in 1216. Both were alive during part of Henry III's reign.)

These arms suggest that the Mallory lion was single-tailed when first granted, and that Kirkby Mallory, although the senior branch, did not receive a coat-of-arms until the practice of differencing by a forked tail was adopted (*see* Origins). The Mallory colours of gold and scarlet may indicate royal service at some time, since these reflect the arms of England.

There is little to give us a picture of Geoffrey; Kirkby Mallory was an important establishment and his relationship with the Earl of Stafford (Botley) seems to indicate that he was a gentleman of charm and means. He was followed by his son, the first recorded Sir Anketil Mallory, lord of Tachebrook Mallory in 1174 and a great warrior. His most exciting moments are told at the end of the chapter, under 'Leicester Castle'. Sir Anketil forfeited his lands for a time.

A daughter, Elgiva, is also recorded. An Elgiva Mallore was a benefactor of the Abbey of St James, founded by the Augustinian canons on the outskirts of Northampton by William Peveral, a son of the Conqueror. Elgiva gives lands at 'Eston', which may have been the modern Easton Maudite, east of the city.

Sir Anketil's eldest son, Robert, succeeded to Tachebrooke in 1186; his second son, Henry, inherited Kirkby Mallory and Walton, and, after Robert's decease, Tachebrook also. Henry retrieved the family lands from King John in 1199, and was followed at Kirkby Mallory and Tachebrook by one of his sons, Sir William Mallory (v. 1216).

In the Swinford pedigree (Nichols), Henry is also given as the father of Simon Mallory of Draughton (Northants.), but Foss states that Gilbert Mallory was the father of Simon, and a Sir Gilbert is given as ancestor of their Newbold Revel descendants. In the descent of Tachebrook Mallory, Gilbert is described as 'son of Henry'. Richard is given as another son, but he seems to have been a son of Sir William Mallory, v. 1216, of Kirby Mallory and Tachebrook. Richard succeeded Sir William in 1221, holding Kirkby Mallory, Tachebrook Mallory, Botley and Walton. Sir Richard gave the land on which Kirkby Mallory church was built (Dugdale, *Monasticon*). His son, Robert, gave lands to the Priory of St David's and to the Knights Hospitaller (recorded in 1279—Nichols). Robert's brother, Sir William, was lord of Walton in 1293. He also held Tachebrook and Botley. Robert's successor, Thomas Mallory (spelled Mallure in the inquisition of 24 Edw. I) held the town of Kirkby Mallory 'of Edmund Earl of Leicester', and other lands previously held by Robert, by the service of one knight's fee, in 1296. Thomas Mallory is noted by Nichols as a knight in 1300. The line of Mallory of Walton (from Sir William's son, Reynold) appears to be straightforward, but at this point the Kirkby Mallory descent is once more confused. Perhaps Thomas was Robert's brother, not his son.

In the 1619 Visitation to Leicestershire (*Harleian Society*, vol. 2, p. 58) a Thomas Malory, 'son of Sir William Malory v. 1293', is given as alive in 10 Edw. 2 (1317). Thomas is erroneously ascribed the daughter of an earlier Sir Thomas in the Visitation. A Thomas Malorie was created Knight of the Bath in 1306, together with William La Zouche. ('Knights of England', below.) Two Thomases appear to be indicated (*see* Pedigrees pp. 135 and 139).

It also seems likely that Sir Thomas, 'son of Sir William Malory', above, was the Sir Thomas Malory of this period who married a daughter of William Lord Zouche, and was the father of Sir Christopher Mallory who founded the branch in Yorkshire that eventually acquired Studley Royal and bore arms derived from Walton or Kirkby Mallory. (Although the spelling of Malorie may have been peculiar to the scribe who penned the citation, the Studley Royal family used it in some generations, and it may have been an instance of a lingering 'folk memory' of that first use of the spelling in their line.)

Another branch of Yorkshire Mallorys was also related to Sir William. He was granted custody of the lands of Anketyn Salvain, a minor, who was the grandson of Sir Anketin (or Anketil) Mallory, lord of Octon in Yorkshire. The dates (1275–1317) imply that Sir Anketil was a younger brother of Sir William (*Early Yorks. Charters* and *Noble Coll.*).

An Anketil Mallory is the next recorded lord of Kirkby Mallory, in 1346 (Rot. 20, Edw. 3). The 1619 Visitation of Leicestershire states that he was a son of John Mallory, lord of Walton, but Nichols gives a Sir Ralph Mallory in the pedigree for Kirkby Mallory as the father of Anketil. In the pedigree for other properties only one Ralph is recorded, not always in the same position. Sir Ralph is noted as a knight in 1300 and again in 1337. He seems to have been sent on a hazardous journey to the north of the country to lead troops which he had been ordered to raise for King Edward's campaign against the Scots, some time between 1321 and 1324 (Cal. Pat.). There is no other news of this event. Perhaps they were diverted to fight for the king at the battle of Boroughbridge in 1322, or they may have been deployed along the chilly watches north of Hadrian's wall after the truce with Scotland in 1321. The truce lasted 13 years. By 1341, Sir Ralph Mallory was back home, enjoying a busy retirement from soldierly duties, for he is recorded as a member of parliament for Leicestershire in that year. In 1361 a Ralph Mallory held part of a Knight's fee at Kirkby Mallory, although Sir Anketil was lord of the manor. It seems unlikely that Ralph was the father of Anketil. A Sir Ralph Mallore was Keeper of Rutland Forest (noted in 1280 and 1300). It has not been possible to ascertain the correct places these Ralphs should take in the pedigree. The Keeper of The King's Forest wielded great power, having authority over all the hunting rights, apportioning the number of bucks a lord could take in a season, controlling the amount of timber allowed for building, and selecting the oaks to be used for the king's own projects, or his gifts. Sir Ralph was a pleasant custodian, frequently issuing pardons to transgressors of the forest laws. The Keeper would scarcely have had time to be a soldier. The appointment was for life: his successor is noted in 1321 (Cal. Pat.) and the Close Rolls for 1326 record an order of the Sheriffs of Leicester to appoint a new Coroner, 'since Ralph Mallore is paralysed and infirm'. (Two Ralphs are indicated.)

The will of Sir Anketil Mallory, written in 1390, was proved on 16 April 1393 at Stowe Park, Lincs. (A Gibbons, *Early Lincolnshire Wills*). It suggests that he expected to die owning very little, although not in unhappy circumstances. He died before his father and had already sold his birthright at Kirkby Mallory, but he seems to have acquired part of the Tachebrook Mallory and Walton properties under the last will of William of Walton in 1389. This, however, was after Sir Anketil, irresistible in his best made-to-measure suit of armour, had married for love. His wife was 'The Lady of Bytham', Alice née Dryby. Throughout her long life, the wealthy, and we must suppose ravishing, Alice, never lacked suitors for her hand, yet she chose to lie for eternity in anticipation of a joyful reunion on Resurrection Day, beside Anketil and not near one of her other richer or more influential husbands, nor by the man to whom she was married at the time of her death (*see* below). The chapter on Northamptonshire furnishes the antecedants of Alice.

The following notes are brief extracts from Nichols (with his page numbers) with corrections from other sources. It should be said that the history of the Mallory family only constituted a minute part of his vast work; small mistakes are not unlikely to have occurred.

1. In the pedigree of Moton of Peckleton (p. 870) the particulars are: 'Sir Robert Touchet, first husband of Alice, daughter and heir of Sir John Driby, was widow by 1494, relict of Ralph, Lord Basset of Sapcote, married to Sir Anketil Mallory of Kirkby Mallory (died before 1394), second husband'.

> *Corrections:* for 1494 read 1394; Sir Anketil was her *third* husband.
> *Note:* Ralph Basset of Sapcote (Lord Basset, writ 46 Edw. 3) asked to be buried at Castle Bytham. (*The Complete Peerage*, vol. 2.)

2. The pedigree of Basset of Sapcote (p. 904), reads: 'Alice, daughter of Sir John Dryby, relict of Sir John Touchet, wife of Ralph Basset'.

> *Correction:* 'Sir John Touchet' should read Sir Robert Touchet. (Alice's will gives him as Robert.)

3. The pedigree of Mallory of Kirkby Mallory (p. 761) reads: 'Alice, relict of Sir Ralph Basset, married to Sir Anketil Mallory (Kt. 1347) and wife of Sir John Bernack, third husband who died 1410'.

> *Correction:* Sir John Bernack was her fourth husband. In her will, probated in October 1412, Sir Anketil is referred to as her 'last husband', implying that Sir John was still alive when it was written. The Bernack family, who were earlier connected with the Dryby family, had an interest in the manor of Upper Isham, which was also associated with the Mallorys of Northamptonshire.

4. The pedigree of Zouche (p. 968), gives Ralph Basset dead in July 1378. The Escheat reference for his manor of Breedon, which he held *jure uxoris* (p. 685), is 2 Rich. 2, No. 8 Leics. So he was certainly dead by 1379.

5. In the Breedon Escheats, Alice is described as 'the wife of Ralph Basset'. It seems that these must have been written with reference to documents which related to her own inheritance and which had not been altered after Bassett died. Sir Anketil died in 1393, Alice in 1412. An Anketin Mallory was Sheriff of Lincoln in 1390, possibly this was Sir Anketil.

Alice's castle gave its name to the Lincolnshire village where now only foundations remain to raise the ghosts of the nightingales and eglantine, the whispers under the moon, of its romantic past. Castle Bytham is about eight miles north of Stamford (*see also* Bramcote notes).

Anketil's will announced airily that wife Alice will pay all his debts, including arrears of wages to deserving servants. He left his complete body armour to son Thomas (aged 12 in 1393) and 'all my other armour' to son William.

In the 1619 Visitation, Sir Thomas is called the 'first sonne' and William, the 'second sonne sine p'le'. This is in the pedigree of the Moton family, and it represents the verbal testimony of members of that family living some 200 years later than William Mallory. It is possible that William may have taken his father's second best battle axe and gone away to make his fortune at Papworth St Agnes, being soon forgotten in Leicestershire. This is discussed further under Cambridgeshire.

Anketil directs that he is to be buried 'at the Church of the Priors Preachers' in Stamford, Lincs. 'Before the altar of the B.V.M. [Blessed Virgin Mary] on the north side.' Alice's will (in which she is called Alice Basset), proved at Sleaford Castle on 26 October 1412, says that she wishes to be buried in 'the chapel of St Trinity' (? The Trinity) 'next to my last husband Sir Anketin Maloree Knight'. Later in the will he is styled 'Anketin Malores'. The supervisors of her will were no lesser personages than the Bishop of Lincolnshire and William, Lord Roos. She built an oratory at Bytham where masses were to be said for the souls of all her husbands. Her bequests are discussed under Bredon and Bramcote (*see also* Isleham). She also mentions her son, 'William Maloree'. The 'Priors Preachers' were Dominicans, the 'Blackfriars' who founded a nunnery for both monks and nuns at Stamford in 1155. It was dedicated to St Michael and St Mary. Sir Anketil was a benefactor of this order and so was Alice Dryby's daughter, Elizabeth, Lady Grey of Codnor, who died in 1444. It is likely that she, too, was buried near Sir Anketil.

The nunnery and its church had been demolished piecemeal by the late 18th century but modern building sites and serious excavations have brought some relics to light from time to time. These include coffins and tomb covers, the identities of which have not been published.

In the 14th century a 'Mallorye Bridge' was recorded in Stamford that ran from All Saints to the Sheep Market north of the castle mound. It may have been provided by Sir Anketil or another Mallory, to benefit the citizens of Stamford, or it may have

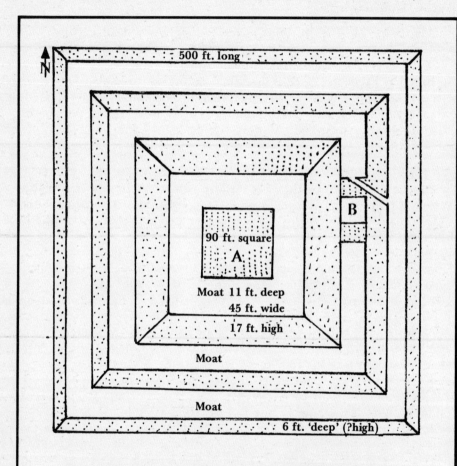

N

500 ft. long

B

90 ft. square

A

Moat 11 ft. deep
45 ft. wide
17 ft. high

Moat

Moat

6 ft. 'deep' (?high)

Fig. 1. Plan of the site of the Mallory manor, Kirkby Mallory. It has been drawn from incomplete measurements in *The Victoria County History*, 1907, which records a 'central plateau, 3 great ditches and triple vallum'. Plateau A was large enough to house a keep and subsidiary buildings similar to Dunvegan Castle on the Isle of Skye. Area B may have been a fish stew. A path, not marked, crossed the two outer aggers. The area has now been ploughed over.

Scale: approx. 10 cm. = 500 ft.

commemorated the earlier Sir Anketil who defended Leicester Castle in 1173. In modern times a culvert was built and the bridge renamed 'Mallory Lane'.

There were two Mallory daughters mentioned in Alice Dryby's will, Margery and Beatrice (*see* Bramcote, Warwcs. and Abkettleby), but an Anketyn Malory gave the manor of Sudborough (Northants.) to his daughter, Ala, in 1360. Professor R. Griffith lists Alice Digges as the first wife of Sir Anketil: perhaps the mother of Ala.

Sudborough recurs in the Papworth St Agnes inheritance. The implications of this, which are discussed under Northants and Cambridgeshire, raise difficulties in deciding the descent of the Papworth Mallorys, although Castle Bytham is the subject of a claim in 1443 that seems to support the Papworth connection with Kirby Malory. (Fines. Leics. 21 H6.) If Anketil and Anketyn were one individual, he must have married twice. One of the executors of the Stowe Park will was the rector of 'Benyfield', near Sudborough. Sir Anketil sold Kirkby Malory to the abbot of St Mary's Abbey, Leicestershire, by 1377.

The house was owned by various families until after the reign of Henry VIII, when the Noel family built a mansion there; the original house or castle already having almost disappeared. In the church (All Saints) there was a window with the Mallory arms. Among the patrons was Thomas Malore in 1301. The park is today the home of a big auto racing circuit. Of the Mallory manor, only the moats and mound remain, which Professor W. G. Hoskins sites to the north of the park. In Nichols' time this was an attractive place with big trees and the moats full of water. The moats are described as 'unique' in the *Victoria County History,* but in spite of this, in recent times part of these great defences has been levelled. (They should not be confused with 'Kirkby Little Moats', in the village.)

Kirkby Mallory was built near to the county town of Leicester, near the junction of the Fosse Way and Watling Street and almost equidistant from the boundaries of the counties of Nottinghamshire, Derbyshire, Staffordshire, Warwickshire, Northamptonshire, Lincolnshire and Rutland. Perhaps this commanding position accounts for the strength of the defences. It is not certain if they predate the Mallory house itself. The situation suggests the residence of a 'Bad Sir Brian Botany' (A. A. Milne, *When We Were Very Young*), but it is to be hoped that the Mallorys did not oppress the villagers, although one cannot be so sanguine about their possible role as border raiders and highwaymen. Certainly a Norman knight who held positions of responsibility needed to be secure, even against his friends.

8 miles W.S.W. of Leicester; Sparkenhoe 100; Nichols, v 4.2.761; *V.C.H.*, v 1.2.3.

Castle Bytham, Lincolnshire (not Little Bytham); 30 miles N.E. of Kirkby Mallory; 12 miles N.W. of Stamford; 35 miles S. of Lincoln.

Walton-on-the-Woulds: Mallory property before 1154 to 1641 (not Waltham-on-the-Woulds, near Walton)

There were two manors at Walton-on-the-Woulds, one of which belonged to Geoffrey Mallory 'in the time of King Stephen' (i.e., before 1154). At some time between 1154 and 1189, Thomas Mallory, Kt., was lord of Walton. His son is not named, but *see* Hyde, below. His granddaughter, Eleanor Mallory, married Sir John Fenton of Fenton, who was allowed to quarter her arms. These were similar to those of Kirkby Mallory, but the lion, given in trick in Harl. MSS. 1400, fo. 12b. in the British Library, has a single tail and was collared Argent. It is obvious from the way in which the property descended that Thomas, alive in the time of Henry II, was 'of' Kirkby Mallory. In 1293, William Mallory of Walton, a son of Sir Richard of Kirkby Mallory, owned the manor (*see* Bramcote, Warwcs.). He also held Tachebrook Mallory and Peckleton. The descent of Walton from 1293 to 1335 is described under Kirkby Mallory. Sir William's (great)-grandson, John, and his heirs, were granted 'liberty of free-warren in all their demesne lands at Walton and at Tachebrook and Bolley [Botley] in Warwick' in November, 1336. (Cart. 9 Edw. 3, No. 10). All these properties were in the Kirkby Mallory inheritance.

In 1346 the king's son, Edward of Woodstock (the Black Prince), was knighted. Levys were made on manorial lords: one is recorded on 'John Malore of Walton'. In 1389, 'William Malory of Walton' was writing his last will and (with others) he enfoeffed Sir Anketil Malory, Knight (this seems to be the Sir Anketil who sold Kirkby Mallory) of 'his manor of Walton-on-the-Wolds, Mimeswould and Saxleby, Co. Leicester; and the manors of Tachebrook Mallory, Botteley and Whitmarsh, Co. Warwick'. Anketil appears to have returned these properties to William's descendants.

There is an indenture dated April 1439, in respect of the marriage of Anthony Mallory, in which his father, John Mallory, is to give him the manor of Walton-on-the-Woulds. Possibly this is the John who married Cecilia Cotton and died in 1490, his wife dying in 1495 (*see* Botley). There are Escheats (9 and 10 Edw. 4, No. 17 Leics.), which name John Mallory seised of the manor 'of the King'. John's son was also a John; possibly the John who sold Tachebrook Mallory in 1496.

Some authorities maintain that John Malory, lord of Walton, died at the battle of Tournay (Terouenne), in 1512, and left five daughters. (Escheat reference, 4 Hen. 8.) The main battle was in 1513. However, he may well have perished earlier in the campaign, which was long and terrible in many ways besides the actual fighting. An account of this period by J. Mackie in *The Oxford History of England*, vividly evokes the perils of that time.

There is also evidence that John had a son, Henry, who died in 1553 and whose five daughters inherited (*see* South Croxton notes). Anne (?Agnes) Malory was the heir general. Her daughter and heir, Ursula Somerfall, had a grandson, John Sison, who inherited the manor of Walton in 1641 and immediately alienated it to a Mr. George Savage (Burton MS.).

These Mallorys also owned lands at Frisby in 1420, a manor in Herbury (Warwcs.) in 1432 and the manor of South Croxton in 1512. There is no description of a surviving manor house at Walton in the accounts by Arthur Mee, Sir Nicholas Pevsner, or in the *V.C.H.*

Nichols' description of the church, St Bartholomew, says that there were three instances of Mallory arms in the windows. All were 'Or a lion rampant queue fourchee Gules'. In the list of rectors, the first is a Hugh Dispenser, 1221. The patrons include a Sir Hugh Dispenser, 'guardian of Henry Malore'. The only Malory monument is one inscribed 'Hic jacet Johe' Malori et Cecilia uxore jus, MCCCCXC'. The arms are 'quarterly Mallory and a spread eagle'. Cecilia was the daughter of John Cotton of Staffordshire. The Cotton arms for Staffs. and Leics. are, 'Azure an eagle displayed Argent differenced' (*see also* Papworth St Agnes, Cambridgeshire).

3 miles E. of Loughborough; East Goscote 100; Nichols, v 3.1.497.

South Croxton

Anthony Malory of Walton was lord of the manor in 1452. In 1512, -. Malory died seised of the manor of South Croxton, with its appurtenances, at Walton. (This was John, but was it 1512?) (Escheat 4, Hen. 8). Henry Malory died seised of it in 1553, leaving, Anne, Eleanor, Elizabeth, Margaret and Katherine, his daughters and co-heirs. (Inq. 1. Mariae n.203.) In January 1583, Frances Cave died, seised of a parcel of land here. (Escheat 26 Eliz.). (The Newbold Revel Mallorys married into the Cave family— *see* Swinford pedigree.)

12 miles S.W. of Loughborough; East Goscote 100; Nichols, v 3.1.234.

Swinford: Mallory property before 1154 until about 1513

Swinford consisted of several manors, each of which was owned by a different family. The Revels of Warwickshire held there in 1183. If the Mallory pedigree given by Nichols (in v 4.1.364) is correct in substance, although the order of the names of individuals may need rearranging, then Swinford has a special place in Mallory annals. This manor is usually listed as a subsidiary holding connected with the Malorys of Newbold Revel and Winwick, yet despite Nichols' own statement that this family was separate and distinct from that at Kirkby Mallory, the first few names in the pedigree are the same as those at Tachebrook Mallory in Warwickshire, and consequently, of Kirkby Mallory.

In particular, we should note Henry Mallory (son of Anketil of Tachebrook) who had two sons according to Nichols' pedigree for Swinford. They were William, knight in 1216, who possibly also held at Tachebrook Mallory, and 'Simon of Drayton'. 'Drayton' was, in fact, the manor of 'Draughton' (Northants.). Simon died in 1277. It is possible that he was Henry Mallory's grandson and the son of Gilbert Mallory, who is recorded at Tachebrook in 1227. Swinford is an early link between the knights of the Red Lion, the three Black Lions, the Ermine shield with the Red Chevron, and the three Boars' heads.

The great lords who held Swinford at the time of the Domesday Survey rejoiced in the names of Alsi and Erneborn, but a Richard Mallore held part of Swinford—a house and land—before 1155, for he gave some of these properties to the nuns of Eaton (Nuneaton) during the lifetime of the founder, Robert Boffu, earl of Leicester, who died in 1155. These grants are confirmed in the records of Henry II's reign (*Vet. member penes Decanum and Capitulum Lichfield*: Dugdale). A Richard Maulore, possibly the same Richard, held at Welton (Northants.) and lands at Bredon before 1189. (*Twelfth Century Survey.*) Richard of Swinford is given as the father of

Geoffrey of Kirkby Mallory in Nichols's pedigree for Swinford. In the reign of King John, Swinford belonged to a later Richard Mallory.

In 1279 and 1296, Roger Mallory (Sir Roger of Draughton) held there 'of the King' and in 1346, Sir Stephen Mallory held the property. He married Margaret Revel who inherited a share of the Revel holdings at Swinford. Stephen and his father, Simon, were also lords of Draughton and Winwick in Northamptonshire. Their near relatives were the Mallorys of Lichborough. The Swinford, Draughton and Winwick properties were inherited by Stephen's son, Sir John Mallory, and his wife Agnes (Alice) Revel, who inherited Newbold Revel (Warwcs.), together with the arms of the Revel family.

In 1317, Miles Vincent held property at Swinford and the family continued there until sometime in the reign of Henry VI. In 1429 Robert Vincent was married to Helen Malory, the sister of Sir Thomas Malory of Newbold Revel. Eventually they sold the property to Sir Thomas, but reserved the right to an annuity which was enjoyed by two generations of their descendants, the Vincents of Thingdon, Northants.

In 1343 Ralph Basset of Drayton held one knight's fee at Swinford (Escheat 17, Edw. 3, No. 59 Leics.). The Kirkby Mallory family married into the Sapcote branch of the Basset family.

Elizabeth, relict of Sir Thomas Malory of Newbold Revel (knight, died 1471), held a life tenure of Swinford. After her death it reverted to 'Nicholas Malory, cousin and heir of Sir Thomas, being son and heir of Sir Thomas, being son and heir of Robert Malory, son of Sir Thomas', and to his heirs. Elizabeth died on 30 September 1479 and Nicholas her 'cousin and heir' was '13 years old, and more'. She held other lands in Leicestershire. (Escheat 20, Edw. 4.) Nicholas was her grandson.

By a grant of Edward IV on 10 October 1480, the custody of the property during Nicholas's minority was granted to Margaret Kelen and Thomas Kyngeston. They held it until Easter 1486. In 1513 'Cope' held the manor of Swinford 'in capite'. (Escheat 7, Hen. 8.)

In 1519, William Vincent, grandson of Helen Mallory, released Swinford to Edward Cave, the husband of Dorothy Mallory, one of the two heiresses who inherited the Newbold Revel properties. (These Mallorys are usually given the spelling Malory.) Her sister married Clement Cave and later, J. Cope (*see* Stanford notes). The Cave family of Stanford Hall held property there until 1780.

Nichols notes that in 1480, one Ralph Wolseley complained that 'long before, Sir Thomas Malory, being seised in fee of the said manor had conveyed the same to H. Sharpe, J. Meneley, Eustace Burnaby and John Malory son of Simon Malory'. From the Warwickshire pedigrees it will be seen that Eustace Burnaby was the husband of Phillipa, the daughter of the Sir Thomas Malory of Newbold Revel who died in 1471. Do nine years constitute the 'long time'? Who was John Malory? There was a Simon in the same family who was Sir Thomas's uncle and might have had a son John.

It has not been possible to find a description of the manor house at Swinford either in the past or in recent times. The only property noted is Stanford Hall. In Nichols's day the church, All Saints, had the coat-of-arms of the Newbold Revel and Draughton Mallorys among the 11 shields adorning the windows. (Burke lists a Maloure of Leicestershire, Temp. Edw. I, bearing the Draughton Mallory arms: *see* Winwick.)

The patrons from 1220 until 1449 were the prior and company of the Knights of St John of Jerusalem in England. (Sir Robert Malory was the prior of this company in the mid-1400s.)

7 miles N.E. of Rugby (Warwcs.); Guthlaxton 100; Nicholas, v 4.1.360.

Bredon (Breedon-on-the-Hill): Mallory property 1378 to 1485

Nichols in his footnotes to p. 364 lists a Richard Mallory, temp. Stephen and Henry II, who held lands at Bredon. He was therefore a contemporary of Geoffrey of Kirkby Mallory, probably his father. He also held land at Welton and at Swinford (*see* appropriate notes). In King John's reign a Richard Mallory also held at Bredon and Swinford (i.e., between 1199 and 1216).

About 80 years later, William Ferrars, earl of Derby, granted Bredon to Ralph Basset of Drayton. After siding with Simon de Montfort in the disastrous battle of Evesham in 1265, Basset was captured and his lands forfeited. In 1306 the manor was inherited by Joan, coheir of the last Lord Tateshall. Joan's first husband was Robert de Driby. Their granddaughter, who received Bredon as a dowry, was Alice Driby, the daughter of Sir John Driby, *see* Kirkby Mallory. (Nichols says 'Robert' Driby and gives her husbands in the wrong order in this chapter.) Her third husband was Sir Anketil Mallory of Kirkby Mallory.

In 1378 Ralph Basset of Sapcote held the manors of Bredon, Holwell and Abkettleby 'as right of Alice his wife as of the honour of Tutbury'. (Escheat 2 Rich. 2, No. 8 Leics.). *See also* the Abkettleby notes.

In 1412, Alice, 'wife of Ralph Bassett, knight', died seised for life of Bredon, with reversion to a Roger Flower and others. Alice (presumably this should read 'Elizabeth', but an 'Alice' should not be discarded out-of-hand), daughter of Thomas Malory deceased, son of aforesaid Alice, wife of aforesaid Ralph, was her 'cousin' and next heir. (Escheat 14 Hen. 4.15 Leics.—Nichols.)

In Escheat 3 Hen. 5. 60 Leics., 'Alice wife of Ralph Basset and later, Malory', died in 1412 seised of Bredon, Somerby, Dalby Parva, Holwell, etc. (*see* Abkettleby notes and Alice Dryby's will). One of the executors of Anketil Mallory's will was the chaplain of Bredon.

Elizabeth Mallory married Sir Robert Ever (Eure), who died in 1480. (C.F.R. 20 Edw. 4.n. 562). Elizabeth appears to have predeceased him, since Bredon passed to Thomas Evere, who died in 1482 (C.I.P.M. 21 Edw. 4.n. 12). P. LeNeve suggests that her aunts inherited. Elizabeth was the daughter of Thomas Malory kt. of Bramcote in Warwickshire, and granddaughter of Sir Anketil Mallory of Kirkby Mallory.

An Escheat of 1 Hen. 7, says that an unidentified Malory died seised of Bredon 'of the King in capite' in 1485. Which Malory could this be? Part of the property passed to a Ralph Constable 'in right of his wife Anne'. He died in 1500.

Although no Mallorys are recorded as having an interest in Bredon after this time, it eventually passed to the Shirley family of Staunton Harold. A Cambridgeshire Mallory married into a branch of the Shirley family in about 1600.

8 miles W. of Loughborough; West Goscote 100; Nichols, v 3.2.685.

Note: Properties owned by Alice Dryby. (See also Isleham.)

Cal. I.P.M. 2 Rich. 2 n.8 on death of Radulphus Bassett de Sapcote Miles, 1379. Dower of wife Alice.

'Rutland—rent only in Ocham (Okeham).

Lincolnshire—
Castyl Bytham, cast. & manner'.
East Bytham, manner'.

Corby manner', South Wytham manner', Careby manner' (non Hunts.), Cheyle manner' in Holland, West Yrkle a house [E. Wallace suggests West Keale].

Leicestershire—
Sapcote manner', Sapcote villa and house, Stanton manner', Bredon Manner', Somerby, Dalby, Holwell Parva, Abkettleby . . . Potters Marshton, land.

Staffordshire—
Chedle manner'.'

'A mysterious inquisition post mortem on the death of Antonius Malory, Chyv, C.I P.M. 16 Rich. 2 n.19, new number C136/75/16. P.R.O., must almost certainly have been in respect of Sir Anketil Mallory of Kirkby Mallory, husband of Alice Dryby. The properties are 'Castle Bytham maner, Corby maner, Somerton maner and Carleton maner in Leicestershire'. The wife's name is Alice and the date, 1393. Both men bore similar arms. (*See* Kirkby Mallory, above, and Papworth's *Ordinary*: Arms of M. Antoyn Mallory, Co. Leicester. 'Or a lion ramp. tail forked Gules.' Willement's Roll, *c.* 1392-97).'

Stanford (not Stanford-on-Soar, which also had a Stanford Hall)

Arthur Mee, in a lyrical description, puts Swinford on the banks of the River Avon; the site of Stanford Hall, which is now a grand William-and-Mary mansion. The Hall was begun by Sir Roger Cave in 1697 on the manor held by his family since 1430.

Sir Ambrose Cave, who was High Sheriff of Warwickshire and Leicestershire and a Privy Councillor to Queen Elizabeth I, acquired one of the queen's garters which she lost while dancing (the Volta?) and vowed to wear it on his arm for the rest of his life.

His brother, Clement Cave, married Margery Mallory of Newbold Revel. They are reported as buried in the church at Stanford where there was a brass memorial inscribed 'of your charitie pray for the soule of Clement Cave esquiyer and his wyfe deceased the last day of November ano 1538 on whose soules Jesu have mercie'.

The brass, in the drawing in Nichols (v 4.1., Fig. 3, p. 356), depicts such a meek and earnest couple that it is hard to imagine them and their relatives indulging in the kind of junketings implied by the garter episode. A painting of Queen Elizabeth I dancing hangs in Penshurst Place in Kent. Could the Caves be among her merry company of courtiers? The drawing of the brass is reproduced in the book by Stanislaus about the history of Newbold Revel. The date of the brass refers to Margaret's death.

7 miles N.E. of Rugby (Warwcs.); Guthlaxton 100; Nichols v 4.1.350.

King's Norton

The manor of King's Norton was held by the Norton family in 1316 but in 1346 it was held by Henry Mallorie (Rot. Aux 20, Edw. 3). By 1368 it had a different lord, William Levere. This Henry Mallorie does not appear in any of the pedigrees and demonstrates the fact that persons other than those recorded in pedigrees did indeed exist.

According to Arthur Mee, the old hall-house was demolished and the house standing at the time when he wrote (1960), was built about 1700. It was known as 'Manor Farm'.

7 miles E.S.E. of Leicester; Gartree 100; Nichols, v 2.2.731; *V.C.H.*, v 5, 256.

Houghton (not Houghton-on-the-Hill; not Hoton)

The manor of Houghton provides a Leicestershire link between the Mallory family and their connections, with the family of great Marcher Lords, the Corbets of Shropshire (*see also* Sibbesdon).

In 1240, Richard Corbet held half a knight's fee at Houghton. In 1301, Richard Corbet of Morton died seised of this manor and Thomas Corbet, his son and heir was nineteen. (Escheat 29, Edw. I.45 Leics.) This Thomas was married to Amici. (Roper MS. Edw. I.) In the Cambridge notes it will be seen that about 130 years later, Thomas Corbet's great-grandson, Sir Robert Corbet of Morton Corbet in Shropshire, married Margaret Mallory, the 'daughter' of Sir William Mallory of Papworth-St-Agnes. These Mallorys bore the arms of the fork-tailed lion.

6 miles S.E. of Leicester; Gartree 100; Nichols, v 2.2.61.

(In the following short notes, the volume references are to Nichols' *Leicestershire.*)

Stormsworth and Westrill: v 4.1; Guthlaxton 100

In 1377 Sir John Mallory of Winwick (Northants.) was lord of this manor. His arms were 'Or 3 lions passant (guardant) Sable'. (Dugdale, Burke. *See* Draughton.) By the next generation this family had adopted the Revel arms (*see* Warwcs.). In 1479, Elizabeth, widow of Sir Thomas Malory, died seised of a house and land in 'Stormfield'. (Escheat 20 Edw. 4, No. 46 Leics.). In 1511 her grandson, Nicholas Mallory, sold the manor to Richard Cave. Richard was presumably the father of Clement Cave and 1511 may coincide with the marriage between Nicholas Mallory's daughter, Margaret, and Clement. Stormsworth was still owned by the Cave family in 1810.

3 miles N.E. of Melton Mowbray (near Abkettleby).

Syston: v 3.1.452; East Goscote 100

In 1512 'Malory' died seised of lands and tenements at Syston, held of the king (Escheat 4. H8). (John Mallory, lord of Walton-on-the-Woulds, died in 1512. *See* Ped. F.) The church of St Peter had amongst its rectors: 1220, Gilbert Malore; 1230, William Malore. (These names, in this order, do not appear to belong to families in the Pedigrees: possibly younger sons of Sir William, v 1216, of Kirkby Mallory and Tachebrook?)

10 miles N.E. of Kirkby Mallory.

Hoton: v 3.1.372; East Goscote 100

In 1277 Simon Mallory possessed two carucates in the village. (Chetwynd MS.) Nichols cites him as the first lord of Draughton (Northants.), but wrongly attributes the following notes to Houghton-on-the-Hill in Gartree Hundred.

In 1293, Nicholas Malore of Draughton, Northants., gave his capital messuage at Houghton (this should read Hoton), to his brother, Roger Malore. These were Mallorys whose coat-of-arms was charged with three black lions 'passant (guardant) in pale'. (*See* Draughton.) The gift gives a glimpse of the way life was lived at that time. In addition to the manor and lands, Nicholas Mallory also 'gave' to his brother, 'John the son of his villein Sampson and all John's goods and chattels and his house'.

In 1369, Henry Beaumont died seised of a moiety of a knight's fee in Houghton (Hoton) and Swinford, which 'Stephen Malore sometime held'.

2 miles N.W. of Walton-on-the-Woulds.

Shearsby: Guthlaxton 100

In 1511, John Charnels sold part of his lands at Shearsby to Nicholas Malory of Winwick, Northants. John Charnels may be the son or grandson, of Margaret Grendon whose second husband was Thomas Mallory of Bramcote, Warwcs. (If this is so, another link between Kirkby Mallory and Newbold Revel is indicated.) Nichols notes a deed of 1660 concerning a re-division of the manor, naming amongst others, John and Anthony Maior.

12 miles S.E. of Kirbky Mallory.

Saddington

Saddington may provide important links between different branches, but there are only two references available. Further research may be rewarding. The first is from Nichols in the chapter on Walton-on-the-Woulds. He says that in 1419, John Mowbray of Newbold Revel and John Mowbray of Walton, Wm. Repyngdon, rector of Kibworth, and Wm. Heynes, rector of Cleybrook, joined in a conveyance of two parts of the manor of Saddington to William Mallory, Esq. and Margaret his wife: from a deed 'in my possession'. There was a William Mallory with a wife, Margaret, at Papworth St Agnes at this time (also a 'William Mallory of Northants, Gent' in the Lichborough line). One could have been the father of 'John Mallory of Saddington'. (*See also* I.P.M. for Elizabeth of Newbold Revel. Obit. 1479.)

The second reference is that a John Malory of Saddington lived about 1435 or earlier, and was perhaps the ancestor of the Malorys who held Saddington in Leicestershire; Glendon and Woodford in Northamptonshire, at later dates. (Material kindly supplied by the Northants. Archivist.) There is also a link with the Mallorys of Holwell (Beds.). (The Papworth family had the same, differenced, coat-of-arms as the Woodford Mallorys.) Nichols gives no Mallory references under Saddington. There is a 50-acre reservoir there now.

7 miles S.E. of Leicester; Gartree 100; Nichols, v 2.2.776.

Hathern: v 3.2.842; West Goscote

In 1270 Eleanor de Vaus, relict of Roger de Quincy, Earl of Winton, held Hathern in dower. Simon Malore and Hugh Nauntell held it under her. (Escheat 55, H3. 36 Leics.) The Bassett family held there at a later date.

Shenton: v 3.2.526; West Goscote

The Corbet family of Sibbesdon held here in 1352. Thomas Corbet of Legh held here in 1420. (*See* main notes on the Corbet family.) Coats-of-arms in the church included one Mallory shield and another quartered with Mallory: 'Or a lion rampant queue forche Gules'. (*See* Sibbesdon.)

7 miles W of Kirkby Mallory.

The Hyde: v 4.2.722; Sparkenhoe 100

A hamlet, where in '3. King John', William Mareschall and Ralph Mallore levied a fine on land here to the use of Richard Fitz-Robert. An early Ralph Mallory who, the author suggests, was perhaps the unnamed son of Sir Thomas of Walton. Liecia of Hyde, alive in 1202, was his wife. It has not been possible to identify this property on the modern map. It appears to be the same property as 'Hyde Pastures', described by Dugdale. (*See* Warwickshire notes.)

Burrough-on-the-Hill (Burrow): v 2.2.527; Gartree 100

The *Victoria County History of Leicestershire* (V1. 64) records the 'Malore' family in Burrough before 1240. In 1250 a Christine 'Malorye' held the property. She may have been the daughter of Henry Mallore and Iseult. In 1243 she gave her possessions in Eaton to the Abbey of Croxton in return for prayers for her soul. (Rot. Hund. Rec. Comm. i, 237). (Her father may have been Henry of Kirkby Mallory, ob. 1199.)

In 1290 Thomas Malore held it and sub-let. In 1346 various tenants held one-tenth parts of a knight's fee 'of Anketil Mallory' (John Dryby is mentioned). The Malorys were still connected with the village in 1347. (Farnham and Leics. notes: Cal. Clo. 346–9, 292). No other Mallory notes are available for this property. There are no houses in the village earlier than 1650; the present mansion was built in 1876. Church, St Mary the Virgin; memorial to a Charnel Cave, ob. 1792 (cf. Charnels + Cave).

10 miles E.N.E. of Leicester.

Thorpe Lubenham: v 2.2.710; Gartree 100

In 1296, Hugh de Luteringto held the town of Thorpe, near Lubbenham, of Gilbert de Neville, who held it of Thomas Malore, who held it of Robert Wyvill, by whom it was held under the Earl of Leicester. Presumably this was Thomas of Kirkby Mallory (Kt. 1300), who inherited Walton. (Lib. Feod. Mil., 24. Edw. I.) Later it also belonged to other Malory connections, viz.: 1391, Robert Basset; 1392, John Vincent and Ralph Basset, with reversion to Thomas, Earl of Stafford (Rich. 2), 1410 John Catesby.

Probably Lubenham, 2 miles W. of Market Harborough.

Scalford: v 2.1.313; Framland 100

Henry Revel, lord temp. Henry II, gave certain lands here and in Swinford to the Knights Templar. In 1439, John Malory of Walton-on-the-Would, Esq., settled lands and tenements in Scalford on his son, John, prior to his marriage to Anne, daughter of Lawrence Sherard. (This appears to be a mistake. The son must be Anthony. See Walton-on-the-Woulds and below.) Church. St Egelwin.

5 miles E. of Abkettleby.

Framland 100, v 2.1.

In 1445 the hundred of Framland, in common with some other manors, was exonerated of part of the taxes due. In the records, Anthony Malory was ordered to pay a reduced tax of only £541 18s. 2d. Presumably this was Anthony of Walton-on-the-Woulds. No village of Framland has been found.

Abkettleby: v 2.1.18; Framland 100

This manor, which included Holwell and Holt, was held by Joan de Dryby (Escheat 17, Edw. 2, 188 Leics.). Her son, John de Dryby, was the father of Alice, who married Sir Anketil Mallory of Kirkby Mallory (above). In 1412 she died seised of Abkettleby leaving her grand-daughter, Elizabeth, heir at Abkettleby and Bredon

(Escheat, 14 Hen., 4.4.15 Leics. and Alice's will). Elizabeth was the daughter of Alice's son, Sir Thomas Mallory (Malory) of Bramcote in Warwickshire. It is interesting to note that there was another Mallory manor called Holwell, in Bedfordshire, which became the property of Sir John Bernard who died in 1451. It was connected with the Welton, Northamptonshire, Mallorys (*see* Welton notes). There is always a possibility of confusion arising concerning these two properties. A 17th-century manor house still exists at Abkettleby. Abkettleby is north of Melton Mowbray.

12 miles W. of Bytham.

Sibbesdon

Sibbesdon manor was the property of the Shropshire Corbets from 1301 until at least 1622 (Nichols). The transcript of the will of a John de Harowden of Sibbesden, proved in 1381, lists 'two sons of Sir John Malore' as beneficiaries (Gibbons). They have not been identified; perhaps they were sons of John of Walton, v 1346. It has not been possible to locate this property on a modern map. It may have been Sibson, near another Corbet property, Barton-in-the-Beans, which lies approximately five miles from Kirkby Mallory. The manor of Snarestone, which was included with the Sibbesden property, is also in this locality. (Harrowden is 7 miles S.E. of Draughton, Northants.) *See also* the manor of Shenton.

Leicester Castle

Henry II was constantly at war, especially against his own sons, who all wanted the throne. His eldest, who was known as 'Young King Henry', rebelled against his father, supported by the Earls of Derby, Gloucester, Norfolk, Leicester, and the Earl of Huntingdon, whose brother was King of Scotland. Sir Anketil Mallory, the son of Geoffrey of Kirkby Mallory and owner of Tachebrook Mallory in Warwickshire, was at that time the Governor of Leicester and Constable of Leicester Castle. By the laws of allegiance to his lord, the Earl of Leicester, he was perforce one of the rebels, too. The history of his career at this period would make good theatre and Nichols's own account is stirring stuff, which cannot be improved upon. There appears below a resumé of the facts as they affect the Mallory story.

Early in 1173, the king took his revenge for the disaffection of the Earl of Leicester by sending Sir Richard de Lucy to take the city. Leicester was burnt and its townsfolk dispersed, but the castle held. The Earl of Huntingdon with Anketil and his knights, marched against Northampton, which belonged to the king. After a great battle with the knights of Northampton Castle and the burgesses, he defeated them and returned home with the spoils of victory. In the meantime, the king had captured the Earl of Leicester and his Countess in Normandy, and taken the town of Huntingdon. While he was there, he ordered the constables of all Leicester's castles to surrender them, with the threat that if they did not comply, their lord, who had been brought to England in fetters (and probably chained to a horse for the journey) would suffer further. The Constables went to the king, an Angevin of uncertain temper, and begged leave to ask for the earl's orders. Surprisingly, this was granted. Leicester was not co-operative and the king flew into a rage and swore on the holy relics that the earl should starve until the castles were handed over. Anketil and his fellow Constables of Mountsorrel and Groby, fearing that the king would carry out his threat, and knowing that the King of Scotland had been taken at Alnwick, finally relinquished their custody.

After this, the rebellion collapsed. In 1177, the king restored to the Earl of Leicester all his property except the castles of Mountsorrel and Pacy and gave him the whole of Leicester and the forest again. Anketil, however, was deprived of all his lands. The family did not regain possession of them until the reign of King John. Perhaps he had displayed too much enthusiasm in his retaliations at Northampton. The castle is close to the River Soar, on the west side of the city.

Chapter Two

WARWICKSHIRE

THE WORK OF Sir William Dugdale on the history of Warwickshire provided much of the information about the manors in this county. Alternative and additional material is also included. The history of Prior Sir Robert Mallory (1430–1440) will be found under Newbold Revel and Balsall.

The lists of the sheriffs of Warwickshire contain the same Mallory names as those given under Leicestershire between the reigns of Henry II and Elizabeth I. The M.P.s for the county of Warwickshire, called to Parliament at Westminster, included:

> King Hen. 5, No. 1 and No. 7, John Malory (of Winwick and Newbold Revel).
> King Hen. 6, No. 5, John Malory (of Winwick and Newbold Revel).
> Also, Thomas Mallory, 1445 (Sir Thomas of Newbold Revel).
> (Note: Dugdale says that the returns for all the parliaments from 17 Edw. 4 to 33, Hen. 8, 'are lost and destroyed'.)

In 1979 only three families remained in the county. They spelt the name 'Mallorie'.

Tachbrook Mallory (Tachebrook Mallory): Mallory property before 1174 to 1496

Tachebrook Mallory was one of two manors in the larger parish of Bishop's Tachbrook. The first Mallory lord of the manor named by Dugdale and in the *V.C.H.*, was Sir Anketil Mallory, who was one of the earliest remarkable members of the Kirkby Mallory family. (*See* the notes on Leicester Castle.) The Tachbrook Mallory inheritance continued to be connected with the Kirkby Mallory inheritance; the various manors which these comprised passing across from one branch of the family to the other, from time to time.

Dugdale is confusing on the origins of the lords of Tachbrook. It is not clear whether Sir Anketil received the estate from a member of the Boteller family, or whether an earlier Mallory received it from a Boteler, temp. Henry I. If the latter, then he was possibly Richard of Swinford (etc.), alive temp. Stephen (1135–54). (*See also* notes on Mauliverer.)

The name Anketil has afforded great scope to the chroniclers of old, who have variously written it as Asketil, Ankitel, Anchitol, and so on. The *Victoria County History of Warwickshire* gives Anchitel, Dugdale preferred Askitell. It has also been written Anketyn. In one Visitation the same individual is called Ankitell on one line and Ansitill, on the next.

There is a very full documentation for Tachbrook Mallory in the *V.C.H.*, where it appears under Bishop's Tachbrook. Most of these references are given below, augmented by those from Dugdale and others. (*See also* pedigree for Tachbrook Mallory, ex. Dunkeswick Mallorys.)

The rebellion against Henry II is described in Hoveden Chron. Rolls Ser. ii, 57.65. The reference for the forfeiture of the property in the time of Henry II is Pipe Rolls Soc. XX, 143 and Hist. MSS. Comm. Rep. iv, 344. The succession of his son, Robert, is in Pipe R. Soc. XXXVI, 127; XXXVI, 115.

Sir Anketil, whose family arms were a gold shield bearing a red rampant fork-tailed lion, died in 1187 and Robert Mallory succeeded, to be followed by the next son, Henry. Henry Mallory evidently regarded Richard I, rampaging off on crusades and wasting the taxpayers' money, as not being an asset to the country and took Prince John's side against the king in 1194. When king, John was proverbially always short of money and the fine of 60 marks that Henry paid him in 1199 no doubt went a long way towards cancelling royal claims to Anketil's birthright for in that year all the rest of his property was restored to the Mallorys. (Pipe Roll Soc. X. 253i Rot. de Obl. et Fin. 23.)

Part of Tachbrook was owned by Henry de Clinton in 1200. He had built the castle at Kenilworth and founded the priory there. His share of Tachbrook, he gave to the canons of Kenilworth, who came to an arrangement with Henry Mallory, by which he held the main village and its tenants and the northern half of the property, for the service of one knight's fee. It seems that the villagers were present at this transaction and that they agreed with it. They also 'agreed' that they were villiens.

The succession for Tachbrook as given by the *V.C.H.* provides further possibilities to consider in conjunction with the pedigrees given by Nichols for Walton-on-the-Woulds, Swinford and Kirkby Mallory (all in Leicestershire). According to the *V.C.H.*, Henry Mallory had at least two sons: Gilbert, who was at Tachbrook in 1227 (Pipe Roll Soc. X, 354.414), and Richard (but *see* Kirkby Mallory). The descent followed from Richard to his son, William, and to William's son, Sir Reynold. (*See also* the descent in Draughton, Northants. and Swinford, Leics.) Sir Reynold's son (or grandson) was a John who, together with his wife, Margery, inherited the manor in 1333. (F. of F. Dug. Soc. XV 1743). This is the John to whom a charter of free warren was granted in 1336 (17 Nov. 9, Edw. 3, Cal. Chart. R. iii, 350). The charter also applied to Walton and Botley (*see* Walton notes). By Pat. 10, Edw. 3, pl. m20, he was granted permission to house and maintain a priest to say mass daily in his chapel at Tachbrook 'for the health of his soul and the soules of Margery his wyfe, with all the faithful departed'. The Mallory family, with their usual attention to organisation, but with uncharacteristic thought for self-preservation, were great builders of chantries, in an age when prayers and gifts to the church were guaranteed to ease a soul's passage through purgatory.

Baronies and knighthoods were not always considered to be such desirable honours as they sometimes are today, and many a medieval gentleman found it extremely inconvenient to be obliged to saddle his horse and gather some trusty friends to accompany him to Westminster, when he could have been better employed at home. Others were unable to meet the financial requirements of a knighthood. It is probably for reasons such as these that the 'King's yeoman' John Mallory of Tachbrook Mallory did not take up his knighthood and in 1336 received a pardon for failing so to do (Cal. Pat. 1134-8, p. 251).

The owner in 1389 was a William Mallory of Walton. Sir Anketil of Kirkby Mallory was an enfeoffee under his will. Five generations of the Mallorys continued to live at Tachbrook for the next 160 years, their other manors of Walton, Botley, Croxton, etc., being divided between successive sons and brothers. In 1489, a John Mallory died (Cal. I.P.M. Hen. VII, ii, 295). His heir was his son, John. With his wife, Joyce, he sold the manor to Benedict Medley in 1496 (F. of F.: Dugdale Soc. XVIII, 2754). Medley was Clerk of the Signet to King Hen. VII, and died, owning Tachbrook, in 1504. In 1613 Tachbrook Mallory was united with Bishop's Tachbrook once more.

Half a mile to the N.E. of the village is Chapel Hill Farm. The house is built on to the remains of a medieval chapel, the chantry which John Mallory built in 1336. (It fell into disuse when the Mallorys sold the manor.) In 1510 the Medleys and the Prior of Kenilworth dispossessed 60 of the villagers at Tachbrook and enclosed their land. Only about four houses remained. There does not appear to be a manor house now, perhaps the house 'of mediaeval origin' known as 'Grove House' in 1931, was built on the site of the Mallory manor. It was to the N.E. of the village. There is an hotel at Bishop's Tachbrook called *Mallory Court,* but it has not been possible to discover its history. Bishop's Tachbrook had a separate, very grand manor house, known as 'Savage's House', in Dugdale's time. The church, which contains memorials to later owners of the manor, is at Bishop's Tachbrook. It is dedicated to St Chad.

Kington 100 (sometime in Knightlow 100); 3 miles S.S.W. of Warwick; Dugdale VI, p. 485; *V.C.H.,* vol. V, p. 162 (Warwcs.), vol. 2, p. 81.3 (Leics.).

Botley: Mallory property before 1154 to 1444

A satisfactory day's hunting may have gained the manor of Botley for the Mallorys, for it was the gift of the Staffordshire baron Robert de Stadford to Geoffrey of Kirkby Mallory, in return for a token payment of one 'Sparhawk', to be renewed between their heirs in perpetuity; in this case for almost three hundred years.

The notes by Hamper on Dugdale's *Antiquities* give an ambiguous date in connection with the Botley charters (*V.C.H.*), but Geoffrey of Kirkby Mallory also owned the manor of Walton 'in the reign of King Stephen' and Dugdale says 'temp. King Henry 2' for Botley as a Mallory holding.

The first Robert de Stadford's home is recorded in 1086, built where his descendants, the earls of Staffordshire, were later to raise castles. He was succeeded by more Roberts, the last of whom died in 1193. It seems that the one who gave Botley to the Mallorys was either the first Robert or his son. A study of their affairs may yield a definite date for Geoffrey.

Edmund, Lord de Stafford, who died in 1308, married the daughter of Ralph, Lord Basset of Drayton (Staffs.). He was a relative of the Bassets of Sapcote, one of whom was the husband of Alice Dryby (before 1378), whose third husband was Anketil of Kirkby Mallory. Stafford is one day's ride from Kirkby Mallory.

Botley was one of the properties included in the grant of free warren granted to John Mallory in 1336, together with Walton-on-the-Woulds and Tachbrook Mallory. In 1389 it was among the inheritances of the Kirkby Mallory family and belonged to

William Mallory of Walton-on-the-Woulds. (*See* Leicestershire notes.) Dugdale quotes a deed, dated 'the Thursday after the feast of S. Michael th' Archangel, 22. Hen 6' (1444/5), by which a John Malore and Anketill Malore, 'his son', alienated the manor of Botley to Richard Archer. It is not clear whether this was the father of John Mallory of Walton-on-the-Woulds, who died in 1490 (tomb), or John of Tachebrook, who died in 1489 (*V.C.H.*), or a separate John of Botley. It is also possible that some or all of these Johns were one individual. There is no other reference to this Anketil in the literature.

Botley Hill is half a mile to the north of Ullenhall, where a rectangular moat still remained in 1945. Was this the site of the Mallory manor? (The moats at Kirkby Mallory are rectangular.) The parish church of Ullenhall, St Mary's, is mostly Victorian. Botley is listed as one of several small manors all grouped under Ullenhall in the *V.C.H.* This account also is ambiguous regarding Geoffrey Mallory, and which Robert Stafford was concerned.

Barlichway 100; Ullenhall, 2 miles N.E. of Henley-in-Arden; *V.C.H.*, vol. 3, 214; Dugdale, v 2.820.

Newbold Revel (Fenny Newbold—not Newbold on Avon); Mallory property 1383 to 1538

Newbold Revel has received more attention from researchers than any other Mallory property, for it was the main house of the Sir Thomas Malory who has been the favourite choice for authorship of *Le Morte d'Arthur*. Although others have written at length about him, a Mallory history would be incomplete without an account of his life. For more detailed reviews there are the prefaces and notes to the works of E. Vinaver, to other standard editions of *Le Morte d'Arthur*, and, more, recently, articles by P. J. C. Field in *Medium Aevum* (1979) and elsewhere. Kelliher and Field present up-to-date arguments supporting Thomas of Newbold Revel as the author, which other scholars find acceptable, but the reader must study them for himself. Circumstantial evidence linking the Winchester MS. copy of *Le Morte d'Arthur* with the Newbold Revel cousins at Lichborough is given under Northamptonshire. The paper by Kelliher is to be found under Lichborough. Arthur Mee's *The King's England* may be more accessible. The volume on Warwickshire describes Newbold Revel under Brinklowe and gives an eulogistic account of Thomas which reaches similar conclusions. The present author has no authority to favour one theory before another but can only provide the alternatives for consideration. (*See* in particular, Papworth St Agnes Thomas.)

The manor, together with sister manors of Winwick (Northants.), Lichborough (Northants.) and Swinford (Leics.), is also famous for the confusion that has arisen in the past from the entirely dissimilar coats-of-arms borne by successive members of the Mallory family from whom Sir Thomas was descended. The family of Revel, who also owned land at Swinford, inherited Fenny Newbold which then became known as Newbold Revel. At least two members of the Mallory family married Revel daughters. The first was Sir Stephen Mallory of Draughton. The Mallorys of Draughton were descended from Kirkby Mallory (*see* Northants.). He also owned

Winwick, and was alive in 1330. He married Margaret Revel of Fenny Newbold, who may have brought part of the Revel holdings at Swinford to the marriage, thus extending the Mallory property there, but this is one area where some confusion exists. Nichols quotes a deed (Escheat 1, Hen. V, 45 Leics.) which implies that Stephen Mallory held land at Swinford as late as 1413, but it is possible that the wording is misleading and that the escheat, which was in respect of a William Beaumont, should have read 'which Stephen Mallory sometime held'. A later Stephen is possible but, if so, this is the only reference to him. He also notes that Stephen's son, John, bore the Draughton coat-of-arms. Dugdale, however, ascribed to John the following arms (from S. Kniveton), 'a fess between 3 boars' heads couped'. Among the heraldic windows he described in the parish church, there were the following arms (some given in trick, some described in the Index to Blazon):

> No. 17. Azure 3 boars' heads couped Or (unidentified).
> No. 18. Argent on a canton a boar's head couped Or (Malory).
> No. 20. Quarterly Azure and Gules in the first quarter a boar's head couped Or (unidentified).

The arms of the family of Swinford (not Mallory of Swinford), all carry boars, or boars' heads. The Swinfords of Devonshire and Leicestershire bore 'Argent 3 boars' heads couped Gules' (Burke). (*See also* Isleham [Cambs.], Lichborough [Northants.], especially the arms on Lichborough deeds 1366/7, and the Mallory arms at Charwelton [Northants.].) It is therefore possible that John Mallory, who was described as 'of Winwick' during Sir Stephen's lifetime, may have used the Swinford arms, differenced, perhaps inherited by marriage when one of his ancestors acquired the Mallory property at Swinford. The shields described above may be those of earlier Mallory–Swinford connections, even though the church is at Monk's Kirby.

John Mallory was knighted in 1363 (Nichols), was twice Commissioner of Peace in Richard II's reign, and was High Sheriff for Leicester (and Warwickshire) in 1392. His wife was Alice (or Agnes) Revel. The Revel male line failed in 1383 and the properties were divided between three sisters, of whom Alice was the eldest. She inherited Newbold Revel and with it the Revel family arms of 'Ermine a chevron Gules a bordure engrailed Sable'. In addition, she was given Esenhall, Stretton, Strod Aston, and the manor of Paylington. She also inherited (or retained) the Revel property at Swinford. At the time of the division of the Revel holdings, Sir John seems to have passed them on to his son (Dugdale), and in 1392 Sir John and Alice consolidated the family's claim to the inheritance (Fin. 15, Rich. II).

Sir John had cousins whose line lived at Lichborough for over four hundred years (*see* appropriate notes), including his own lifetime, when he himself owned the Lichborough property; probably an expedient to keep it in Mallory hands since Lichborough Mallorys were frequently 'persona non grata'.

His son, known as 'John Mallory of Winwick' during his father's lifetime, succeeded to all the estates. It seems that Winwick was usually the residence enjoyed by the eldest son at this time. He was probably the first Mallory to use the Revel arms, inherited from his heiress mother. The Lichborough deeds mention another son, Nicholas (Baker).

A deed dated 1422, signed by 'John Malory de Wynwyk' and sealed with the Revel seal, was exhibited by A. T. Martin in 1897. (*See* Cambridgeshire notes.) On the deed, John Malory is called 'armiger', but Dugdale says (V. I, p. 83) that he was one of the knights of the shire called to Westminster in 1413. Stanlislaus says he was M.P. (i.e., knight of the shire for Warwickshire) in 1413 and 1420. *See also* Feudal Aids, 1428, Lichborough. He took typical Mallory responsibility for the running of the county, being also Sheriff of Leicestershire and Warwickshire in 4 Henry V (Rot. F.4, H5. In dorso, m. 12). In 1420 he was appointed to the unenviable task of persuading the people of both counties to lend money to the king (Pat. 7, H5, m. 12), and while the king was away enjoying martial and marital victories in France, Mallory was one of 'thirteen notable men of the county such as did bear arms from their auncieters', called to the Great Council at Westminster to arrange for the defence of the realm in the king's absence. (Penes. Camer. Scac.) He was also escheator for both counties and in 1425 was sheriff again (Rot. F. 3 H6. m. 10). He was a commissioner for the peace from 1419 to 1433.

His wife was Philippa Chetwynd from Grendon Park, a property within a day's ride of several Mallory manors. A Thomas Mallory married into the Grendon family at about the same time and the inheritance of his family provides possibilities for making some Mallory links, as will be seen in the notes on Bramcote manor and Paylington.

In the church of All Saints at Grendon (Warwcs.) there was once a series of stained glass windows, memorials to members of the Chetwynd family. Sketches of these appear in Dugdale (p. 1105), and they have been reproduced in several books and papers since, including Stanislaus and Matthews. One window depicted John Mallory and Phillipa Chetwynd. The sketch shows the couple kneeling, the wife behind; her mantle and the knight's surcoat bore the Revel coat-of-arms. In the key, Dugdale lists this as the Malory arms. The inscription under the figures is 'Orate pro Iohe Malorey et Philippa uxore cius'. Shield No. 10 on the same illustration is of the Revel (Malory) arms impaling Chetwynd: 'Ermine a chevron Gules a border engrailled Sable impaling Azure a chevron between 3 mullets Or'. Humphery-Smith gives the following arms for Mallory, taken from Harl. MSS. 1404 fo. 62: 'Ermine a chevron Gules between three trefoils slipped Argent. A border engrailed Sable'. In Glover's *Ordinary* they are incorrectly described and ascribed to 'Sir Piers Mauloure. Leics.'. Stanislaus also gives these as: 'The Mallory Arms'. (It is not possible to comment further.) Another variation ascribed to Malloree is: 'Ermine on a Chevron Gules a 3 foil slipped Or a border engrailed Sable'.

Also living at this time was Robert Mallory, the prior of the Hospital of St John of Jerusalem in England, an influential man who had Henry VI's ear and was in the forefront of the country's affairs. He was also Preceptor of Grafton and Balsall (Warwcs.) and of Clerkenwell Priory in London. He was nominated in a Bull of Grand Master Fluvian as Grand Prior of the Knights of St John in 1433 (correspondence with the library and museum of the Order). Field suggests that he was a close relative of the second John Mallory of Newbold Revel. (*Jo. Eccl. Hist.*, V. 28, No. 3). He led a seaborne expedition to rescue Rhodes (passport was granted on 29 June 1435, records of the Order) and must have been familiar with the formidable fortress there and have made incredible journeys in his lifetime. (*See* Balsall.)

Other Mallorys of this period were also connected with the Knights of St John and were buried in Clerkenwell Priory in London. In the chapel of the Knights Templar the burial of a John Mallory, Knight of the Order, and possibly a prior, is listed by Stow. (*Survey of London, 1598.* Ed. H. Morley.) He may therefore have been dead before 1312 when the Templars were disbanded, but Field suggests a later John Mallory of the Order. Stow also lists the burials of a Simon Mallory, obit. 1442, and a William Mallory. These would have been connected with the order of the Knights Hospitaller. For a study of Prior Robert and more information about the 'Holy' Mallory knights and brothers, *see* P. J. C. Field. A John Mallory was Commander of Baddescroft between 1468 and 1481 (Museum Records).

The Newbold Revel inheritance passed next to John's son, Thomas Mallory. Dugdale says that John was a commissioner for the peace in 1434, but some authorities say that Thomas succeeded to the property in 1433, suggesting that John was already dead in 1434.

Thomas himself provides material for the greatest puzzle in Mallory history. Many scholars have discovered facts about 'Thomas Malory', perhaps we shall never know how many of them really apply to this one. His affairs were mixed up with those of at least one other Thomas—Thomas of Papworth St Agnes—and it has been suggested that in Warwickshire there might have been another Thomas, 'bad Thomas', whose blacker deeds have become confused with the fairly reprehensible escapades of our hero. There is also the much more likely possibility that some of the charges he faced were the result of what would be described in modern terms as a 'frame-up'.

One school of thought favours the view that he brought his unacceptable ways back from the Hundred Years war, in common with many of his contemporaries. Perhaps with the examples of his terrible Uncle Robert and his pillar-of-the-establishment father before him, young Master Thomas took himself off to France to sample a little roistering before the heavy duties of his house descended upon his shoulders. He could equally well have been commanded, as a suitable young man representing the honour of Warwickshire, to accompany his lord the earl on an expedition abroad. Certainly he is listed as one of the 69 young esquires who followed the Earl of Warwick to Calais. Matthews gives a reference to the Hatton papers in the Bodleian, which includes documents concerning the Earl of Warwick (Richard Beauchamp) 'from 1414 onwards'. Dugdale also quotes these papers as giving the Earl's retinue *pour la demeure a Caleys sur l'enforcement de la ville et les marches illoeques'*. This has been interpreted as meaning 'for the seige of Calais', for which more than one date is possible. The two most favoured dates are 1415 and 1436. Applying one or the other of these would imply different dates for Thomas's birth.

In 1436, Warwick 'crossed the Channel to protect Calais from a threatened siege by the Duke of Burgundy' (*Dictionary of National Biography*), so Thomas may have been on that expedition. On the other hand, in addition to the 1415 campaign, early in 1437 Beauchamp took over the regency of France (based in Calais), from the retiring lieutenant, the Duke of York. The list of those who would have been required to serve with him as the occupying force may have been prepared some months previously. At all events, Thomas and his small party of men-at-arms are listed as follows:

> *Thomas Mallory est retenuz a j launce et ij archers. pr sa launce ove j*
> *archer XX marcs par an bouche de court et pour lautre archer X marcs*
> *saunz bouche de court.*

For the lance and first archer he was allowed a retaining fee at the rate of £20 per year and food. For the remaining archer there was only half that sum and no food at all. (It is surely a marvel that archery enjoyed sufficient popularity to survive to the present day!)

We do not know when he returned to England and it is possible that during his absence others at home may have annexed some of his belongings, as was customary at that time, when no man's property was safe from the depradations of his neighbours.

Thomas was knighted by 1445 (Rot. f. 23, H6, m. 10) and was then known as Sir Thomas Malory of 'Newbold Revel, Winwick and Swinford'. This suggests a possible age of roughly 16 years in 1436, which would be reasonable. His sister, Helen Mallory, married Robert Vincent of Stoke d'Abernon and Barnake. They occupied Swinford (*see* Leics.).

In 1445, Sir Thomas was M.P. for Warwickshire at Westminster, seemingly well set to pursue the career of a reliable Mallory. He also may have been knight of the shire for two West Country properties (*see* Dorset). However, after this phase of respectability, he appears to have settled down to a life of remarkable irregularity that demonstrated an unbelievable capacity for survival. He was repeatedly hauled before the courts throughout the rest of his life, being imprisoned at least eight times. He was accused of a succession of crimes: of stealing, assault, taking cattle and property supposedly rightly belonging to his neighbours, his relatives, and the Church, and even of attempting to murder the Duke of Buckingham on the king's highway. (The first duke, Humphrey Stafford, who was troublesome to the family at Bramcote.) For a full account of his transgressions, see Matthews, p. 91.

Newbold Thomas appears to have been the despair of his gaolers. The governors were liable to stiff penalties if he should escape. No doubt their captive was an unruly charge, taking delight in guard-baiting in the time-honoured custom of imprisoned British soldiery. In 1451, on Royal Warrant, he was arrested by the Duke of Buckingham, Sir Edward Grey of Groby, the Earl of Warwick, and the Sheriff of Warwick, and imprisoned in Coleshill Manor. From there he staged one of his most dramatic escapes, which culminated in the best romantic tradition with him swimming the moat. On another occasion, in 1454, he fought his way to freedom from Colchester Castle gaol. Noble dukes frequently stood bail for him. At later dates he spent varying amounts of time in the Marshall, Ludgate and Newgate prisons, and in 1455 in the Tower. In 1456, while in the custody of the Lieutenant of the Tower, he requested a Royal Pardon. (A Robert Malory is recorded as being the Earl of Worcester's lieutenant in the Tower at about this time; perhaps he was able to ameliorate his unhappy kinsman's plight.) He was soon to be taken inside again, this time for alleged debt.

A Sir Thomas Malory is on the list of the 59 knights who besieged the castles of Alnwick and Bamborough during Edward IV's campaign in 1462. As the fortunes of politics made it expedient, many people altered their allegiance during the Wars of the

Roses, not least the next Earl of Warwick, Richard Neville 'the Kingmaker'. It is likely that Thomas followed Warwick and transferred his support from Edward (York.) to Henry VI (Lancs.) at the same time, no doubt without any choice in the matter. It is also possible that more than one Thomas Mallory took part in these campaigns. When Edward was firmly on the throne he extended no fewer than four general pardons to his opponents. In autumn 1461 those pardons included *'Thomas Mallory, miles, alias dominus Thomas Mallory de Newbold Ryvell'*. The next two pardons in 1468, excluded 'Thomas Mallarie, Knight' and 'Thomas Malorie, *miles'*. Were both or either of these, Newbold Revel Thomas? It is usually assumed that they were. Not only was Thomas a master of the art of escape, he was also on many occasions acquitted of the crimes laid at his door, and despite the times when his luck was out, the extensive Mallory estates remained intact. Do we see the hand of an influential connection here or is the impression of Thomas as an impossible scallywag not the true picture? Every student of his life soon becomes aware of the fact that he probably had enough time on his hands in gaol to have written *Le Morte d'Arthur*. His larger-than-life personality also suggests that he may have been capable of the feat, although some aspects of his character may seem to be at variance with the chivalrous sentiments of its author and an old campaigner does not seem to be a person who would take the discipline of the pen.

He was in gaol in 1468 but it is not known where he died. It is likely that he might sadly still have been in Newgate, for after a splendid procession and grand funeral, he was buried near there in the chapel of St Francis the Apostle at Greyfriars church (Bibl. Cotton). He was laid to rest alongside four queens, several heralds, the treasurers of England, and many other famous persons (Stow), in a marble tomb. His epitaph reads: *'Dominus Thomas Mallare Valens Miles Obitt 14 MAR 1470 De Parochia Monkenkyrby in Comitatu Warwici'* (Stanislaus). Martin says, 'obit 12 March 1471, his heir Robert aged 23 years'. Dugdale gives 'Robert obitt vita patris', but Robert seems to have died in 1479 (Cal. Pat. 19, Edw. 4, p. 183). The chapel was among those secularised by Henry VIII. The contents, including the memorials, were sold by the Lord Mayor of London in 1545. Does Thomas Mallory's marble still lie in some London garden? New research is frequently published concerning Thomas and the book he may have written. (Readers will enjoy Miss M. Bradbrook's *Sir Thomas Malory*, 1968.)

Of his children there is only mention of his son, Robert (second son according to Martin), born in 1448, and daughter, Phillipa, who married Eustace Burnaby. (*See* Swinford.) His wife, the Lady Elizabeth, although barely mentioned, emerges as a typically capable medieval chatelaine, surviving her trouble-starred husband and keeping a firm hand on the domestic reins and estates through all the vagaries of his fortunes. She died September 1479, having borne the grief of the deaths of Thomas and two of her sons, leaving the Mallory property to Robert's son, Nicholas, then only a child of 13 years. (Martin: I.P.M. 20, Edw. 4, No. 46.) This inquisition states that Newbold Revel was held 'of the Duke of York who held in right of Lady Mowbray, his wife'. (*See* Saddington, Leics.) Dugdale gives a birthdate of 1468 for Nicholas.

The Swinford estate was granted to Thomas Kyngeston during Nicholas's minority (*see* Swinford notes) and throughout his lifetime, the Lichborough cousins

continued to occupy his manor there. At his death Lichborough returned to the ownership of that line. He married Kyngeston's daughter. (*See* Wiltshire.) Nicholas lived from
1436 until 1513. In 1502 he was High Sheriff of Leicester, and from 1502 until 1513,
justice of the peace for Warwickshire. His heirs were his two daughters, who shared the
properties. Dorothy, the elder, had married Edward Cave, the brother of Margaret's
husband, Clement Cave. (*See* Stanford notes.) Both sisters married twice, Dorothy's
second husband was George Ashby, Margaret's was J. Cope. Dorothy, who had two
daughters, received Winwick manor, Swinford, Stretton-under-Fosse and the manor
of Paylington. She also held lands at Newbold Revel which she sold to Thomas Pope
in 1538. Margaret inherited the manor of Newbold Revel, Easenhall, and part of the
Winwick lands.

Margaret had no children. In October 1538 she sold Newbold Revel to Thomas
Pope and died the next month. Thomas Pope soon sold Newbold Revel to Sir William
Whorwood, and it passed through a succession of aristocratic owners to the Skipwith
family who were to live there for 300 years. The Mallory manor was replaced by a
handsome mansion, completed in 1716 by Sir Fulwar Skipwith, Bt. (All the properties
of this Mallory line were sold by 1538 except those inherited by the Cave family
descendants.)

Dugdale sketched seven armorial shields that were once in the parlour windows.
The first one, which has no trick, shows a rampant fork-tailed lion, apparently the
Kirkby Malory arms. The second and third shields were the same lion impaling a
quartered coat which had not been identified. If these quarters could be named,
they might throw some valuable light on to the Mallory connections. The central
shield is also a mystery, described in the *Index to Arms* as 'Gules, 3 barulets with a
bendlet Arg'. It was not named. The fifth shield is of unidentified arms impaling
quartered Whymall and Davall arms (Nichols), presumably from the Chetwynd family.
The sixth shield has the Revel arms, and the last one shows the arms of Malory of
Draughton, the early owners of Winwick. The arms of one of Dorothy's daughters are
in Charwelton church (Northants.) and are described below. The identification of
the Newbold Revel shields by P. J. C. Field is given at the end of this section.

The house changed hands many times, eventually ceasing to be a private dwelling.
For some years it belonged to the Sisters of Saint Paul, who very kindly provided
material about Newbold Revel for this chapter. In 1978 it was sold to the Post Office
and is now a staff training college.

The parish church for Newbold Revel is at Monks Kirby (*see* John Mallory, above)
and is dedicated to St Edith. Among the armorial windows were the arms of Malory
of Draughton, two 'Revel' shields (one differenced by the addition of 3 gold stars
to the chevron), and the shield with boars' heads already discussed. There was also a
shield with Malory of Draughton quartering Revel arms. Sir Anthony Wagner ascribes
it to 'Sir Thomas Mallory, obit 1471'. He gives 'lions passant'. Similarly in Dugdale's
sketch of the parlour windows, the tomb at Charwelton, the Parliamentary Roll and
Erdeswicke, 1295. Dugdale's sketch of the arms in the church, and Burke, have
'passant guardant'.

Knightlow 100; 6 miles E. of Coventry; *V.C.H. Warwickshire,* v 6, p. 175.

Dugdale, p. 81, etc. (Monks Kirby is 1 mile N. of Newbold Revel.)

Sir Anthony Wagner, Garter Principal King of Arms, *Historical Heraldry of Britain* (1972 edn.).

The museum of the Order of St John, the chapter house, library, etc., may be visited. It is located at St John's Gate, Clerkenwell, London, E.C.1. A garden and meagre ruins of the Greyfriars' church still remain, near St Bartholomew's Hospital at Newgate, E.C.1.

Note: The reader's attention is directed to a paper by P. J. C. Field: 'The last years of Sir Thomas Malory'; vol. 64, No. 2., *Bulletin, John Ryland's University Library,* 1982. It augments some of the information in this book since it identifies most of the arms in the parlour at Newbold Revel and the relationship of the families to the Mallorys. There is fresh speculation about matters relating to that Sir Thomas, and the claim that he was the author of *Le Morte d'Arthur,* which may be compared with papers supporting the Papworth man. There are some new names of spouses suggested for the Malory pedigree. However, although these appear to be satisfactorily accounted for, they do require that the artist employed to decorate the parlour made mistakes (not unusual, since mistakes occur elsewhere). The discrepancies should be noted since they raise a doubt respecting Baker's description of the arms at Charwelton. (*See* that chapter.)

Dugdale's *Index to unidentified Arms* states that a shield on his p. 83 was 'Sable a lion rampant Or'. He does not specify which shield nor describe the lion's tail. This Field ascribes (correctly) to Kingston. The lions on 'page 83' all have *double* tails, however, and the Kingston lion of the relevant branch of that family has a single tail. (*V.C.H. Berkshire* and Burke). In the second and third shields, the double-tailed lion is impaled with the quartered arms of Childrey (P.J.C.F.). This implies that it was intended to represent Kingston.

The central shield ascribed with good reason to Walsh (P.J.C.F.) is only an approximation of their arms. The Walsh(e) arms are 'Gules two bars gemellee Argent a bend of the last' (Dugdale, V.3., pt. 2, p. 1097, shield 11, and Burke), and are not the arms depicted. (*See* Newbold Revel.) The combined evidence of all the descriptions of the lions at Newbold Revel and Charwelton is confusing. It does not, however, affect the descent of these houses as given in the pedigrees below.

Bramcote: Mallory property 1407 to 1466 (with a reference to Peckleton, Leics.)

The history of the manor of Bramcote provides one convenient focus for considering several Mallory muddles, and the possibility of perhaps resolving them through connections which begin with Alice, née Dryby, wife of the Sir Anketil Mallory who sold Kirkby Mallory (Leics.) in 1377, but other appropriate sections should also be read. Further work is still required to establish all the correct relationships.

Bramcote, near Grendon in Warwickshire, was a Grendon family holding in 1086. Early in the 15th century it was inherited by Margaret, daughter of Sir Thomas, the last male Grendon. She married twice: her first husband was William Charnells of Snarkeston in Leicester; her second was Sir Thomas Mallory, the eldest son of Sir Anketil Mallory and Alice Dryby (*see* Kirkby Mallory, Bredon, etc.). Kirkby Mallory is only 10 miles from Grendon. Thomas and Margaret were married by 1407, for he is called 'Thomas Malorei, lórd of Bramcote' in F. of F. Warw. 8, Hen. IV. Five years later they were at law about Bramcote with 'John Mallory' and 'Robert Mallory'. (F. of F. Warw. 13, Henry IV.) John Mallory of Newbold Revel and his relative, Robert, prior of the Knights Hospitaller, were both alive at this time. John's wife was Phillipa Chetwynd of Grendon Park. Perhaps the dispute was with them and thus may confirm a close kinship between these branches of the Mallory family at that time.

By 1412, when Alice Dryby died, Thomas was apparently already dead. His daughter and heir was Elizabeth Mallory. Alice Dryby's second husband, Sir Ralph Bassett of Sapcote (whose mother's name was Isabella), had two daughters by his first wife, Sibilla, daughter of Giles, Lord Astley. Alice ('Sibilla's daughter', aged 30 in 1379) married as her last husband, Sir Robert Moton. Their grandson (? son), also a Sir Robert Moton, lord of Peckleton (Leics.), died in 1456. Peckleton is just to the east of Kirkby Mallory; the properties adjoin. Sir Robert Moton's first wife (deed 1397, Nichols) was Margery/Mary/Margaret Mallory, a daughter of Sir Anketil Mallory and Alice Dryby. In her will, Alice Dryby mentions her daughter, Elizabeth Bassett, who married Lord Grey of Codnor in Derbyshire. Elizabeth's daughter, Elizabeth Grey, married Richard, the brother of William Lord Zouche of Harryngworth (obit. 3, Hen. V). The Mallorys were also connected by marriage with the family her Lord Zouche (Yorkshire notes).

Reginald Moton, son of Sir Robert Moton and Margery Mallory, died before his father, as did many young representatives of knightly families in those days. There were two daughters, but Sir Robert married again, and the inheritance passed to his new male heir.

In 1296 the 'town' of Peckleton was held by a William Malore, presumably either William, lord of Walton, or William of Lichborough.

The escheat reference for Alice Dryby in respect of Bramcote is 14, Hen. IV, No. 1, 15 Leics., and for her other manors of Bredon, Holwell, etc., 3 Hen. V, No. 60 Leics.; Elizabeth Mallory was her heir.

The age for Elizabeth given in the I.P.M. in respect of Alice Dryby is the one most likely to have been correct, and implies a birth date of 1401. I.P.M.s elsewhere imply dates ranging from 1391 to 1401 (I.P.M. 14, Hen. IV, No. 15 Leics.). There may have been lawyer's reasons for these discrepancies.

The Anketil Mallory whom Alice Dryby married has much in common with the Anketil Mallory whose son inherited Papworth St Agnes, although their antecedants vary according to different authorities (*see* Cambridgeshire and Bedfordshire).

In 1428 John Charnells of Snarkeston, the son of Margaret Mallory's first husband, William Charnells, was granted Bramcote. This was confirmed by deeds of 7, Hen. VI and F. of F. 8, Hen. VI.

Elizabeth Mallory, daughter of Thomas of Bramcote, married Sir Robert Ever. (*See* Bredon, Leics.). Sir John Mallory of Studley Royal married Anne Eure. Another family comes on the scene, the Bruyns. In the Duchess of Cleveland's *Battle Abbey Roll,* there is mention of Bramcote being the dowry of Joan Bruyn for her marriage with Sir Nicholas Burdett, Great Butler of Normandy. He died in 1439. Joan Burdett was heir to Henry Bruin who owned Ab Lench in Worcestershire. The Duke of Buckingham, Humphrey Stafford (the same man whom Thomas Mallory of Newbold Revel was accused of attempting to murder in 1450) took Bramcote by force and handed it over to Joan. (Chanc. Proc. 31, No. 149). However, William Charnells (assumed here to be the son of John Charnells and grandson of Margaret Mallory) contested Joan's right to the manor, and it was proved that Joan Burdett and her son, Thomas Burdett, had forged documents to substantiate their claim. (Cal. Pat. 1446-61). The influence of her sponsor no doubt obtained the pardon she received for this deception. Was there a reason for her thinking she had title and what lay behind the apparent animosity between Buckingham and the Mallorys?

Banks' *Baronies in Fee* notes that Elizabeth le Bruyn (another Bruyn heiress) married a William Mallory, Esq., either as her first or third husband. Her third marriage would have been after the battle of Bosworth in 1485, when her second husband, Sir William Brandon, was killed. (Their son, Charles Brandon, became the Duke of Suffolk and married Henry VIII's darling sister, Mary Rose, who gave her name to the king's flagship which has been returned to us after 437 years in a watery grave, together with all who sailed in her.)

It seems unlikely, although not impossible if we consider a child marriage, that any of the known contemporary William Mallorys could have been Elizabeth Bruyn's first husband. There is, however, a very eligible young man for a third husband in the person of William of Papworth St Agnes. He was the third son of (Sir) Thomas of Papworth and his brothers were wards of the king after his father died in 1469. He was born after 1457. He seems to have been dead by 1492, when his next brother, Anthony Mallory, inherited Papworth. (Cal. Fine Rolls.) There remains the possibility that her husband may have been an otherwise unrecorded William Mallory. (*See also* the Visitation to the North. 1480/1500: Ped. Wingfield: 'W. Brandon Miles married Elizabeth, daughter M. Branze, postea nupta Malory' . . . 'W. Brandon knighted by King Hen. VII at Bosworth 1485'. Surtees Soc. Pub., 1930).

The fact that the Mallorys of Kirkby Mallory and the Papworth Mallorys were both allowed the red rampant lion coat-of-arms, indicates a common ancestor. They share this coat with the Yorkshire Mallorys, the Northampton branch, the Mobberley Mallorys and some smaller branches and more distantly, with the Warwickshire branch. Further discussion of the Mallory puzzle is continued in the sections on the manor of Sudborough in Northamptonshire and other Cambridgeshire Mallory properties.

By 1446 Joan Burdett had died, and in that year the Burdett family made another move to acquire Bramcote, for William Charnels appears to have felt himself obliged to enfeoffe her son, Thomas Burdett, of the manor (F. of F., Warw. 6, Edw. IV). Burdett was attainted for treason in 1474 and in 1477/8 he was arrested on a charge of sorcery and beheaded. By a strange irony his bones lie near those of Thomas Mallory of Newbold Revel, under the floor of the Bluecoat School, which was built on the site of the desecrated church of the Greyfriars in London. (Not the Blewcoat School in Westminster, founded 1709.)

Bramcote Hall was rebuilt in the 18th century. In 1823 the Burdett family were still lords of the manor. The site of the house is near Polesworth railway station and should not be confused with Pooley Hall, the manor of Polesworth.

Hemlingford 100; 3 miles N. of Grendon; Dugdale, vol. 2, p. 1122; *V.C.H. Warwcs.*, vol. 4, p. 189 (not Bramcote in vol. 6).

Ansty

Although not a Mallory holding, this manor has two indirect points of contact with the family, which it may be useful to note. In 1184 it belonged to Roger de Burcheville. In 1243 the heiress of the family, Agnes de Boschevill, married Thomas FitzLucien de Donmore, known as Thomas le Greys. Ansty is near Newbold Revel. The Newbold Revel family of Mallorys came from Winwick in Northants and the first names on their pedigree are Simon Malory of Draughton, married to Beatrice de Bokervyle (Simon was alive between 1264–1277). (*See* Draughton for a further discussion of these names.)

Wootton (Leek Wootton)

Baron Stadford, who gave Botley to the Mallorys, was also lord of Wootton, which encompassed several manors. One of these, the manor of Lower Woodcote, belonged to the Mallory family in Dugdale's time. They are recorded as still holding the manor in 1730. A Robert Harvey Mallory held it in 1783. His daughter inherited and sold it in 1851 and the house was demolished shortly after. The death of Robert Harvey Mallory seems to mark the end of one line of the family which has not, at the time of writing, been traced back to the main branch. The church (All Saints at Leek Wootton) contains a tomb bearing the following inscription: 'Here lyeth Mr John Mallory of Woodcote. Obit. 22.1.1713 aet 66'. (Dugdale). Charities were endowed by Samuel Mallory in 1713 and by his son, Robert, in 1759 (*V.C.H.*) Leek Wootton is 5 miles north of Tachebrook Mallory.

Hyde (Hyde Pastures)

Dugdale notes that in the third year of King John's reign a William le Mareschell, Ralph Mallore and his wife, Liecia, levied a fine on land to the use of Richard FitzRobert. (1202, F.F.) The Bassets of Sapcote also held land here which eventually passed to the descendants of Alice Dryby and the Moton family. Hyde was once in the hundred of Knightlow, but is now absorbed into the Leicestershire parish of Hinckley in the hundred of Sparkenhoe. *See also* Leicester notes under 'The Hyde'.

Easenhall

This village came to the Mallorys with Newbold Revel. Margaret (Mallory) Cave inherited it and sold it to a Sir Walter Smith. It is 7 miles east of Coventry, south of Newbold Revell.

Stretton-under-Fosse

This property came to the Mallorys with Newbold Revel. Dorothy (Mallory) Cave inherited it and it passed to her younger daughter, Margaret, heir to Edward Cave. At Margaret's death it passed to her son and heir, Edward Boughton (Escheat 8, Eliz. I). It is 2 miles north-west of Easenhall.

Paylington (Pailton)

Pailton came to the Mallorys with Newbold Revel. A John de Charnells owned part of a knight's fee at Pailton in 1297 (Escheat 25.E. I. n.51). This would be the same family as the Charnels whose widow, Margaret of Bramcote, married Thomas Mallory of Kirkby Mallory in about 1407. (*See* Bramcote and Grendon notes.) Dorothy

(Mallory) Cave inherited Pailton and it passed eventually to her grandson, Edward Boughton. Part of the village was owned by Roger Corbet of Morton Corbet in 1461 and passed to his descendants (*see* Papworth Mallory notes, etc.).

1 mile N. of Easenhall; Knightlow 100.

Nun Eaton

In King Stephen's reign a Benedictine monastery was founded at Nun Eaton, and amongst the endowments were lands at Swinford in Leicestershire and the rents from a house in Leicester, all of which were the property of a Richard Mallore (Dugdale). This Richard may have been the father of Geoffrey of Kirkby Mallory (*see* Swinford).

Hemlingford 100; about 8 miles N. of Newbold Revel and 7 miles S.W. of Kirkby Mallory.

Balsall

Dugdale recorded the arms in the windows of the church at Balsall. They included one shield showing the Revel (Warwickshire Mallory) arms of 'Ermine a chevron Gules, etc.'; one with the arms of Weston, a Lord Prior of the Knights Templar, and one which he did not identify. This was 'Gules, a St George's cross Argent' (a red shield with a silver 'cross of St George'). Silver in this context could be the equivalent of white. The arms of the non-combatant Knights Hospitaller from their inception, were the silver eight-pointed cross of St John worn upon a black habit. Their militant members, a division formed in the 13th century, wore red with a white 'straight cross' (Boutell); i.e., in the shape of a St George's cross. The Weston arms included the 'St George's cross' in chief. Robert Mallory, Prior of the Knights Hospitaller (*see* Newbold Revel) held Balsall, amongst his Preceptories. Field gives evidence of both the Kirkby Mallory lion (which he dismisses) and the Revel arms, as being associated with Sir Robert, the latter, more recently, from the Prior's own seal, thus enabling a Warwickshire descent to be postulated for him. In the records of the order, and still displayed in the Chapter Hall on Sir Robert's stall, his arms are the familiar Red Lion, but with a single tail.

The Revel arms were present in several Warwickshire churches. Some must have been memorials to the Revel family itself, some to the Mallorys. The Balsall shield seems to have commemorated Prior Robert. The 1618 Visitation to Warwickshire notes the confirmation of arms to Robert Mallory, '5th in descent from Sir Gilbert Mallory, Kt.' by Camden's deputies. (Burke.) These are the Revel arms and may refer to Prior Robert and may also confirm the placing of (Sir) Gilbert, v 1227, as ancestor of the Draughton/Newbold Revel line. It may also confirm Sir Robert as a son of Agnes Revel. There are, however, six generations between them in the pedigrees suggested here, if this is so. The church is dedicated to St Mary (the original was built by the Templars in 1290).

7 miles W. of Coventry.

Woodcote

This manor, which originally belonged to the Boetler family, was in the possession of the Mallorys in Dugdale's time (*circa* 1650).

Coleshill (Colshill)

It is not clear which of the several manors in Coleshill was the scene of the aquatic escape of Sir Thomas of Newbold Revel. There are at least three sites today with the remains of dry moats, but Maxstoke, the Earl of Huntingdon's formidable castle, still rises from its moat two miles to the north-east of the village. The castle, chapel, manor and parks were the property of the Duke of Buckingham. Another manor in the vicinity was Kingshurst, also moated, the seat of the de Mountforts. The present house dates from the 17th century. The stained glass windows of the church, St Peter's, included four showing the Revell (Mallory) arms. It is 8 miles east of Birmingham.

Chilvercotton (Chilverscotton)

One shield in the windows of the church depicted the Revel (Mallory) arms. It is 1 mile south of Nuneaton.

Kenilworth

The Visitations to Warwickshire also give evidence of an unidentified Mallory who resided at Kenilworth after 1646. The pedigree of 'Gramer of Mancetter', Helmingford 100, 'noe arms exhibited', commences with 'Francis Gramer of Kennilworth. Obit 1625. Married Anne Hansard'. One of their grandchildren, Mary, married Mallory of Kenilworth. (Visitation 1682/3). (*Note*: It has not been possible to visit all the churches in Warwickshire. Some of the armorial windows noted by Dugdale may still be in place.)

Chapter Three

NORTHAMPTONSHIRE, RUTLAND, NORFOLK

THE TWO HISTORIES of Northamptonshire which supplied many of the facts on which this chapter is based are by George Baker and by Bridges (ed. Whalley). Some material also emerged from studies of the history of Mallorys in other counties. Confirmation of the antecedents of Alice Dryby from *The American Genealogist* were supplied by Mr. E. Miller. I am indebted to Professor R. Griffith for details of Sloane MS. 779 (his letter to *The Times,* 1978) and a copy of the manuscript. Miss Verena Smith kindly sent me a translation of the Lowick indentures.

Members of Parliament for the county of Northamptonshire given by Bridges include the following:

> 24, Edw. 3 at Westminster: Peter Malore (? Sir Peter of Winwick).
> 9, Rich. 2 at Westminster: Giles Malore (Sir Giles of Lichborough).
> 11, Rich 2 at Westminster: Giles Malore (do.).
> 16, Rich 2 at Winchester: Giles Malore (do.).
> 2, Hen. 4 at Westminster: Giles Malore (do.).
> 4, Hen. 4 at Winchester: Giles Malore (do.).
> 4, Hen. 4 at Winchester: John Cope (*see* text).

Banks notes that Sir Peter Mallory of Winwick, judge, was frequently called to parliament from 1291 to 1309. Sheriffs of Northampton include the following:

> 25, Edw. 3. Peter Malore (? Sir Peter of Winwick).
> 16, Rich. 2. John Malore (? Sir John of Winwick and Newbold Revel).
> 4, Henry 4. Giles Malore (? Sir Giles of Lichborough).

Also, in Henry V's reign, members of the Grene family, who were married to Mallory ladies, held this office. In 1980 there was only one Mallory family in Northamptonshire.

Northamptonshire and Rutland

There were Mallory holdings in Northamptonshire at the time of the *Twelfth Century Survey,* some of which appear to have become confused with properties that belonged to Fulcher Malsoures, reputed to have been a Breton knight who came at the time of the Conquest and who is named by some authorities as the original Mallory in England (*see* Origins). If ownership of the manors and lands held by families named Malsoures and Mallory are studied, it will be seen that these do not provide a basis for making that assumption.

The county of Rutland may also be mentioned in this connection. Fulcher held Oakham, where there was also a Mallory interest, but this had no connection. Alice Dryby, the wife of Sir Anketil Mallory of Kirkby Mallory, held a small property in Oakham which it is believed she inherited from Margaret de Clare, the Lady of Oakham, in 1316. Lady Clare, granddaughter of King Edward I, seems to have been the grandmother of Alice Dryby. In 1280 a Ralph Mallory was given life custody of Rutland forest by King Edward I (*see* Kirkby Mallory, Leics.).

The boundaries of the Northamptonshire hundreds were changed from time to time. In addition, there are several instances of there being more than one Northamptonshire township known by the same name. The results of combining the accounts and maps in the *Victoria County History,* the Domesday Survey, *The Twelfth Century Survey of Northamptonshire,* Baker's *History and Antiquities of Northamptonshire* and other sources, follow.

In 1086, Fulcher held Thorpe (called Alidetorp), later known as Thorpe Malsor, in Gravesend hundred (also called Rothwell hundred at one time). It was two or three miles west of Kettering and near the Mallory holdings at Old and Draughton. It has been mistaken for Thorp (spelled Torp), which was held by the Mallorys at a later date. Torp was held as part of the Welton, Torp and Staveton inheritance: all three are listed by Nichols as belonging to Anketil of Kirkby Mallory (V. 4, p. 762), and later to Sir John Mallory of Welton, whose daughter and heir also inherited Holwell in Bedfordshire (*see* Isleham, Cambridgeshire). The section on the manor of Welton provides a more detailed account of these properties.

There are no references to the name Mallory (in any form) in connection with the history of the manor of Thorpe Malsor, which descended clearly through unbroken generations of Malsoures, nor are Mallorys connected with any other property held by the Malsoures family, with the exception of the manor of Walgrave. It is a very misleading exception, however, since the property came to the Mallorys by a marriage nearly five hundred years later than Fulcher. Sir Richard Mallory, Lord Mayor of London (*see* Cambridgeshire) married the widow of the Lord of Walgrave in 1565. She held the manor jointly with her sons (by her first husband) at the time of the marriage. (Walgrave Hall dates partly from 1630.)

The first Northamptonshire manor known to have a Mallory connection was Welton. In the *Twelfth Century Survey,* Richard 'Maulore' held land at Welton (spelled Weletone) and because of the way the properties descended to successive Mallorys, he is thought to have been the same man as he who held at Swinford (Leics.) and at Bredon. He was contemporary with Geoffrey of Kirkby Mallory, probably his father, as Nichols' pedigree for Mallory of Swinford suggests. There is an overlap in the histories of the properties held by these Mallorys, since the manors eventually converged into one inheritance. Repetition of some of the facts is unavoidable. An inquisition of 1383 records that an Anketil Mallory had an interest in the manor of Exton, Rutland. Other families connected with the Mallorys held there from time to time: Bruyns, Bassetts, Greens and the First Lord Zouche of Harryngworth—none with any connection with the Malsoures. (*See* Drayton, Joan de Bruys, 1358.)

Northamptonshire

Welton, Thorp and Staveton: Mallory property from early 12th century to 1484

Welton, Thorp and Staveton were owned by Sir Anketil of Kirkby Mallory and were held of him 'as of his manor of Kirkby Mallory', by Sir John Mallory of Welton, in the reign of Edward III (1327-77). In Domesday, one Leofric held 'Weleton' and an area called 'Thrup', marked 'Thrupp Grounds' on a Domesday Book map (1086). Thrupp was written 'Torp' and subsequently 'Thorp', but it has not been located on a modern map. It was immediately south of Welton. In the register of the abbey of St Mary de Pratis at Leicester, it is called 'Thorp Wylby'. It was certainly not Thorp Malsor (but *see* Delapré and Earls Barton, below). Welton was in the hundred of Alwardsley in the corrected Domesday map given in the *V.C.H.*, but in Gravesend hundred in Domesday (Baker placed it in what he called Fawsley hundred). If all the locations are combined, only one Welton is possible, near Long Buckby Wharf (not the village of Long Buckby).

Staveton, also a property of Leofric in 1086, is a village south of Daventry. The monks of Daventry held most of Welton in the 12th century. In the abbey charter of Henry II's reign (1154-89), 'Richard Mallorie and his heirs' were charged 40s. a year for land at Welton and Torp. (A Richard Mallore, possibly the same, held at Swinford in the preceding reign.) Later these lands became part of the Mallory manor of Welton. In the *Twelfth Century Survey* (*V.C.H.*), the name is spelled 'Maulare' and 'Maulore' and refers to a Richard who was alive before 1189.

In the reign of Henry III the returns for the period 1247 to 1256 give a Robert Mallory as Lord of Welton. (Testa. Nev. fo. 170, says 'Lord of the town under the earl of Leicester'.) In 1247, Robert (spelled Malore) gave the advowson of the chapel at Welton to the Daventry monks. He was the son of Sir Simon Mallory of Holwell (Beds.) and was also lord of that manor, a seat of the Mallory family from the time of Henry II, when Bertram Mallory held it.

Baker complains that there is little information about the Mallorys of Welton. This suggests that for many years their main home was at Holwell. Robert's eldest son, John Mallory, was lord of Welton, Holwell and Wold, in 1285. There were two other sons (*see* Holwell). A grant of arms for the branch of the family at Welton has not been found.

The Mallory family were represented in many of the major conflicts in England; it is therefore surprising that there is no mention in the literature of their involvement in the battle of Evesham (1265). Their friends, the Bassets and others, were deprived of life and possessions because they supported Simon de Montfort. The Mallorys, throughout history, generally fought on the side of the monarchy, excelling themselves in the Wars of the Roses by fighting for both kings. By the rules of chivalry, some were bound to follow their overlord, the Earl of Leicester. Since he opposed the king, the Mallorys would have been in a dilemma regarding their position vis-à-vis the '65 Rebellion.

Baker furnishes only three more notes on the Mallory lords of Welton: John Mallory of Welton 1315 (Nom. Vi11). Sir John Malore of Welton 1329 (Title deeds of Whilton Mill) and Sir John Malory of Welton (witness to a deed). Each of these different spellings may represent one individual. It will be seen from the chapter on Isleham that a Sir John Mallory of Welton was succeeded by his daughter, whose grandson, Thomas Peyton of Isleham, sold Welton in 1484 to William Catesby of Ashby St Ledgers (home of the Gunpowder plot) and Welton passed from Mallory History. (Cal. Pat. 1485, 275.)

An undated reference mentions a Simon Malore who granted 'six acres of land and his rights to the chapel at Welton to the Priory' (Daventry). Possibly this was one of the early Simons who were descended from Bertram of Holwell. The arms of that branch of the family were probably either 'Argent a demi-lion rampant Gules' (Elena Mallory) or 'Or a demi-lion rampant double tailed Gules' (William Maulare)—*see* Isleham.

Recent particulars about the house have not been verified, but according to Baker, in his day it was still extant and known as 'Churchill House' situated on the Daventry side of the village. Arthur Mee only refers to a Georgian manor house, and Sir Niklaus Pevsner describes a 16th-century house known as 'Norton'. The fate of this house would surely qualify it to feature in a Mallory history since it was 'blown up' in 1945. The church is dedicated to St Martin; the village is in Aywoldsley (Fawsley) hundred (Fawsley in Gravesend hundred). For further information, *see V.C.H. Northants.*, V.1.

Welton, N.W. of river Nene; 4 miles N.W. of Daventry; 25 miles from Kirkby Mallory, 5 miles from Winwick.

Thorp, S. of Welton (but *see also* Thorpe Lubenham, Leics. Owned by a Thomas Malore in 1296. It is about 10 miles north of Welton. No further comment is possible).

Staveton, 2 miles S.W. of Daventry; church, St Mary.

Old (alias Would)

This manor lies near to the early Mallory holding of Draughton and was possibly owned by them from the beginning of the 12th century. The only reference to it is as part of the inheritance of Elena Mallory of Isleham, whose father, Sir John Mallory of Welton, held it in 1427. (Cat. Anc. Deeds 4, p. 176.) Her grandson, Thomas Peyton, sold it to one Catesby in 1484 and it eventually came to the family of Isham, who still hold it. The Isham family, some of whom were Mercers, were friends of the Mallory family in Tudor times; notably John Isham and Sir Richard Mallory, Lord Mayor of London (*see* Cambridgeshire).

Church, St Andrew; Orlingbury hundred; *V.C.H. Northants.*, V. 4; 2½ miles S of Draughton; 12 miles N.E. of Welton.

Draughton (not Drayton): Mallory property from circa 1264

By the year 1220 the name Draughton had evolved from the Domesday spelling of Dracstone, although in the *Twelfth Century Survey* it appeared as Draiton (*Place-Names of Northamptonshire*). It should not be confused with Drayton, also sometimes called Draiton, in Fawsley hundred, which is now a suburb of Daventry, nor with

Drayton in Huxloe hundred, which gave its name to Drayton House at Lowick and which has different Mallory connections.

It is also possible to confuse the first recorded lord of Drayton in Huxloe hundred, Simon de Drayton, with the first recorded lord of Draughton, Simon de Draughton. Simon de Drayton was not a Mallory. He was alive in 1264. Simon Mallory appears in Nichols's pedigree for Swinford (Leics.) as lord of Draughton in 1277, and as the son of Henry and grandson of Anketil of Tachebrook Mallory (Warwcs.). Anketil is given, probably incorrectly, as the brother of Geoffrey of Kirkby Mallory. He seems to have been Geoffrey's son. Some individuals appear to have been recorded twice in this pedigree. A. T. Martin's notes enable them to be correctly placed with some confidence. It is also possible that Simon was the grandson of Henry (*see* Winwick). In addition, Simon owned land at Houghton (Hoton) in Leicestershire which passed to his descendants. By 1283, Mallorys were lords of the manor of Hoton.

The arms of Mallory of Draughton were 'Or three lions passant guardant in pale Sable' (a gold shield charged with three horizontal black lions in a vertical column). What story lies behind the granting of this coat-of-arms, for these are the royal lions of England with the colours changed? *See* Newbold Revel: discussion of 'passant' versus 'passant guardant', *also see* Winwick.

Simon married a lady of property, Beatrice de Bokervyle, who was coheir with her brother, Stephen, to the manor of Winwick, which she must have brought to her marriage, since the I.P.M. on her son, Sir Peter Mallory (4 Edw. II, No. 6: Martin), states that he and his brother Stephen held it by feoffment of their mother. An inquisition of 16 Edw. I on the holdings of Elias Rabayn and his wife Maude, who later married Sir Peter Mallory, states that Stephen and Peter 'Maulore' held 'Wenewick: 1 messuage, 12 virgates, water mill and rents of them by the service of half a knight's fee'. (Perhaps these were two houses consituting the whole property, as at Tachebrook.) There is also an undated note in the *V.C.H.* taken from Halstead, which records that Beatrice de 'Blokervyle' gave lands at Drayton near Lowick to a chapel which was attached to a church at Islip, belonging to the abbey of St Mary.

Beatrice may have been a member of the Burchville family. The similarity between Bokervyle and the following names may be significant, although one is reminded that conclusions based on spelling may be unreliable. The manor of Ansty, near Newbold Revel, belonged to Roger de Burcheville in 1184 (Dugdale). By 1243 that family's name was written Boschevil. Leland notes a name inscribed on one of the Battle Abbey Rolls, of which he says 'Basseville or Bosevile, who were great lords of the North and probably derived from Boschervile near Honfleur'. The son of Agnes de Boschervill (temp. Henry III) married into the family of Charnels, who also had connections with the Bramcote Mallorys.

Simon and Beatrice were blessed with five sons of whom at least three were knighted. Sir Roger Mallory, born in 1250, seems to have been the eldest. He was a knight in 1283 (Nichols) and became lord of Draughton after his father, who died in 1286. The second son, Nicholas, sometimes called 'of Draughton', held the manor of Hoton in 1293. There was a son, Stephen (named for his uncle), a fourth son, Sir Peter of Winwick; another was Sir William, lord of Lichborough in 1280. There are no other references to Stephen and Nicholas. Sir Peter died in 1310 and Winwick passed to Sir Roger, whose son, Simon, inherited Draughton, Winwick and Swinford. Several dates from 1313 to 1333 appear by his name on Nichols's pedigree. Simon's son, Stephen, a knight in 1333, was lord of Draughton, Winwick and Swinford, and married Margaret Revel, who may have owned a property at Swinford (*see* Swinford and Newbold Revel). According to Nichols, their son, Sir John Mallory, a knight in 1363, bore the arms of Mallory of Draughton. Dugdale, however, ascribed to him arms probably inherited from Swinford. He also married a lady of the Revel family, Alice, who inherited Newbold Revel in 1383, and with it the Revel arms. Their son, John Mallory of Winwick, took his mother's arms, and there is no further mention of Draughton in the Mallory inheritance. The fortunes of the family are continued under Newbold Revel, Winwick and Lichborough.

Rodwell (Rothwell) hundred; 7 miles E. of Winwick; 6 miles S.W. of Kettering;
11 miles W. of Lowick and Drayton.

Winwick (Wenewyk, Wynwyk); Mallory property circa 1250–1538

The history of the manor of Winwick, owned by the Mallorys for almost three centuries, is told partly in the notes on the other manors which the Mallorys of Draughton held. The chief of these, towards the end of their history, was Newbold Revel in Warwickshire. Their earliest major holdings were at Swinford in Leicestershire and at Lichborough in Northamptonshire. The notes on Draughton give the probable details of the acquisitions of Winwick by Simon Mallory, lord of Draughton about 1277. One of his many sons, Sir Peter Mallory, was styled 'lord of Winwick'. He also held lands at Dodemerton and the town of Melcombe, in Dorset.

Edward I appointed Sir Peter Mallory a judge of the Court of Common Pleas in 1292. (Pat. 20 Edw. I.) From that date he served continuously until July 1309 (E. Foss: *Judges of England.*) In 1293, as Commissioner of Array, he was ordered to choose, arm and send, footmen (soldiers) in Nottinghamshire, Derbyshire, Lancashire, Cambridgeshire, Westmorland (?) and Yorkshire, to Chester to fight against the Welsh. He was summoned regularly to parliament from 1295 until his retirement the year before his death, including to the parliament called at Salisbury in 1296. Foss notes that the spelling of Mallory varies considerably in all the documents relating to Sir Peter; in one he is called 'de Malore'. This emphasises the truth of the contention that differences in surnames rose chiefly as the result of scribes' and copyists' personal preferences and have no genealogical significance in many instances. Foss also records that he was descended from 'Gislebert, a follower of the Conqueror, and of Anchitel, temp. Henry II' (i.e., between 1154 and 1189). This startling statement, which appears to also identify the first Mallory in England, is made without a qualifying reference. It may be so, although a Gislebert temp. 1066 has not so far been discovered in any other record of Mallorys in history.

The pedigrees for Tachebrook Mallory and Swinford, however, provide a more likely identity for Gislebert. If the remark that he was 'a follower of the Conqueror' is disregarded, he could be placed as Gilbert Mallory who appears in the Tachebrook pedigree as the son of Henry Mallory and grandson of the great Sir Anketil Mallory who died in 1187. The dates are possible: Gilbert is noted in the Pipe Rolls as owning land at Tachebrook in 1227, although his brother, Richard, was then lord of that manor (*V.C.H.*). A Gilbert Mallory appears in the Cal. Chart in 1270 and one in the Cal. Pat. in 1289. *See also* Sir Gilbert Mallory, kt., in the Balsall notes.

The Tachebrook Mallorys were descended from the Kirkby Mallory family. The first Simon of Draughton must have been Tachebrook Gilbert's son, not as Nichols's pedigree for Swinford states, the son of Henry. Sir Peter of Winwick was therefore probably the grandson of Gilbert and the great-great-grandson of Anketil.

Erdeswicke's Roll for 1295 blazons the arms of 'Sire Petrus Malaure' as 'd'Or 3 lupards passaunz de Sable' ('leopard' was sometimes synonymus with 'lion' in ancient heraldry). It is not clear whether these arms were granted to Sir Peter directly as representing England on the bench, or whether he was allowed them by right of an earlier grant. Burke gives them as the arms of Mallory of Draughton and the family continued to use them until Newbold Revel came into their possession together with the Revel arms, which they then adopted (*see* Newbold Revel).

Sir Peter married Matilda (Maude), daughter of Baron John de Bayeux and co-heir with her brother Stephen. The family, which came from Normandy, ranked as 'Great Barons'. They held many properties in Lincolnshire and the West Country. In addition, Matilda was the widow of the powerful Constable of Corfe Castle, Elias de Rabayne. He was a distinguished soldier, who fought in the Gascon War of 1251, and became notorious for having appropriated from the woods and quarries of his neighbour William de Canville, the materials to carry out his far-seeing improvements to the castle. When de Canville took him to court, Elias dismissed the charges with cheerful insoucience. The Sheriff did not regard the trespass in quite the same light, but in mitigation of de Rabayne, history reveals that his additions to the defences of the tower resulted in a stronghold which was to remain impregnable until the siege cannon of the 1640s reduced it to the impressive ruin which still stands guard over the pass between the downs.

Sir Peter held Winwick 'of his mother', but de Rabayne and Matilda also owned a house there (*see* Draughton). Matilda was his wife by 1303, for they both paid £1,000 to the Pope on behalf of Edward I in March of that year. In return, Edward was to pay them £60 annually, for the next 11 years 'from Bayeux Manor in Lincolnshire'.

In 1300 Sir Peter was summoned to fight the Scots. He was also one of the judges called to try Wallace (Turner), a stern duty in those harsh times. He was called to attend the king's coronation in 1308. Peter and Matilda were childless. When he died in 1310, his manor of Winwick passed to his elder brother, Sir Roger of Draughton, who was then aged sixty. (I.P.M. 4, Edw. II, No. 6). Sir Roger's son, the second Simon Mallory of Draughton and Swinford, succeeded to Winwick. The history of Winwick from 1313 until 1383 is given in the Draughton notes.

After 1383, this branch of the Mallory family adopted the Revel arms. They retained the manor of Winwick, probably as the main home of the heirs to Newbold Revel. Nothing further is known which treats of daily happenings at Winwick. Further research should being more anecdotes to light to add to the chapter on Newbold Revel, which covers it as a subsidiary holding until the time of Henry VIII. In 1513, Nichols Mallory, the last Mallory lord of Newbold Revel, died, and his properties passed to his two daughters. Each of these ladies married twice. The eldest, Dorothy Mallory, whose heirs were also daughters, inherited Winwick manor. Dorothy's eldest daughter by her first husband, Edward Cave, was Katherine. She took the manor of Winwick to her marriage with Sir Thomas Andrews of Charwelton (Northants.). Properties in the West Country (which are discussed under Dorset) also belonged to this branch of the Mallory family. The younger daughter, Margaret Cave, was married first, to Thomas Boughton of Causton (Warwcs.).

Dorothy Mallory's sister, Margaret, who inherited Newbold Revel manor, married as her second husband, one J. Cope. In 1978, the owners of Winwick had the same surname: 450 years lie between. The writer is indebted to Mr. Dennis Cope for his kind interest in this work and for supplying particulars relating to the manor. The original mansion was considerably larger, but even in its diminished grandeur the exterior presents the well-preserved and gracious picture of a Tudor manor house; gabled, stone mullioned, with fascinating chimneys and diamond panes. Parts of the interior date from the 14th century. The main staircase is medieval. There are no recognisable Mallory embellishments, like those at Papworth St Agnes. The moulded ceiling in the saloon is decorated with a fleur-de-lys and the initials 'P.H.', the history of which has vanished with their owners, although there are rumours of a Carolean connection.

The long years of loving care devoted to the yew hedges, parterres and lawns, provide a charming vista through the remarkable entrance arch, embodying all the traditional beauty and peace of England's ancient pleasure grounds. Sir Thomas Mallory of Newbold Revel walked here and lived from time to time in the house. If he were the author of *Le Morte d'Arthur,* part of the book may have been written at Winwick.

Church, St Michael and All Angels; Guildsborough hundred; 7 miles S.E. of Newbold Revel (Warwcs.); 10 miles N.W. of Northampton.

Charwelton

The church of Charwelton dreams quietly in a flowery field at the end of a narrow country lane some way outside the present village. It contains an exciting collection of Mallory arms on tombs of the Andrews family. Unfortunately, the oldest one is not clear enough to photograph well. There is, however, one very clear set of carved arms on a later tomb. The blurred arms appear to be of a forked-tail lion rampant, but it is by no means certain. No colours survive. Baker, in 1822, said these arms were 'Or and Gules' and identified them as Mallory arms.

The manor of Thorney at Charwelton belonged to the distinguished family of Andrews, who married into at least two other families who were also connected with the Mallorys. These were the family of Cotton (*see* Leicestershire) and Isham (*see* Cambridgeshire). The fourth Sir Thomas Andrews (Sheriff of Northamptonshire 3, Edw. VI, and twice in the reign of Philip and Mary) who died in 1563–4, married twice. His first wife was Katherine, eldest daughter of Edward Cave and Dorothy Mallory, co-heiress of the Newbold Revel and Winwick Mallorys.

Fig. 2. Winwick Manor House, home of the Newbold Revel Mallorys. Impression by S.V.M.S. after a water colour by J. S. Barry (both descendants of George Mallorie of Kilham, v. 1629).

Katherine died during the reign of 'Bloody' Mary. She is buried with Sir Thomas and his second wife in a life-sized alabaster tomb in the north chapel of the church. The figures are beautifully carved and dressed. Sir Thomas wears a collar of 'Esses'. Katherine, in a delightful Tudor costume, has a coif enclosing her hair, chains and a locket around her throat, many finger rings and pretty shoes with Tudor roses carved on the soles. Seven sons kneel at their father's feet, three daughters before his lady. The inscription round the tomb, where it refers to Katherine, reads as follows:

> Sub isto tumio jacet Domina Katerina Andrews prima uxora Thoma Andrews mit. Una filia et heredum Edwardi Cave Armiger Que quidem Katerina obit Octavo die Augusti ano millimo quinquenstesimo quinto (etc.).

The arms on the tomb, carved in shallow relief and a rather galumping style, are in roundels and are seen to be as follows (colours given by Baker): 'Gules a saltire Or surmounted by another Vert' (Andrews) impaling 'Azure fretty Argent on a fess Or a greyhound courrant Sable (Cave of Winwick) impaling quarterly four coats-of-arms', viz., 'Ermine a chevron Gules a border engrailed Sable' (Revel and Mallory of Newbold Revel and Winwick), 'A lion (possibly) double-queued', 'Or 3 lions passant in pale Sable' (Mallory of Draughton and Winwick), 'Argent on a fess Azure between 3 boar's heads couped Sable a lion passant Gules' (Mallory ?). The latter is thought to be the arms of Mallory of Swinford and may represent the most correct description of their arms (*see also* Isleham and Newbold Revel).

Katherine's son, Sir Thomas Andrews the fifth (obit. 1590), also married twice. He produced 12 children. He was also Sheriff of Northamptonshire. His first wife was Frances, daughter of Sir John Cotton of Cambridgeshire, who died in 1567. His second wife was Mary, the daughter of Gregory Isham, who died in 1589. They are all remembered on a fine alabaster wall plaque at the west end of the church. It repeats many of the arms. On this memorial the lion has a single tail: Baker described it as 'Sable a lion rampant Or'. It seems to be the correct arms of the Kingston family and confirms P. J. C. Field's identification of the arms at Newbold Revel. (The double tailed lion does not rest easily, however, even so).

Katherine and her relatives owned property in the West Country (*see* that chapter).

The church has, as its only neighbour, a farm which belonged to the Buckingham Priory of Bittlesden. A Henry Mallory was abbot of Biddlesden in 1241. Biddlesden is on the border, four miles north-east of Buckingham, 20 miles south-east of Charwelton (*see* Holwell, Beds.).

Church, Holy Trinity; Fawsley Hundred (*see* Welton); 10 miles S.W. of Winwick.

Lichborough (Lychebarrowe): Mallory property before 1280 to 1572

A younger son of the first Sir Simon Mallory of Draughton, Sir William Mallory, was lord of Lichborough in 1280. He founded a line of men whose reckless deeds vie with those of their famous Warwickshire cousin. The manor was long in the possession of the family. They owned it before Winwick and Newbold Revel and after both those houses passed out of Mallory hands. It has a further interest for scholars since, in recent years, it has been suggested that the library there may have contained one of the manuscript copies of *Le Morte d'Arthur* (Kelliher).

Sir William's son, who was styled 'Richard of Lichborough' in 1315, died in 1329. His young son and heir, Peter, born after 1308, was under age at that time (Baker) and a Geoffrey de Cornwall claimed to be his guardian—a remunerative responsibility entitling him to dues from the estate and other perquisites. Peter's uncle, Simon the second of Draughton, quickly refuted this claim by proving that the Lichborough family were his enfeoffees from times past. They enjoyed a position which brought them favours from members of the royal family.

Peter was eventually knighted, but frequently found himself on the wrong side of the law. Fortunately, he had good friends who often successfully interceded on his behalf. His guarantors included the Black Prince and King David of Scotland, but in spite of such influential backing, he saw the inside of The Fleet and Newgate. In 1363 he and his son, Sir Giles, were released from the latter. Three years later, he found himself obliged to transfer all his properties at Lichborough to his cousin, Sir John of Winwick. It appears to have been a gentleman's agreement, possibly to protect the Mallory inheritance from his creditors, for he was accused of owing money even to the queen. 'Sir John, Agnes his wife and their son Nicholas' were granted the rights of the property 'for their lives' in return for paying the annual dues to the overlord of the barony of Burford, a nominal 'broad arrow if required' (*see* Escheat 6, Edw. VI, below) and a yearly sum of £10, together with a peppercorn rent of 'a single rose', to Sir Peter and his heir, in perpetuity.

Sir Peter's descendants, when available, continued to inhabit the manor. Baker describes the seals attached to the relevant deed, which was stamped with two coats-of-arms. One an unspecified 'cross', perhaps referring to a connection with the Knights Hospitaller and one, 'a fess between three boars' heads couped', which reinforces Dugdale's description of the arms of Sir John of Winwick. (*See* Newbold Revel and Charwelton.) It has not been possible to place a John Mallory who was rector of Lichborough church in 1349.

Sir Giles Mallory, whose career apparently suffered no reverses from accompanying his father to gaol in 1363, married the heiress of a wealthy Herefordshire knight, Sir Richard de Baskerville. Giles held important positions in the Earl of Warwick's household. He was M.P. for Northamptonshire in 1386, 1388, 1393, 1401 and 1403, and was a credit to his house during the reigns of two kings, although in 1381 a commission was sent to the Sheriff of Hereford about the 'Wastes and destruction' alleged to have been committed in the king's castle and lordship of Erdesley, Hereford, by Giles Mallory, kt.; this was followed in 1385 by a warrant for his arrest. Taken with him, to appear before the king and council, were Canon William Weston, Sir Warin Lucy, Thomas the Parson of Bruynton, and the Priors of Canons Ashby. Sir Giles of Lichborough is the only man of that name to be found in the contemporary Mallory pedigrees. If he were the one who figured in such depredations, and if the charge, which recalls those levelled against Thomas of Newbold Revel, was not malicious, his behaviour is difficult to explain. A later namesake at Greens Norton was even more improvident (*see* below).

Feudal Aids notes that in 1428 the next Sir John of Winwick levied a fine on Sir Giles's son, Richard of Lichborough. Field accredits this Richard (a cousin of Sir Thomas of Newbold Revel) with at least two sons, John of Lichborough who had no descendants, and a William, styled 'of Northants, Gent.' who was certainly alive between 1435 and 1438. Baker lists a Robert Mallory, alive in 1471, who is next in the history of the manor. He may have been a third son of Richard. The will of a William Mallore, probate 1438 (Guildhall MS. 9171/4), gives a Robert Mallore as executor. (Transcript courtesy N. Rogers). Beneficiaries were Roger Poynant, Robert Dysse and Richard Cabull. Commissary Court of London.

The erratic and baleful doom, which periodically influenced Mallory fortunes, manifested itself once again in the affairs of Robert's son John and others of his Mallory relatives. When Henry VII came to power in 1485, he imprisoned his most likely rival, the Earl of Warwick, and hastily called parliament to confirm the crown to himself and his heirs. Two years later a conspiracy was launched to put young Lambert Simnel on the throne as a fake Earl of Warwick. The rebels were defeated at Stoke in November 1488. The pseudo-Warwick's supporters were attainted of treason. Lambert Simnel was pardoned, but Henry amused himself by putting the poor child to work as his scullion. Among the ringleaders taken were 'John Mallary of Lichbarrowe, Robert Mallary of Fawsley, Gyles Mallary of Greysnorton and William Mallary of Stowe in Northamptonshire' (Rot. Parl, V6, p. 397). A Sir Robert Mallory was beheaded at Coventry in 1498. Was he Robert of Fawsley paying a traitor's debt 10 years later? Fawsley is 4 miles N.W. of Lichborough.

John of Lichborough fared better. He was only to endure a year in gaol, although his pardon did not return him to his original status. Henry VII seized the manor in 1489, together with other Mallory property. John died in 1521. The Newbold Revel branch of the family relinquished their rights over the manor after his death since their male line had ended with the death of Nicholas of Newbold Revel in 1513. Henry VIII magnanimously returned Lichborough to John's son, Thomas Mallory, Esquire (Pat. 13, Henry VIII). The patent refers to Lichborough, Farthington, Sewell and Blakesley.

Thomas Mallory, Esq., was of a steadier disposition. He married Anne, who outlived him, having produced at least four children. He added to the family estates, benefiting from Henry VIII's distribution of monastic lands in the same way as the Cambridgeshire Mallorys. He was King's Escheator and Commissioner for the Peace. In addition, he had the care and administration of the great forest of Whittlewood. He was a Lieutenant of the Forest in 1535, the year Elizabeth I was born.

Kelliher connects the family at this time with ownership of the Winchester manuscript copy of *Le Morte d'Arthur*. (Article in *Brit. Lib. Journal*, August 1977, and *Aspects of Malory*.). This suggestion reinforces the view that Thomas of Newbold Revel was the author of *Le Morte*. However, the Winchester manuscript is generally acknowledged to be only a copy of a previous manuscript and to be in two handwritings. It may therefore have originated elsewhere. Professor Griffith discovered a fascinating document at the British Library in 1978 whilst researching correspondence between Caxton and Lord Rivers. It is a single sheet of scribbles and verses, probably written not later than 1550, considerably over-written with the names 'Thomas',

'Thomas Malory', and one clear statement which says 'Thys hys robert Malory hys book'. (Sloane 779, fo. 155V.)

A William Risley is connected with the ownership of this document. He was at school with a grandson of the Sir William Mallory of Studley Royal (and Hutton Conyers) in Yorkshire, who owned Sloane 706, from which it appears that he was a collector. An earlier Sir William of Hutton Conyers had a son, Thomas, a younger son, Robert, and a grandson, Robert, alive between the years 1430 and the early 1500s. Sir William of Studley's grandson was Thomas Malory, rector of Northenden in Cheshire, born 1566, whose brother Robert was alive before 1594. The Papworth St Agnes (Sir) Thomas, possible author of *Le Morte*, had a son, Robert, who died in 1492. There are other names present on the sheet, which may be equally well connected either with Papworth or Lichborough. Alice Dryby, probably the grandmother of Thomas of Papworth, collected books. She bequeathed three of them in her will, probated 1412.

Thomas of Lichborough died in June 1552, still under an implied obligation to produce a broad arrow for his rental. (Escheat 6, Edw. VI, No. 53.) His will was proved on 19 July 1552. The following year saw another controversial Mallory lord of Lichborough in the person of Robert, Thomas's eldest son, aged 25 years in 1552. (Robert had a brother, Richard, and a sister, Susan, who careers have not been followed.) He married Ursula. Their first child, Thomas, was born in 1550 at Lichborough. Two years later, brother Richard faced a charge of committing a robbery in Bedfordshire, as a result of which he was fined and consigned to the Tower. He seems to have found the money to pay his way out, but the Patent Rolls for 1557 record that he became involved in a case of perjury regarding a Parson White's claim to Lamport Rectory, against John Isham. The matter was taken to the Star Chamber. Mallory lost the suit, which the shaky Lichborough finances could ill afford. There seems to have been a deal of bad feeling between the Ishams and the Mallories despite their earlier connections. In 1568 he sold off some of the Lichborough lands to a Nicholas Phyppes (Cal. Pat.). By 1572 Robert's financial troubles obliged him to part with the rights of Lichborough, which he sold to a William Stone and John Grey. The manor later passed to a Sir James Needham, but Baker states that the Mallorys continued to live at Lichborough 'in indigent circumstances' into the 19th century.

No coat-of-arms has been described for this family. Burke and other authorities list the following arms, vaguely described as 'Mallory Co. Northants'; 'Purple. A lion rampant Or collared Gules. Crest A Nag's head Or'. (Presumable a single tail?) These arms might apply to Lichborough (*see* Woodford). A differenced Draughton or Swinford coat-of-arms would seem to be more appropriate, however.

The church, dedicated to St Martin, contains no recognisable Mallory memorials. It is possible that part of the house may be extant, incorporated in 'Lichborough House' which dates from the 17th century. Baker, however, said that it was known as 'The Spinney' and had been demolished in about 1800. *Note*: The paper by Hilton Kelliher in *Aspects of Malory* contains many documented proofs of the Lichborough descent and should be studied by persons whose particular interest lies in this family. There are more anecdotes about the various escapades of this branch.

Fawsley Hundred (*see* Welton); 12 miles S.W. of Draughton.

Woodford-on-Nene (Denford, not Woodford Halse): Mallory property from at least
     1558 to 1622: also Saddington (Leics.) and 'Clendon' (Northants.)

The coat-of-arms of the Mallorys of Woodford given by Burke, is 'or a lion rampant double queued Gules collared Argent. On the shoulder a fleur-de-lis of the first. Crest. A Nag's head Gules crined Or (Gold mane), charged with a fleur-de-lis of the last'. (But *see* 'Symon the Elder's' tomb, below.) These arms are similar to those of Mallory of Studley Royal (Yorks.), with differences, and those of the Cambridgeshire Mallorys, although there the collar is a coronet. All derive from Kirkby Mallory, but only those from Yorkshire (including their descendants in Cheshire), and Cambridgeshire, bore the crest.

The only continuous pedigree for the Woodford family is for the years 1513 to 1618, although a descent from Mallorys alive in 1419 may be suggested, based partly on a pedigree researched by the Rev. H. Longdon about 1920, partly from Bridges and Baker. It will be helpful to repeat part of the information from the section on the manor of Saddington in Leicestershire (above).

The first Mallory in the pedigree for Woodford is John Mallory of Saddington. In the Leicestershire notes it will be seen that a William Mallory and his wife, Margaret, held Saddington in 1419. John seems to have been a descendant, probably their son. Papworth St Agnes (Cambs.) can provide a Sir William and Margaret alive at that time whose family bore suitable arms, but the Cambridgeshire pedigrees only lists one son, Thomas. A Sir William and wife, 'Marger', held at Bytham (Lincs.) in 1443 (possibly the same). Another William Mallory, alive in 1435, was a Lichborough descendant of the Draughton Mallorys (*see* Lichborough coat-of-arms). These are the only possibilities available if the arms are to be taken as the most significant criterion, although the omission of names in pedigrees may perhaps be disregarded.

There is a possibly misleading trail to follow based on Christian names. Five Mallorys of Woodford were all named Symon. This name was popular with the Mallorys of Draughton and the Mallorys of Holwell (Beds.). In neither case would the arms support a connection with either of these, however.

The next name is Symon Mallory, styled 'Symon Mallory of Saddington co. Leics and Clendon co. Nhants, Gent. Son and heir (of John)'. His will, dated June 1513, was not proved. (*Arch. Northants.* 1st series A216.) His wife was Joan Perwick, daughter of Richard or John Perwick of Lubbenham, Leics. They had four sons: Robert, William, John and George. Only the line of the heir has been followed up. Robert is styled 'of Clendon.' Saddington seems to have gone from the inheritance, perhaps to one of the other sons. Robert's wife was Elizabeth, daughter of John Norwich of Brampton, Northants. Following the fashion of their day they christened two of their living sons by the same first name. There were six other children, the order given in the 1564 Visitation is different from that given by Longdon, who appears to have researched further into the particulars. (*Northants. Archivist.*)

The first son, known as 'Symon the Elder' lived to a great age, if we are to believe his brass memorial to be a portrait. He is recorded in John Isham's account book (*cf.* Rich, Lord Mayor of London) as a Mallory who paid his debts. He married Elizabeth, daughter of Jeremiah Alday of Ashe in Kent, but she brought him no offspring and when he died in 1580, the property was inherited by Symon No. 2, 'heir to his brother'. There were four other brothers; Phillip and John also died childless. Anthony 'of Southampton' married Alice Lambert. The records do not follow them. The last brother, Robert (second in the Visitation), is also only a name on the list. There were two daughters: Margaret, who married Richard Williams of Carlton, and Katherine, married to John Cotes of Islip.

'Symon the Younger' took to wife Dorothy, daughter of Maurice Tresham, Esq., of Newton (Northants.) by his second wife, Margaret Tanfield. Dorothy wrote her will on 30 March 1633, but she was to live six years more. Probated in 1639; Sir Rowland St John, K.B., her brother, Maurice Tresham, and her cousin, Robert Tanfield, were her executors. Dorothy's pleasant nature seems manifest in her bequests, the number of her children, and the wording of her epitaph. Her life was sufficiently joyous for her to anticipate the hereafter with pleasure, even after rearing no fewer than 15 little Mallorys (*see* below).

She bequeathed a 'guitter bole' to her first born, Symon. Perhaps it was a musical instrument, obviously regarded as a treasure.* Symon the fourth was lord of Woodford in 1618, so Dorothy was widowed about twenty years. Eight years previously he had married at Slipton a lady with the delightful name of Kate Garter, daughter of Bernard Garter of Brigstock. Of his 14 siblings, only two brothers and six sisters are recorded in Dorothy's will. The boys were William and Thomas, who may have had descendants.

Symon's little son, Symon the fifth (aged six in 1618 and mentioned in his grandmother's will), and his two daughters, Elizabeth and Dorothy, are the last members of the family to appear in the pedigree so far researched for the manor of Woodford (*see* Goddington, below).

The manor comprised several smaller manors, which the Mallorys acquired and sold at different times. They were already lords of the main manor of Woodford in 1558. Symon is recorded as 'Lord of the chief manor of Woodford' in 1570. (Sale of Trailley Place by Simon Norwich to Symon Mallory.) The other properties were a manor known as Piells (or Vaux), Thorleys manor (where Symon owned land in 1562) which he bought in 1585 from the son of the first Lord Vaux, and a manor called Clements.

After more than half a century, the Mallorys relinquished all their properties in Woodford, when Symon and Kate sold them to Baron Bletso. It seems their fortunes may have suffered a reverse. The last few years of the reign of King James (I and VI) provided several opportunities for Mallorys to become embroiled in doubtful enterprises.

At least one of the houses (Vaux) was still standing in 1930, but it has not been possible to identify the other manors from among the several ancient houses in the village. Rectory Farm which dates in part from the 13th century is known as 'The Old Manor House' (Pevsner). The manor of 'Clendon' was probably Glendon, now shown on the map as 'Glendon Hall', near Draughton (which returns us to the question of origins for Woodford Mallorys) and which was listed in the Doomsday Survey. It belonged to the manor of Rothwell and the Abbey of St Mary of Gretstain 'of the King'. The church held outright a miserable little community of peasants, consisting of 'four villagers, four small holdings and land for two ploughs and one slave to pull the plough'. There is no mention of the Mallory family holding there until about three hundred and fifty years later. The Corbet family also held land at Glendon.

There are two individuals who might have been Woodford descendants. In 1709 a William Mallory lived at Rushden, which is five miles from Woodford, and in 1777 another William Mallory lived at Wellingborough, which is eight miles away. The extant parish registers for Woodford commence in 1680. These have not been consulted, neither have the bishop's transcripts. Both may furnish more information in respect of this family.

In the church, St Mary's, there are two Mallory memorials. 'Symon the Elder' is commemorated in a brass some six feet in length, set in the floor south of the altar rails. (It is by far the most rewarding to a brass-rubber of all the Mallory brasses.) He is dressed in a very fancy suit of armour, the design of which repeats the pattern of the ruffs at his throat and wrists in curious frilly extensions of the shoulder guards. There are picot edges to the plates, which are ornamented with tiny flowers; frivolous decorations which are in contrast to the efficient-looking sword and dagger he carries and the sharp spurs at his heels. The face is a portrait, showing the lined visage and broken nose of an old warrior. He has curly hair, carefully combed moustaches and a smooth divided beard. He lies on his helmet and above his head is a beautiful shield charged with a fierce rampant lion whose tail is forked. Buried in the florid 'seaweed' and tassels of the mantling of the crest is a helm, the visor closed, surmounted by a somewhat inebriate horse's head. The inscription reads:

> 'here lyethe symon malory the elder efquyer, who dyed the — daye of —
> in the yere of our Lorde God MCCCCCLXXX and whos soule is in the
> greate marcye of Jefus Chrift our favyor'.

It will be noted that both the day and the month of his demise are omitted. This suggests that he died away from home (in battle, in gaol?) or perhaps in an epidemic. The coat-of-arms does not bear the distinguising fleur-de-lys noted above. This cadency mark, indicating a sixth son, may refer to another descendant of the Saddington line. The nag's head and the lion's seem to have collars, but these are frills rather than circlets or coronets and may only be further examples of the exuberant style of the carver. There is some doubt as to the correct order of Symon's brothers. Since there were six in all, the differenced arms may even be those of 'Symon the Younger'.

On the floor of the north side of the church, near the altar rails, is the tomb of the amiable Dorothy. Only 59 years separate the two brasses, but they represent totally different schools of lettering. Symon's is carved in medieval script, Dorothy's is inscribed in beautifully clear Roman letters and the date is given in numerals. It reads:

HERE VNDER THIS STONE RESTETH IN HOPE OF A IOYFVLL RESVRECTION
THE BODY OF DOROTHY MALLORY THE WIFE OF SYMON MALLORY ESQVIRE
OF WOODFORD IN THE COVNTY OF NORTHAMPTON WHOE HAD 15 SONNES
AND DAUGHTERS AND WAS BVRIED THE 5 DAY OF IVNE IN THE YEARE OF
OVR LORD GOD 1639

Fig. 3. Simon Malory 'The Elder', died 1580,
from Woodford-on-Nene church, Northants.

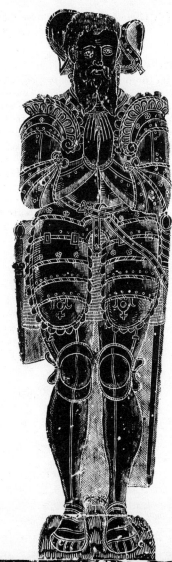

The whole is enclosed in a decorative border. It will be noted that the name Mallory is spelled with one 'l' in 1580 and with two in 1639.

In 1558, 'Symon the Elder' was granted the advowson of St Mary's. It was still granted to Symon (V. 1618) in 1622.

Woodford, Navisland 100; 10 miles E of Draughton (Northants.); 22 miles W. of Papworth St Agnes (Cambs.); 7 miles W. of Shelton (Beds.), owned by P.S.A. 1387–1714; 28 miles N. of Holwell (Beds.).

Saddington (only two buildings on modern map), Gartree 100; 10 miles S.E. of Kirkby Mallory (Leics.)

Glendon (only Glendon Hall on modern maps), Rothwell 100; 5 miles N.E. of Draughton (Northants.).

Note: 'Guitter bole':

If 'guitter' is the noun and 'bole' the adjective: (1) *'Guittern. Cet instrument apparüt dans les ecrits du Proche-Orient du IX-ieme siècle, possède une forme rond. L'instrument occidental a un dos plat'.* R. Fabrizio, *Instrumental Musik des Mittleaters.* (2) 'Cittern: an instrument similar to the lute'.'Gittern: medieval instrument similar to the guitar'. R. Illing. *Penguin Dictionary of Music.* (3) 'But cithern string and glittern player, Their merry mirth could ne'er recall'. 'Pearl', anon, 14th-century Elegy. Trans.: Tolkien. (4) 'Chitarrone. A long-necked lute developed in Italy in the early 17th century' (? 'Guitter bole' a corruption). 'Made of rare woods often lavishly inlaid with ivory, certainly a treasure'. John Isaacs. Lute maker. Private correspondence.

If 'bole' be the noun and 'guitter' the adjective: (1) 'It may be a bowl made of precious materials or a rare object of interest. Possibly a gold-mounted cup similar to the coconut cups of which several survive.' Keeper, V. & A. Museum. Private correspondence. (2) However, in Papworth St Agnes wills, we have mention of a 'gilte salte' (not guilte) and a bowl is described as 'my pot of silver and gilt' (1584).

Notes:

Calendar Fine Rolls:
    1497, Feb. 24. Writ to Escheator. Emmot Malerey, widow, co. Northants.
    1498, Nov. 16. Commitment to Simon Malory, etc., to hold Gedyngton, Northants for 40 years.
London Marriage Lics. St Barts.-the-Less. 1631, Dec. 2. (Harl. Pubs.).
    Simon Malory of Newton by Goddingtin, co. Northants. Aged about 20, son of Simon Malory of the same Esq., and Mary Melhuish of the same, daughter of John Mellhuish of the same, draper.

Northampton and Norfolk

Drayton with Lowick and Isham (not Draughton): (Mallory ladies and cousins)
    Felbrigg(e) Hall, and Blackfriars' Hall, Norwich

The histories of all these properties are included here because the same individuals are connected with them all. In 1328 the manor of Drayton was owned by the family of Drayton, who had changed their name from de Vere before 1211. The first lord of the manor was Simon de Drayton whose daughter married Sir Henry Green (Grene, Greene), Lord Chief Justice of England in the time of Edward III. He was a grandson of Thomas de Boketon (Boughton) and Lucy, a daughter of Eudo Zouch(e) of

Harryngworth, a family with Mallory connections elsewhere. Sir Henry Green died in 1369, succeeded by his eldest son, Sir Thomas Green of Greens Norton, whose lands were respited, passing to his brother, another Sir Henry Green. The manors of Boughton and Isham also belonged to this family, their descendants establishing separate branches as time passed (*cf.* grandson of Dorothy [Mallory] Cave, Warwick-shire notes). *See also* Halstead, *Succinct Genealogies.*

Sir Henry married Matilda, daughter of Sir Thomas Maudit of Wiltshire, their descendants continued as lords of Drayton and Lowick. One of Sir Henry's sisters, Margaret, also married into the Zouche family. Her husband was William Zouche of Harryngworth and Totnes (Devon). Henry's brother, Nicholas of Isham, was husband of Joan de Bruys, a descendant of Robert the Bruce. In 1358 she eloped from the convent of Nun Eaton to marry Nicholas. She was the rightful heiress to the Rutland property of Exton. Nicholas was contemporary with the Thomas Green of Isham who married Ala Mallory (*see* Sudborough). There were many Thomas Greens in this family. The pedigree for the Green family may be built up only from Inquisitions, etc., associated with their many houses. Some of the properties are described quite separately and many of the wives are not named. The families at Isham, Boughton, Greens Norton and other Green properties, seem to be closely related. Some of the Thomases holding at one, may have been the same Thomas holding at another. If Ala's husband was only 'of Isham' during his father's lifetime, it is possible that she was an ancestor of Henry VIII's last wife, Catherine Parr.

Sir Henry Green forfeited his properties after the defeat of Richard II. His sons, Sir Ralph and John, successfully petitioned for restitution of all the manors. 'John married Isobelle' whose son, Thomas, successfully acquired Sudborough (below), was the son of Ala and Thomas. Sir Ralph Green married Katherine (Catherine) Mallory in 1415 and settled Lowick (including brother John's share) on her, for life. (Cal. Pat. and Clo. Rolls 3, Henry V.) Two short years later, Sir Ralph was dead. Katherine ordered a superb tomb in 1418, in which she intended to join him when her time came. The instructions to the 'Kervers' indicate that she was entitled to bear arms (*see* church below). The arms have disappeared from the tomb chest now. There was armorial glass at Lowick church in 1685 (Halstead). 'Or a lion rampant Gules', single tail, appears (? Mallory). Her second husband, Sir Simon Felbrigg, appears to have been a sterner, older man; one wonders if she was allowed to refuse his hand? The history of Lowick is interrupted for a convenient digression to Felbrigg.

Katherine's father was an Anketil Mallory. There was an Anketil in the Cambridge-shire Mallory line who might have been he, but to assume this strains the dates rather. The guidebook to Felbrigg church (Norfolk) states that he was 'Anketil Mallory of Winwick'. Unfortunately, no Anketil is to be found in any pedigree associated with Winwick (Northants.) or its branches. Another Anketil appears briefly at Botley in 1444 (Ped. F). The author spent many months, helped by the staff at Felbrigg and at the Strangers' Hall in Norwich, unsuccessfully seeking to establish the arms of Katherine Mallory and therefore of her father's house. If she inherited arms and was an heiress, there is less support for a connection with Papworth.

Sir Simon Felbrigg, knight of the Garter (with a Garter stall plate still to be seen in St George's Chapel) was a knight banneret and standard bearer to Richard II. (Sir

Henry Green, executed by Bolingbroke in 1399, was also a friend of King Richard.) Felbrigg's beautiful estates in Norfolk, with a well-furnished mansion built upon the cellars of his manor house, are now owned by the National Trust. Sir Simon had been married previously to Margaret, daughter of the Duke of Teschen, a close relative of King Wenceslaus and his sister, the first of King Richard's queens. He was related to the Bigods and Scropes.

Simon Felbrigg fared better than Henry Green, he not only kept his head, but retained the pension granted to him by the usurped king, and continued to serve under Henry IV and Henry V, fighting in the wars with France. Later in life he and his wife devoted themselves to the Dominican Order in Norwich. The remains of the extensive friary, known as Blackfriars and St Andrew's Hall, are open to the public today. Sir Simon, who died in 1442/3, was buried before the altar in the chancel. The site has been covered by the floor of the Victorian 'improvements' and the tomb hidden from view. Lady Felbrigg was a co-benefactor of this order. After her death a tower was raised, embellished with their coats-of-arms (guide book to the abbey). In 1712 the tower collapsed and no record remains of Katherine's arms, although a pair of fine corbels, low on the cloister walls, may represent Sir Simon and his lady.

There is a letter written in 1445 to John Paston, their neighbour in Norfolk and another benefactor of the Blackfriars, by Richard Clere, who was a member of the royal household. He rejoices that the sad, mad king, Henry VI 'is well amended'. He asks to be remembered to 'my Lady Felbrigg'. She died in 1459 (or 1461) just as the Lancastrians were rallying again. According to some authorities, she, too, was buried in St Andrew's Hall. She and Sir Simon share the distinction of having two tombs each (see below). John Wymondham (Windham), who features as a considerable villain in the Paston letters, acquired Felbrigg by an arrangement with Sir Simon, who directed that Katherine should retain it until her death. The Windham family built the present gracious house which was lived in by their descendants until 1969.

The history of the Northamptonshire properties is now resumed. After the death of Sir Ralph Green, Katherine held Drayton and Lowick 'of the Queen'. In 1428 Sir Simon Felbrigg held lands that had once belonged to Simon de Drayton. He also held part of a fee at Isham, which he shared with Thomas Green and others. He retained an interest in the Green property in 1442/43.

Drayton manor house, absorbed into Lowick, has expanded continually as the centuries passed. The present moated pile still contains part of the original house which Simon de Drayton was granted permission to crenellate in 1328. The Mordaunt family (see Sussex) held it in the late 15th century and it remains the home of the Earls of Peterborough. It may be visited by arrangement. The church, which is at Lowick, is dedicated to St Peter. The Greens built much of it. Their main family church at Greens Norton once contained tombs and memorials to a great number of Greens. (See V.C.H. Northants., V.1 for identification of tombs.) Once again, Victorian enthusiasts smashed these priceless artefacts and records of our history and piled them up in disarray outside.

At Lowick, however, their memorials survive, so that we are able to go there today and marvel at the work of Thomas Prentys and Robert Sutton, who for £40 carved the lovely effigies of Sir Ralph and Katherine. The order and instructions for the tomb are still extant. The alabaster tomb chest upon which they lie, touchingly hand-in-hand, a comely knight in impeccable armour, and a slender young lady of fashion. She wears a graceful gown with buttoned sleeves, a sideless surcoat or cote-hardie (some writers say both, but books on costume do not agree about these garments), a mantle with flowing cords, and rings on all her fingers. At her little feet sit two pet dogs, one with bells on his collar, one with a ruff. The long night's dream was to be perfumed with censers, swung by the two angels who guard her pillow. She wears a jaunty head-dress, her hair puffed out above each ear in golden nets. A coronet of flowers on her brow carries a veil at the back. The memorial to the 5th Earl of Arundel in the Fitzalan Chapel is very similar. The stone gablettes and his lady's costume are the same, except for the countess's coronet. The tomb is contemporary with the one at Lowick. Not young lovers, their hands are folded in prayer.

Note: It has not been possible to discover the identity of 'Gyles Mallary of Grenysnorton' attainted in 1487/8 (*see* Lichborough), nor his family connections with Greens Norton. Sir Thomas Green, last of the Green family at Greens Norton, died in 1506.

Drayton, Lowick: Huxloe 100; 7 miles N.E. of Kettering (Sudborough further north).

Greens Norton: Fawsley 100; 25 miles S.W. of Kettering, 5 miles S. of Lichborough.

Isham: Orlingbury 100; 3 miles S. of Kettering.

Fitzalan Chapel: Arundel Castle, Sussex.

Boughton

Possibly the site where the Wentworth family built their hall in 1844. (Not Boughton House, the home of the Duke of Buccleuh, at Geddington, near Kettering.) The churches at Greens Norton, Isham and Boughton have not been visited.

Felbrigg Hall: at Felbrigg

The church, dedicated to St Margaret, is in the pastures which surround the house. It contains a wonderful succession of brass memorials. Sir Simon Felbrigg appears with his first wife, surrounded by an impressive array of arms. His personal arms include a red rampant lion with a single tail on a golden shield, confusingly similar to the arms of the Mallorys. (Perhaps it should be noted that Papworth's *Ordinary of Arms* gives a lion salient, not rampant, for the arms of Felbrigg. However, all extant Felbrigg artefacts depict a lion rampant.)

15 miles N. of Norwich; 2 miles S.W. of Cromer.

Sudborough: Mallory property from 1341 (passed as dowry)

The ownership of the manor of Sudborough was in dispute for years between members of nearly all the early branches of the Mallory family and demonstrates how their affairs were intertwined. This account is, in consequence, involved and disjointed in order to draw together all the individuals concerned. Many are the subject of quite different histories in other chapters, to which the reader should refer. The Green family is described in greater detail under Lowick, etc. (above).

The Mallorys acquired one-third part of Sudborough from Sir Nicholas de la Beche, who died before 1341. By 1358 there were two Mallorys dealing with this property (Rate grants). One was 'William Mallory of Sudborough', the other, an 'Anketyn Mallory'. 'William of Sudborough' died in 1360. A William Mallory, son of Richard Mallory of Holwell (Beds.), also died in 1360. His brother held Welton (Northants.). It seems likely, therefore, that these Williams were one. Welton was part of the Kirkby Mallory (Leics.) inheritance. Sudborough was later to be in the Papworth St Agnes inheritance, and Sir Anketil Mallory, last lord of Kirkby Mallory, is thought to also have been the first Anketil Mallory connected with the manor of Papworth St Agnes (Cambs.). It seems that the 'Anketyn' connected with Sudborough was perhaps also Anketil of Kirkby Mallory, although if this were so, he filled in inordinate number of roles. All the dates, however, make this identification just probable (see Cambridge-shire). When 'William of Sudborough' died, the property passed to 'Anketyn' who immediately settled it on his daughter, Ala Mallory, and her husband, Thomas Green of Isham, and their heirs.

In 1445 Sir William Mallory of Papworth St Agnes (the son of Sir Anketil) died seised of Sudborough, which he left to his son, Sir Thomas of Papworth St Agnes. His right to inherit it was challenged by the descendants of the Green family. After his death, Sudborough was granted once and for all to his cousin, Thomas Green (I.P.M. 9 and 10 Edw. IV, No. 16).

One-third of Sudborough was given to Sir Ralph Green as part of the dowry of his wife, Katherine (Catherine) Mallory, daughter of another Anketil Mallory. The V.C.H. describes her as 'another daughter of Anketil', implying that she was Ala's sister, but Katherine did not die until a century later, and Ala, to have been married in 1360, would have been born some hundred, or more, years before Katherine's demise (see Lowick). The third and final portion of Sudborough was owned in 1345 by Sir Thomas Wake, who sold his share to the Drayton family who preceded the Greens at Drayton (Lowick). The Wake family appear from time to time elsewhere in Mallory history. The complete Sudborough property became absorbed into the Lowick inheritance sometime before 1534 and there is no recognisable separate manor house today.

Huxloe 100; Church: All Saints; *V.C.H. Northants.*,V.3, 246.

Delapré Abbey

The abbey was founded during the reign of King Stephen as a house for Cluniac nuns. It was south of the river Nene on the outskirts of Northampton. Two Mallory ladies became Abbesses of Delapré, Emma Malore, who was elected in 1274 and died in 1282, and 84 years later, Joan Mallore, who died in 1394. (Linc. Episc., Regs.). The nuns of this sisterhood held rather independent views, earning reprimands from their male superiors for frivolous behaviour. In 1538 the abbey was surrendered to Henry VIII. It suffered many alterations, especially in the 19th century, and today it functions as the County Record Office.

Earls Barton, etc.

The Abbess of Delapré held the manor of Thorp at Earls Barton in 1349; known as Thorp-by-Barton in 1375. In the same hundred is the village of Holcot, where a Thomas Mallory was rector shortly after 1450. Although unlikely to have been a knight, he would no doubt have received an education sufficient to have written *Le Morte*. Nothing further is known of him, however, and he is unplaced in the Pedigrees. The church, St Mary and All Saints, was in the gift of the Knights of St John.

Hamfordshoe 100; all near Wellingborough, south of Draughton.

Chapter Four

CAMBRIDGESHIRE AND HUNTINGDONSHIRE

MANY REFERENCES in this chapter are from material in the Cambridge City Reference Library. The work of A. T. Martin, Professor R. Griffith, documents in the P.R.O. and private correspondence with Sir John Corbet, Bt., Professor Griffith, the Welsh Herald Extraordinary, the Lord Mayor's office and the Guildhall Library, provided other information. Professor Griffith also kindly made available transcripts of the 'Proof of Age' and the will of Thomas of Papworth. There are no Mallory papers deposited in the Cambridge County Record Office. This chapter also provides details of the family of another distinguished Papworth Mallory, Sir Richard, who was Lord Mayor of London in 1564 and Sheriff of London in 1558. The Huntingdon Record Office provided some additional Mallory information.

The *Notable gentlemen of Cambridgeshire and Huntingdonshire* included Sir William Mallory of Papworth St Agnes, Knight of the Shire in 1433; Anthony Mallory of Papworth St Agnes, High Sheriff (1506, 1515, 1516, 1517, 1519, 1532); (Sir) William Mallory of Papworth St Agnes, High Sheriff, 1564 and 1565; and a member of the gentry of the county (1564, 1575), Sir William Mallory of Papworth St Agnes. In 1980 no family surnamed Mallory remains in either of these counties.

Papworth St Agnes: Mallory property 1416 to 1635/37

The manors of Papworth St Agnes (Nether or Lower Papworth) and Papworth Everard (Upper Papworth) are on opposite sides of Ermine Street. The boundary between Cambridgeshire and Huntingdonshire runs through the house at Papworth St Agnes. For convenience, these manors will be written as P.S.A. and P.E. in this chapter. Early in the 13th century, P.S.A. was known as 'Russell's Manor'; the name was altered to P.S.A. when it became the property of the Papworth family, and it has been so called ever since. An Agnes de Pappewarda lived there in the 13th century.

In 1415 William Papworth 'Chyvaler', lord of P.S.A., died (I.P.M. 3, Henry III, No. 28, new number C/138/12/28). He appears to have been acquainted with an Anketil Mallory ('Anketyn Malore Chyvaler') as early as 1387. (*See* Shelton, Beds.) Some pedigrees suggest that this Anketil's family descended from the branch that held Holwell (Beds.) and which may also have held Sudborough (Northants.). There is no record of a later relationship existing between the Bedfordshire branches.

The Papworth Mallorys owned Shelton before Papworth and continued to use the house at Shelton long after they had passed from the Cambridge scene.

The descent given for the Mallorys of Holwell provides a succession which seems to agree with that of Sudborough, a property in the later P.S.A. inheritance, but the arms of the P.S.A. Mallorys favour a descent from Anketil of Kirkby Mallory, rather than a direct father-to-son inheritance from Holwell, where there is some evidence to suggest that the arms borne by the heirs of Holwell may have been a demi-lion rampant (*see* discussion under Isleham). It is possible that since the Shelton and Holwell Mallorys were earlier related through Kirkby Mallory (*see* Welton, Kirkby Mallory and Bramcote), that Anketil received Sudborough by a sideways relationship with William Mallory of Holwell (obit. 1360). No contemporary documents referring to this William have been seen by the writer. Sudborough was a source of periodic family disputes and was legally the property of their relatives, the Greens.

Sir William Papworth's widow, Alice Papworth, died a year later (I.P.M. 4, Hen. III, No. 24, new number C/138/19/24). They left the manor of P.S.A. to 'William Mallory, son of Sir Anketil Mallory, and in case of failure of heirs to William Mallory, to Elizabeth daughter and heir of Thomas Malore now defunct. Elizabeth aged 20 years'. These words describe the family of Kirkby Mallory Anketil at that time and it would seem to be too much of a coincidence, even for Mallory history, to expect that there were two sets of contemporary characters fitting that specification.

From the wills of Anketil and Alice (Dryby) Mallory it may be deduced that their son, William, was still alive when his father died and would have been at least 22 years old in 1412 when his mother died. This agrees reasonably well with P.S.A. William Mallory who was 'aged 30' in 1416 when Alice Papworth died. The will of Alice Dryby also contains a reference to 'Elizabeth daughter of Sir Thomas Maloree Kt.' (*see* Bramcote, Warwcs.).

What the origins of the P.S.A. Mallorys may have been and what the connection was between the Papworths and the Mallorys, remain inscrutable, but two solutions may be suggested by the inclusion of Papworth arms in the quartered shields in the house. An earlier Mallory may have married a Papworth, or William may have been brought up in the Papworth household and a child marriage arranged with an unrecorded Papworth daughter who died young. This is not unlikely in view of the acquaintance known to have existed between the two families, and the customs of the time.

In the Noble Collection, a son of Sir William and Alice Papworth is noted in manuscript. He was John Papworth, who seems to have died in 1376, possibly an infant.

In the Leicestershire Visitations, 1619, Ped. Moton, William is noted as having no legal heirs, perhaps it was a legal protection of the inheritance of the Kirkby Mallory family.

The wills and description of arms, appear to confirm the descent of the Papworth Mallorys from Anketil of Kirkby Mallory. If P.S.A. William Mallory was the second son of a man (Anketil of Kirkby Mallory) who had been dead for more than 20 years and whose mother had re-married and if he had removed to another county, it would not be surprising if he was overlooked in the Visitation of Leicestershire in 1619. If Alice Dryby were his mother, her own connections in Cambridgeshire become more significant (*see* Isleham). She was the 'Lady of Bytham' (Lincs.). Nichols's footnotes on Swinford record that a 'Sir William Malory and wife Marger'' 'held at 'Castel Bytham' (Fines, Leics, 21. H.6) in 1443. They could be the P.S.A. family.

P.S.A., held 'of the King in Chief' became the principal seat of the head of the family. The Mallorys led restless lives, continually journeying between their houses and having much business in London. Many of the family's children born in Cambridgeshire were baptized at Shelton or at neighbouring Deane.

William Mallory, who inherited from Alice Papworth, was born in 1386 (aged '30 and more' in 1416). He served as Knight of the Shire for Cambridgeshire in 1433; he died in 1445. He may have had more than one wife, the first being perhaps a daughter of the Papworths and mother of Margaret Mallory (*see* below). His last wife's name was also Margaret. The length of time that elapsed between the probable date of birth of his first recorded daughter, Margaret (inferred from the date of knighting of her own son, Thomas Corbet), and the date of birth of William's son, Thomas, suggests that a common mother for all William's children is unlikely. His 'daughter', Margaret Mallory, married Sir Robert Corbet of Moreton Corbet in Shropshire in about 1400. Since Margaret (Mallory) Corbet's eldest son, Thomas, was knighted in 1422, a date for her birth in about 1385 is indicated. (Perhaps, child marriages being the custom, Margaret had married at a tender age.) This suggests that she was perhaps Sir William Mallory's sister and not his daughter.

The Corbet family, great Marcher Lords who came with William the Conqueror, built one of the defensive border castles, Castle Caux, and another castle at their present seat in Moreton Corbet. Considerable ruins of the latter and subsequent building still stand next to the church in the centre of the village. The main line of Corbet barons descended from the union of Sir Robert and Margaret Mallory. Their eldest son, Sir Thomas Corbet (knighted in 1422 according to Corbet family records, but called 'Esquyer' in 1432 and 'Knight' in 1433 elsewhere), died in 1436, before his father. Their second son, Sir Roger Corbet, inherited after his father's death in about 1439. 'The Corbet family were staunch Lancastrians' (A. Corbet). Robert was ancestor Q. 115745 of the Prince of Wales, generation XVII (Paget).

The mother of Sir Robert Corbet, husband of Margaret Mallory, was another Margaret. She was the daughter of Sir Giles de Erdington of Shawbury, and she owned the manor of Shawbury, the manor of Upton Waters and other properties. She died in 1395 (I.P.M. 19, Rich II, No. 12 and other refs.). The properties of Shawbury, Upton Waters and land in Moreton Corbet were held in 1428 by Sir William Mallory of P.S.A. (*Feud Aids*).

With the 'Proof of Age' (C. 139/144/45. M.2) and (C. 54/301. M.2) submitted by Sir William's son when he claimed his inheritance, it is possible to recreate the day of his birth. The Mallorys were at Moreton Corbet for the Christmas season. Sir William and his immediate family apparently having ridden, on wintry roads, all the way from Cambridgeshire (or perhaps from their Shelton home) in a jingling, creaking cavalcade, to spend the festival with their illustrious relatives. Sir William Mallory (the records only imply one William) was now married to a lady named Margaret. She must have been very thankful to have reached the comfort of the Corbet house, for on 6 December 1425, their son, Thomas Mallory, was born.

Fig. 4. A sketch of Moreton Corbet, Salop, by Mary Hey, a descendant of Peter Mallorie, v. 1562, of Dunkeswick. From 'The Castles and Old Mansions of Shropshire, 1142-1660' (1868). Camden thus describes it: 'Moreton Corbet, anciently a house of the Turets, afterwards a Castle of the Corbets, showeth itself, where within our remembrance Robert Corbet, carried away with the affectionate delight of architecture, began to build in a barraine place, a most gorgeously and stately house, after the Italian model; but death prevented him, so that he left the new work unfinished, and the Castle defaced'.

The weather was atrocious. Neighbour William James recalled that Thomas was born and baptized 'on the day aforesaid' because that day the gale was of sufficient strength to blow him from his horse and break his right leg; not to be outdone, Geoffrey Wright said his great barn was blown down; another friend's house was 'struck by lightning in the great storm and burnt to the ground'; a long catalogue of 'memorable' events was supplied by friends and relations to support Thomas's submission.

In spite of the weather, the huntsmen of the household were out finding game for the Christmas feasts, and 'John Bonley' was fortunate enough to sight and slay a 'great stag and presented the head to Margaret, mother of Thomas Malory on the same day, lately lying in childbirth'. No doubt as a token of the general rejoicing for both achievements. The new mother on her couch of furs, lying by the fire in the guest bedchamber, must have been a little startled by such exuberant good wishes. But there it all is, solemnly set down and sworn to, before the King's Escheater, John Whitchecote, for us to see to this day. Other affidavits, such as Sir William Mallory sending for the wife of John Badeley to be nurse to Thomas, and a servant, Lewis, being despatched to Shrewsbury to fetch Mistress Margery Thornes to be the child's godmother, are more sober confirmations of the event. Thomas was baptized at Moreton Corbet church a week later, on 11 December. There was another daughter born to Sir William Mallory, called Anne (in Thomas Mallory's will).

Who was Margaret, mother of Thomas Mallory, and why did the Corbets give Sir William property that would normally be passed on to descendants of Margaret de Erdington? Was his wife perhaps an unrecorded sister of Sir Robert Corbet? The determination to ensure that Thomas should be born at Moreton Corbet may support this. The Margarets of P.S.A. give rise to as much speculation as the Alices, Williams and Thomases. (The reference to Sir William's properties are to be found in the Lay Subsidy Rolls, Salop, 1666/67, 6, Hen. VI, Fine Rolls 23, Hen. VI; I.P.M., 23 Hen. V, No. 10, also I.P.M. in respect of Hunts. and Northants. and I.P.M. 29, Hen V. No. 45: Martin: A. T. Martin, 'The Identity of the Author of Le Morte d'Artur', *Archaeologia*, 1898.)

In Augusta Corbet's history of her family, written in 1919, there is a Thomas Palmer mentioned, 'servant to Robert Corbet' (v 2, p. 247). Thomas Mallory married a Palmer lady, or so it is inferred from his will, which mentions his 'brothers', Thomas Palmer, William Palmer, and Robert Palmer. They are all described as 'Esquires'. Perhaps these two Thomas Palmers are the same. The Palmer arms are quartered with Mallory and Papworth on the ceilings at P.S.A. (*see also* Shelton, Beds.).

The Palmer family were lords of Stoney Staunton (Leics.) early in the 14th century. A branch held Carleton in Rutlandshire. In 1412, Alice, the widow of Anketil Mallory of Kirkby Mallory, died seised of one-third of the manor of Stoney Staunton. The Corbets, in the person of Roger Corbet of Caus, who owned the Leicestershire manor of Sibbesdon, settled it on himself, Amice his wife, and heirs, in 1301 (Comitat. 2 Edw. III, L.1, n.22). Sibbesdon remained the home of younger sons of Castle Caux. In 1381, a John de Harrowdean of 'Sibeston' left a legacy to 'The two sons of John Malore Kt.' (Gibbons). Who these young men were has not been determined. Thus the Corbets, the Palmers and the Mallorys, were all close neighbours in Leicestershire from the earliest times, their descendants often marrying into branches of their neighbours' families. Nichols provides many instances, too many to include in this book.

To continue with the life of Thomas Mallory: such lurid signs and portents may well have presaged the arrival of a phenomenon, even if only half of them were true. It will be seen that he was born at the right time to have grown up to be the author of *Le Morte d'Arthur*.

In 1542, within 100 years of Caxton's publication of the book, the much-travelled historian, Leland, recorded that he had a conversation with 'a Mallory'. According to Martin (*Archaeologia*, 1898), in 1544 'tradition' said that Leland also said that Malory was from Mailoria, but, tradition aside, some four years later, Bale also made a similar statement and remarked further that Thomas was an Englishman.

Mailoria or Maelor, which means 'Land of the Prince' (Maellawr), is a stretch of country in the region of the river Dee. It is partly in Wales and partly in England. English Maelor (Maelor Saesneg) is just south of Flint and is close to Moreton Corbet. The similarity of the word Maelor and Mallory is one of the useless coincidences that dog Mallory research and does not of itself confirm the 'Welshness' of the author of

Le Morte. It does, however, indicate that Thomas of P.S.A., who was born in this area, might indeed have been the man to whom Leland referred. (In this connection it may be of interest to consider the possibly misleading fact that the pardon issued under Edward IV, which excluded 'Thomas Marlarie Knight', also excluded the defenders of Harlech Castle, Letters Pat. 1468).

It is unforunate that the careful collection of documented facts and convincing argument given in Martin's paper were eclipsed by the identification of the Warwickshire Thomas with the author, because one vital piece of evidence was missing. It was not to be forthcoming for almost ninety years.

That Thomas could have had access to the learned community which was to become the University of Cambridge, already some 200 years old and with 300 'bokes' in its library, only an hour's ride from Papworth, has never been considered. The fact that the P.S.A. Mallorys and Caxton were all members of the Mercers' Company was also overlooked until recently.

In Vinaver's second edition of *Malory: Works,* we read that Caxton said he received the working manuscript of *Le Morte* during the year 1469-70 and finished printing it in 1485. (This was after he had returned to England from Bruges.) In Caxton's printed book there were notes, written in the third person, summarising the contents of the chapters and uttering little prayers for the welfare of 'Sir Thomas Mallory (spelled several ways) Knyght. A servant of Jesu bothe day and nyght.' At the end of the book, the notes are in the third person, but the prayers are written by the author himself in the first person singular: 'I pray you all Jentylmen and Jentylwomen that readeth this book', etc., 'Praye for me whyle I am on lyve that God send me good delyveraunce. And when I am deed I pray you all praye for my soul.' One might infer that *Le Morte* was almost complete when disaster struck, and that it was not written in prison.

Although many legal documents existed relating to Papworth Thomas, in none of them was he described as anything more exalted than 'Armiger'. Furthermore, in 1934 a manuscript copy of *Le Morte* was discovered at Winchester, copied by two scribes a little later than Caxton's publication, with additional notes that Caxton seems to have deliberately omitted. In these, Mallory is called 'a knyght presoner'. The only Thomas Mallory then known to scholars who was certainly a knight and who qualified with convincing regularity as a prisoner, was Thomas of Newbold Revel.

What can give us a picture of Papworth Thomas as a person? His access to the great mountains and shining seas of his birthplace, to the magical atmosphere of Merlin's country, and an acquaintance with the poetic Welsh storytellers around him, could well have inspired the young Thomas to write the legendary tales of Arthur with the compelling grace displayed in *Le Morte.*

One recorded incident reveals a facet of his character which is comparable to that of his more rowdy contemporary in Warwickshire. The early Chancery proceedings contain a complaint that in 1456 Thomas Mallory and 'four other riotous and misgoverned persons arrayed as if it has been a land at war' pounced upon Richard Kydd, the vicar of P.S.A., and carried him off on a long rough ride into Northamptonshire, during which 'in fear of his lyfe' he was persuaded to relinquish some church land and money to Mallory. As in the case of Newbold Revel Thomas's escapades, this story can be interpreted in two ways. Was Kydd one of the greedy medieval clergymen so familiar from popular stories of Robin Hood, retaining property to which he had no right? Thomas was under age when his father, Sir William, died in 1445, and he was declared a ward of the king in the guardianship of Leon Louthe (I.P.M. 23, Hen. VI, No. 10). He was not legally given his lands at Papworth until May 1469 (Clo. Roll, 9 Edw. IV, 4 m.2). Parson Kydd could have been in wrongful part-possession during these unsatisfactory years. Thomas was at P.S.A. in 1459 and 1460, for he was granted the fishing rights on the river Ouse from Huntingdon to Holywell (Cal. Pat.), about ten miles of waterway today. In 1463 he was assessor for the county. He had a close interest in the priory at Huntingdon which demonstrates that he was not entirely without respect for the church.

At that time there seems to have been some forest in the region and perhaps a cottage industry at Papworth where the villagers were kept busy carving the' many 'wooden trenchers' that formed the rents due to the Bishop of Ely for the manors of Grandesden, Hilton and Toseland. If his people ever resented spending their spare time in wood chiselling, Thomas could always have reminded them that the villagers of Wisbech were put to collecting 3,000 eels every year to pay their lord's due to Ely (Domesday).

Thomas married a Palmer lady. Their first son and heir, John, was born in 1452, and their last child, also christened John, although John I was still alive, was born in 1469. Five other sons and three daughters are recorded in the intervening 15 years. Thomas wrote two wills. The second, written on 16 September 1469, carries a conviction of impending doom, for he makes very careful provision for the welfare of his children. He was dead by 27 October when the will was probated at Lambeth (Will. Godyn 28, 1469). In it he asks for his body to be buried in 'the chapel of the Blessed Mary at Huntingdon' (the now-vanished priory of Huntingdon), and he provided for masses to be said daily for his soul and those of his wife and parents 'now departed'. Payment for this service was by the gift in perpetuity of 'a little grove called Trappes [or Crappes] growing with wood'. 'Crappes' may be the medieval 'Crab Bush Field' which was north-west of P.E. church. It was about half a mile long and a quarter of a mile wide (*see On the Road*, by Rowland Parker).

He made arrangements for the guardianship and education of his sons: John was to learn law, Robert to be sent to study with the abbot of Sawtry, William to be 'apprenticed to a London draper'. The other children's future was also provided for, and his new infant son, John No. 2, was to be found a nurse, for in the middle (or because) of the troubles that precipitated the making of this will, his wife had just died. He leaves her 'green gown' to his sister Anne (green, the colour of faery: was Lady Mallory a mistress of herbs and simples, a white witch?). Other precious (Mercer's) trinkets he leaves to his 'kinswoman', Margaret Stewkley and 'The wife of John Wakys'. He left money to repair the causeway to P.S.A. church and for Stukeley church. There are many names in the will, executors, etc., which suggest avenues of exploration to find more information about Thomas. His daughters were Alice, Ellen, and Elizabeth (*see* Isleham—wife of Herald Sir Christopher Carhill, below).

He was returned to the list of possible writers of *Le Morte* in 1972 when Professor Griffith published his discovery of an escheat record found in the Public Record

Office in respect of Palmer/Mallory holdings in Rutlandshire. It bore the all-important designation of 'Myletis' after Thomas Mallory's name (*Ventures in Research*, 1972). Professor Griffith also revealed that Anthony Wydville (Woodville), the Earl Rivers, owned manors near Papworth. This man, a Yorkist and brother of Edward IV's queen, was a famous patron of the arts and of Caxton in particular. He also fought in the Northern Campaign of 1462. Griffith developed arguments in support of a friendly relationship existing between Rivers, Caxton and Papworth Thomas and his relatives, and demonstrates that a coterie of learned noblemen with an interest in literature also resided in that area of the county.

One of Caxton's little notes says that the story of the 'Sankgreal' was 'cronycled for one of the trewyst and holyest that is yn thys worlde'. Does this refer to the patron himself? Anthony Wydville enjoyed a reputation of great honour and popularity. He would certainly fit the terms of the dedication. Griffith is of the opinion that Mallory may have been a victim of Warwick's vengeance on the family of Wydville and his supporters. He may have been taken to the Tower with other unnamed knights who are known to have been executed by Warwick just too soon for Edward IV's final victory to save them. Thomas was only 44 years of age when he died. (At the end of *The Dolorous Death of Arthur,* Malory states that the book was finished in the ninth year of the reign of Edward IV; i.e., between March 1469 and March 1470.)

It should be noted, however, that it has been demonstrated elsewhere that Rivers could equally well have been acquainted with Thomas of Newbold Revel. There is a good probability that Rivers may have commissioned *Le Morte d'Arthur* and could have arranged with Caxton for its publication. Thomas, the author, may have been the victim of ill health, confined to his bed. The self-description of 'prisoner' may have been poetic. Such a man may well have taken to writing stories.

Present information suggests that Thomas of Papworth is the only man fitting the criteria required to qualify for authorship who may have direct male descendants living today. What the immediate result of his death was at P.S.A. we do not know. Perhaps 'Sister Anne' took over the running of the household and the care of the younger children until the son-and-heir John could manage his responsibilities. John, however, died, aged 18, in 1471 still a ward of the king. Robert succeeded him, but he, too, died without issue, aged 35 years. William also died early, and the fourth son, Anthony, born in 1466, inherited the property. William may have been married to Elizabeth Brandon (*see* Bramcote notes). Antony married Alice Lynne. In the Visitation of Bedfordshire, 1634, he is described as a mercer. He was Commissioner for the Peace in Huntingdonshire for the years 1510, 1513, 1514, 1520, 1522 and 1523, and Sheriff for Cambridgeshire and Huntingdonshire in 1506, 1515, 1516, 1517, 1519 and 1532. His will (Prob. 11/27 R.H. 254—L.H. 255, f. 32, P.C.C. Byngley fo. 32), probated in London in October 1539, recommends his wife Alice to cut and sell off timber in the woods at Papworth to pay his debts and provide money to rebuild the church. The will was written in 1530. The only children mentioned were his heir, Henry Malory, William Malory, and his daughter, Audre. There is a Richard (whose surname does not seem to be Malory) who appears to have been a servant. He also had a daughter, Ellen, and probably a son, Richard (*see* below), whose existence is deduced from the wills of later Malorys. Antony asked to be buried on the north side of the chancel in the church at 'Papperworth Anneys'. It is curious that he also stipulates 'before Saynt Peter the patron of the said church'. The church at P.S.A. is dedicated to St John today; St Peter is the patron saint of Papworth Everard. His wife was buried near him. They also owned the Lynne manor at Bassingbourn until 1538/9.

Henry Malory died without issue, and William, his brother, succeeded to Papworth. He was twice Sheriff of the County and was listed in the Gentry of the County: usually referred to as a knight, he styles himslf 'Esquiyer' in his will. However, he did not die until eight months later. (Noted as 'Armiger' in 1555/6.)

Part of Sir William Mallory's splendid improvements at Papworth still stand. Several of the rooms retain their glorious plaster ceilings decorated with the lavish armorial display proper to the chief seat of a medieval lord of the manor. The glass in the windows, which he bequeathed to his heirs 'to remain in the house for ever', is still in place. The exact message of the coats-of-arms on the ceilings is controversial in the light of the pedigrees, but the arms were acceptable to the Heralds who visited the manor.

Another member of this house, possibly Sir William's cousin or his younger brother, was Sir Richard Mallory, a prosperous London mercer, one of the greatest exporters of cloth from London in his day. (Stow and Fullers' *Worthies*.). He was an alderman of the City of London, serving on the committee responsible for the water supply and sewage. The Fleet river was their constant concern. In 1559 he is described as a 'merchant Venterer'. (Cal. Pat.) The peak of his career was his election as Lord Mayor of London in 1564. That year, in one of the great frosts, the Thames froze solid from London Bridge to Westminster. Queen Elizabeth I herself walked forth on the 'yce', in places 18 feet thick, if the reports are to be believed. Her ebullient lord mayor would surely have escorted the royal party on this adventurous and historic occasion. At the completion of his year in office, he was knighted.

In 1565 he also served, for the third time, as Master of the Mercers' Company. He was Sheriff of London in 1557-8, and had earlier been treasurer of Barts Hospital. His private trade was with the East; with Russia, Persia and Cathay (will). He was also a landowner in Northamptonshire. Another mercer, John Isham (who shipped cloth in *The Mayflower*) kept account books which have survived. Several Mallorys had transactions with him, including 'The Lady Mallory, wife to the Lord Mayor' and 'Symon Mallory Esquire of Woodford in Northants.'. These entries are from 1565-1572. Further details may be read in the description of the account books by G. Ramsay, published by the Northants. Record Society.

The arms of Sir Richard Mallory, from the records in the Guildhall, are: 'Or a lion rampant double queued Gules within a bordure Gules', similar to those of the branch at Shelton. Burke gives a slightly different description: 'Or a lion rampant Gules collared Argent. A crescent for a difference' (Visit. Devon, 1620). The crescent is the cadency mark for a second son, which may be appropriate. The *Genealogical Quarterly* gives a coat-of-arms which appears to combine both the above, and describes the lion as 'guardant' (possibly a misprint). *A Book of Knights,* by W. C. Metcalfe, gives 'Or a lion rampant within a border Gules' and a crest that seems to connect Sir Richard with Papworth St Agnes: 'A horse's head Gules, the face and ears Argent, maned and ducally gorged Or'.

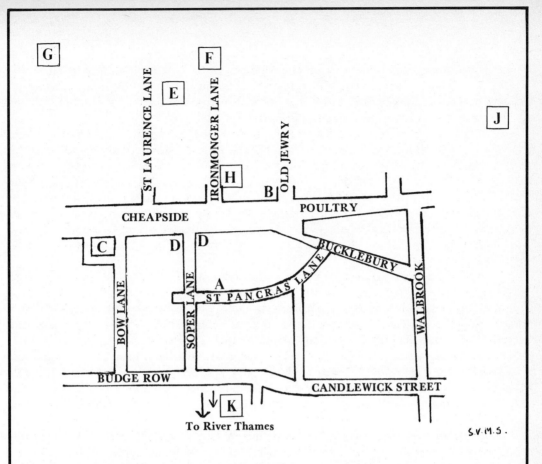

S.V.M.S.

Fig. 5. SIR RICHARD MALLORY'S LONDON
(after N. Partington - Sketch of area *c.* 1666)

KEY: See text p. 66.
A   St Pancras church, Soper Lane - destroyed in Great Fire, not rebuilt.
B   St Mary Cole church, The Mercers' Chapel - Destroyed in Great Fire, not rebuilt.
C   St Mary le Bow - extant.
D   Possible sites of 'The Sign of the Golden Key'.
E   Guildhall - extant.
F   Girdlers' Hall - extant.
G   Haberdashers' Hall - extant.
H   Mercers' Hall - extant - rebuilt, with new Chapel after 1941.
J   Drapers' Hall - extant.
K   Vintners' Hall - extant.
Soper Lane - probably became Queen Street.
St Pancras Lane - part still survives.
Candlewick Street - became Cannon Street.

OTHER MALLORY-CONNECTED SITES WITHIN ONE MILE:
Clerkenwell - extant.
St Bartholomew's Hospital - extant.
Stationers' Hall (Scriveners) - extant.
Greyfriars Chapel (then Bluecoat School - only ruins extant - removed to Horsham).
Headquarters of Order of Knights of St John - extant.
Strand - extant.

See also: *An Encyclopaedia of London*, W. Kent, revised G. Thompson, and *Mediaeval London*, T. Baker.

His main house in London was at *The Sign of the Golden Key,* at 'Soper Lane End, Cheapside' (Stow). This was possibly his house of business, for he mentions another property at Tottenham, in his will. He employed servants in both establishments. They and his apprentices are remembered in his will.

Sir Richard's first wife, Anne Smythe, sadly succumbed to childbirth when Thomas, her seventeenth child, was born in 1560. By the time Sir Richard began to write his will in 1565, he had married again. The will was not completed until 1566 and may have been made because his eldest son was about to reach his majority. His second wife was Elizabeth, daughter of the M.P. for London, Robert Pakynton, and the widow of John Lane, lord of Walgrave in Northamptonshire. Lane died in 1547, when Elizabeth inherited Walgrave and other property jointly with her two sons, William and John Lane. One of Sir Richard's sons, Clement, born in 1552, does not appear again in the records.

Of his 17 (or more) children, 13 are named in his will (Prob. 11/49–R.H. 69–R.H. 70, fo. 9: P.C.C. 9. Stonnarde, March 1567). The sons were (1) Andrew, (2) William, (3) Mehezadeck, (4) Ffrancis, (5) Richard, and (6) Edward. In 1565, all were apparently still under 21 years of age, but by June 1566, Andrew, William and Richard were old enough to be named as executors. Edward was still a child, not at school, having been born in 1557. All appear to have been unmarried, or at least childless at that time. On 27 March 1567, only Andrew and William were available to probate the will. (The original document appears to be dated 15 'sexagisimo sexto' [or 1566] at probate, but the records state that Sir Richard Mallory died in 1567.)

The daughters were: Julyane, the eldest, married to mercer Richard Sharpe; Anne, married to Thomas X, a girdler; Scholastica, married to William Rolph, an haberdasher; three younger unmarried daughters, Elizabeth, born in 1554, Dorothy, born in 1555, Barbara; and one small daughter, Sara, born in 1565, the child of Sir Richard and Elizabeth. Elizabeth had lost their first child, Robert, in 1562.

Two revealing bequests were money to provide new shirts for every man, woman and child who should be cured at St Bart's Hospital and money to provide a grand dinner for all the Aldermen and Wardens of the City of London, all the Liverymen of the Mercers' Company and all their respective wives, after his decease. He asked to be buried near to Anne in the Mercers' chapel at Cheapside. The Mallorys enjoyed entertaining their friends. An undated contemporary account (Noble's Coll.) describes the rejoicings at the marriage of one daughter to a London vintner at St Pancras church. 'Here was goodly singing and playing'. The aldermen were guests, arrayed in scarlet. They ate a 'great dinner' and 'at night a supper' followed by a masque and mummers. They were all presented with gloves, the recognised Elizabethan compliment, to the tune of 100 pairs.

Melchisedack Mallory, who is not mentioned again, is recorded in the Patent Rolls for 1575 when he accused Yeoman Edward Smalley of trespass, and, by virtue of being his father's son, was able to have the unfortunate man brought before the then Lord Mayor and Aldermen of London in the Guildhall (Cal. Pat., Vol. VI, Eliz. 2768).

Sir William of Papworth owned property at Papworth St Agnes, Papworth Everard and elsewhere—he does not mention the Shelton property in his will. He left money to pay for a mourning ring, to 'my cozen Richard Malorye'. Sir Richard used the spelling 'Malorye' in his own will, which he says he wrote, signed, sealed and bound himself. He began it in June 1566 and signed it exactly a year later. Round about Christmas he appears to have cut himself a new pen and to have adopted more fashionable spelling for some of the words. He spells his name 'Mallory' towards the end. Sir William's will, probably not written by himself, spells his surname 'Mallory', but his sons' are written 'Mallorye' and 'Malorye'. The word 'cozen' was applied to all manner of relatives at that time, especially to nephews. Two of the witnesses to the will were Richard Malorye and Edward Malorye. No son, Edward, has been recorded, neither in the Registers nor in the Visitations. A son, Richard, appears in the 1619 Visitation, probably born after the will was drawn. It therefore seems that 'cozen Richard' was the same individual as the witness and that both he and Edward were the (now) grown-up sons of Sir Richard Malorye (now) deceased.

Pages of goods and land are itemised. The treasures were a gilt salt, 'my pot of silver and gilt', silver spoons, silken sheets and silk curtains. Some of his land he had purchased from Henry VIII.

His wife, Joane (Joane Chambers), had a daughter, Jane Grange, by a previous marriage. Joane died in 1597. Sir William wished to be buried near to his parents in Papworth church; his will clearly calls it the church at Papworth Agnes. He died in 1586 (Probate 11/69 R.H. 345—L.H. 347 f. 44).

Sir William's children named in the will were William 'my first son', who was heir to Papworth; (2) Peter, whose descendants lived at Shelton (Beds.); (3) Nicholas; (4) John, who appears in the parish registers 'of Papworth', possibly Papworth Everard. Other sons, recorded in parish registers or Visitations, were Henry 'son of William,' born in 1563, and a William, born in 1585, who is difficult to place. Four of the sons are known to have had offspring. His daughters were Anne 'my eldest daughter', Jane and Dorothy, in his will, also an Elizabeth in the parish register. Sir William also provided for an Ellen Burkenshaw, his sister Ellen's daughter.

Sir William was succeeded by his eldest surviving son, William Mallory, who married twice, firstly Elizabeth Gregory of Barkway, Herts. in 1578. Their marriage is in the P.S.A. parish register. The parish registers of Papworth St Agnes, Papworth Everard, Shelton and Dean and the Herald's Visitations together supply most of the details of the family from this date. Elizabeth Gregory had two daughters and four sons. The last, Gregory, was born in 1602 on the same day that Elizabeth died. Three years later William married another Elizabeth, styled Mrs. Elizabeth Arden in the register. (This may have been a fashionable convention, and not imply that she was a widow, as all ladies are entered as 'Mrs.' at this time.) There was a Visitation in 1575. William Mallory died in 1614 leaving his son, Henry Mallory, as his successor. There was another Visitation in 1619, that confirms as the Mallory arms the following coat: 'Or a lion rampant Gules impaling Paly of six Or and Azure a Canton Ermine'. These are Mallory arms impaling Sherley and must only refer to Sir Henry's own arms. His wife was Judith, daughter of Anthony Sherley of Preston Manor in Sussex. (Recorded as Preston, Essex, by J. Clay in *Harleian Society*, vol. XLV, 1897. This is a mistake in transcribing.) Sir Henry's first son was Anthony, born in 1613. He removed to London and was buried at Richmond in 1640. There were two more sons and five daughters. The Mallorys of this period maintained their ancient role as patriotic supporters of the monarchy. The P.S.A. family, with their London interests, moved in court circles still. They would certainly have been acquainted with Cromwell's flamboyant uncle, Sir Oliver Cromwell of Hinchingbroke (Hunts.), a rollicking gentleman who entertained King James I. He had no sympathy with his solemn nephew and after selling the family estate, died in 1655 leaving such huge debts that his body had to be buried immediately and secretly to avoid it being confiscated by his creditors. To ascertain whether he had any direct influence on the fate of Sir Henry and his family would make an interesting study. Sir Henry also had three brothers (pedigree) whose history has not been studied.

On 27 April 1605, the Lord Lieutenant of Cambridgeshire and the Isle of Ely (the Duke of Suffolk), received returns of the forces furnished by certain knights of the county. Sir Henry Mallory was a captain and the officer commanding a troop of cavalry which consisted of 12 lancers, 60 light horse and 35 petronels (horsemen armed with heavy pistols). In May of the same year he was knighted by the king at Richmond. The cobbled yards where they once mustered at Papworth and the dim cellars where the brimming barrels of ale they quaffed were stored, have vanished beneath the waving grass. Who was his dashing young lieutenant, 'William Norton, Gent'? In 1513 Francis Norton of Ingleby in Leicestershire owned 15 acres of woods at Papworth Everard, 'all ashes elms and okes' (Palmer). The cost of training, equipping and maintaining such a considerable number of men, together with paying the king's 'Ship Money' tax, may have contributed to the fact that shortly after 1635 Papworth St Agnes was sold.

In 1637 another family was in possession. There is a bell in the church inscribed 'Thomas Norris made me: Thomas Catar Esquire 1637', which indicates that the Catars were lords of the manor by that date. They were followed by the Cotton and Pigott families (*Magna Brittania*) and later, Sperling.

Where the Mallorys went to after 1635 is for the moment unknown. Sir Henry may have been removed by any one of the calamities of war after 1642. Perhaps he was taken by Huntingdon Ironsides and imprisoned with other local Cavaliers in the courts of St John's College in Cambridge. If he survived, he may have shared the fate of other Royalists who, though alive and solvent at the end of the war, were fined so heavily by Cromwell's regime that their families were completely ruined (*cf.* Studley Royal).

Papworth Everard had been sold in 1599 to one Adam Thorougood, by a Henry Mallory. Perhaps this was 'Henry, son of William, born 1563', and not Sir Henry, who must have been born rather later (after 1578) and may have been too young to own the property.

Sir Henry's second son, Captain Henry ('Henery' in the Visitation) Mallory, went to his mother's family home at Preston Manor, near Brighton, to join the Royalist forces there. His adventures are continued under Sussex. After 1623 there are no further entries in the Papworth registers, but the history of other members of the family is extended rather sketchily from the Shelton (Beds.) records until 1714.

Papworth St Agnes has, in modern times, joined the increasing number of dying East Anglian villages, while Papworth Everard has expanded and continues to flourish, famous especially for the wonderful work carried out in its hospital.

The Mallory manor at P.E. no longer exists, although moated earthworks remain near the Victorian Hall. P.S.A., however, holds the greatest Mallory treasure hidden in its leafy lanes. The great Tudor house, built by (Sir) William, has in part survived, with a section of the moat which surrounded the earlier house. Sir Nikolaus Pevsner was of the opinion that part of the house dated from the reign of Henry VII. Demolitions and additions in later centuries have greatly altered the original grand concept, but the most important rooms remain, with their huge fireplaces and elaborate plasterwork. The very special fact about this house is that it seems to be the only manor house to retain evidence of Mallory occupation, and because of this, and the possibility that *Le Morte* could have been written somewhere within its boundaries, it is an important living part of our national heritage.

The plan of the pleasure gardens where (Sir) William and his lady took their ease, the fishponds that supplied the household with its Friday carp, the terraces and the outlines of earlier buildings, can all be traced under the turf of years, a solitary lavender bush evoking the herb garden and that gown of elfin green. There is also a

Fig. 6.   Sketch of cartouche on plaster ceiling in manor house at Papworth St Agnes, Cambridgeshire. By L. M. V. Smith, a descendant of George Mallorie of Kilham, v. 1629.

charming brick dovecote. Inside the present house are walls and windows that were once on the outside. In the kitchens a large 'squint', cut through the thickest wall, resembles 'the Porter's squint' underneath the Strangers' Hall in Norwich, which dates from 1320. If the 'squint' at Papworth is of the same period, then a fragment of Thomas Mallory's home may still be standing. Several of the Tudor rooms, including the parlour and state bedrooms have plaster ceilings. There are cartouches showing the Mallory lion on a curious shield which may incorporate a mercer's bolt of cloth in its design. The single lions exhibit an interesting error: the Mallory lion is rampant, these Papworth lions have their forepaws in the salient position. In the house at Hutton Conyers in Yorkshire there is still an armorial plaster ceiling, described by Walbran (*circa* 1876) as being 'incorrect'. He wrote that the position of the lion was 'rather more salient than rampant'. It is tempting to suggest that the same artist/plasterer had been employed at both houses, implying close contacts continuing from times past between these branches of the Mallory family. The Mallorys of Hutton Conyers and Studley Royal also maintained a London house and fought for King Charles. However, the error, if error it is, seems to have been repeated in the now rather blurred coat-of-arms on the tomb of the last Studley Mallory, in Ripon cathedral. In Ormerod's *History of Cheshire* (VI, p. 421), the arms allowed to the Mallorys of Mobberley are drawn. The lion's forepaws are again in the salient position. This coat-of-arms was inherited from the Studley Royal Mallorys. Are we to conclude that the original Mallory lion was characterised by this realistic rampant position? The lion engraved on a church brass memorial to a Northampton-shire Mallory in 1580 has what we regard as the 'true' rampant stance as it is understood today. (It should be noted, however, that the arms of other families that date from an early period of heraldry are also charged with lions whose paws are in curious positions.)

Some ceilings at P.S.A. have splendid quartered arms depicting the full achievement, complete with helm, crest, mantling and gay tassels. The initials 'W.M.' are on either side of the shield. The entire design has been reversed by the plasterer, appearing to confirm his unfamiliarity with the requirements of heraldry. The crispness of the work, the unusual pendants and the decoration of the cornices have retained their original beauty in spite of later dilapidations. It is possible that the work was carried out for (Sir) William's son and that the artist was Italian.

The ceilings have unfortunately been whitewashed, destroying the original colours, but it is possible to identify the quarterings as follows: first and fourth; 'Or a lion rampant la queue forchee Gules', Mallory: second; 'Gules a fess dancetty Argent', Papworth: third; 'Argent on a bend Sable five bezants', Palmer. (Bezants are usually gold.) The crest is a Nag's head couped. This was usually plain 'Gules', for Mallory, but in this case may be the one listed as 'parti-coloured' (for a personal difference). It rises from a ducal coronet which may indicate that some special service to a king was commemorated. (It is not an indication of rank.)

Two sets of strange corbels have a disturbing aura which would quickly be dispelled if fires roared on the ample hearths and music and laughter replaced the silent echoes of the hall. The corbels do not appear to be in their original positions. They may have come from the earlier house, the church, or even from Huntingdon Priory: there is 12th-century and medieval masonry lying in the grounds of the house. The corbels exhibit a likeness in style and similar curious strength and intimations of lurking devilry, apparent in some of the creatures decorating Beverley Minster (Yorks.). If contemporary with those, it is possible that their faces may have given Thomas food for thought, even if he may never have looked through the 'squint'. The flat tops suggest that they may have been lamp brackets, in their present position.

Another interesting feature of the house is a little isolated painted chamber set high up in the gable end; one of the oratories the Mallorys were so fond of building. It appears likely that the Tudor house was never completed. There were further additions later.

Modern conveniences have from time to time been installed with minimum disturbance of the remaining fabric, and in its present state both the house and its surroundings are in prime condition for careful archaeological exploration. There is a unique opportunity for the site to yield up more of its secrets and for Mallory relics to be discovered in the moat, the wells, the garderobe, and in the thickness of the walls. The walls and stairway were once panelled, covering an inaccessible room over the hall, perhaps a priest hole.

The present lord of the manor has set himself the enormous task of revitalising the village. One day soon, perhaps, we shall see the re-flowering of the house itself.

The church at P.S.A. is dedicated to St John the Baptist. The church that Anthony Mallory rebuilt over four hundred years ago has been replaced, with the exception of the west doorway, by another, built in 1848, and it has not been possible to trace the dimensions of the medieval buildings, nor the certain site of the altar. The church stood empty for many years, its roof slates falling and the organ removed to another village. This site must contain Mallory relics under the floor and perhaps outside. Maybe an inscription, 'son (or daughter) of SIR Thomas Mallory'? The writer had hoped to instigate an archaeological excavation of the floor, but the roof was unsafe. Recently the church has become the property of the Friends of Friendless Churches, who have undertaken a splendid restoration, but Thomas's children, Anthony, William and all the others are now buried under concrete. They are, however, safe for the attentions of a later investigator. The church at P.E., dedicated to St Peter, is also Victorian.

Papworth 100; P.S.A. and P.E. 8 miles W.N.W. of Cambridge; 12 miles N.W. of Huntingdon; 16 miles N.E. of Bedford; *Magna Britannia*, Vo. 2:1; Inventory by *Royal Comm. on Historical Monuments, West Cambs.* (H.M.S.O.).

Huntingdon

Little Grandesden

No reported trace of Mallory occupation remains.

Toseland

A dying village. Very few houses remain.

Yelling

A thriving community. No Mallory residence. Profits from the Yelling rectory and land belonging to Huntingdon Priory were given to Anthony Mallory at the time of the dissolution of the monasteries. The Piggott family held Yelling and Papworth St Agnes in 1770 (*see V.C.H. Huntingdonshire*).

Little Stukeley

The lords of this village were the de Swyneford family (*see* Swinford notes), and the Stukely family, whose chief seat was at Great Stukely (*see* Thomas Mallory's will and arms in Isleham church).

All these villages are near Papworth St Agnes

Cambridgeshire

Isleham

The history of the lords of the manor of Isleham provides much of interest in connection with Mallory history, through the marriage of a great Mallory heiress in the 15th century. She was Elena, daughter of Jane and Sir John Mallory, the last Mallory lord of Holwell in Bedfordshire. This manor she had inherited from her father by 1437, together with the manors of Welton (Northants.) and Wold (Northants.), (Clo. R. 5, Edw. IV, 21). His ancestors held these properties 'of Sir Anketil de Mallory, as of his manor of Kirkby Mallory' (Nichols). Elena Mallory's second husband was Sir John Bernard, lord of Isleham; a descendant of Crusader Sir Godfrey Bernard (obit. 1275), the first of the family at Isleham.

It is to be expected that Elena Bernard would have also inherited arms derived from those of Kirkby Mallory: 'Or a lion rampant queue fourche Gules' (a gold shield charged with a red rampant fork-tailed lion). The possibility of an earlier Mallory coat-of-arms charged with a single-tailed lion should be borne in mind (*see* Walton).

There is a splendid array of armorial shields in the church at Isleham and several accounts which describe them. Unfortunately, not all these agree, and one or two of the earliest shields have lost their charges. Snares lie in wait for the unprofessional student of heraldry, even if he consults recognised authorities, and views original artefacts, for first impressions can be misleading. Some arms, considered in retrospect, will be seen to have been really charged with 'three herring Gules'. An attempt to understand the arms of the Isleham families is necessary, however, since they may lead to the discovery of the arms of the Holwell Mallorys, their descent and, *inter alia,* that of the Papworth St Agnes family, whose arms are certainly derived from those of Kirkby Mallory. Isleham church will attract many Mallory tourists, and, for that reason, the arms are described both in heraldic terms and in plain modern English, although this is cumbersome. The following discussion may appear to have been made unnecessarily complicated, but all the alternatives are included to ensure that future researchers shall not lack what might prove to be an essential fact. The only

1. Castle Bytham, Lincolnshire: part of the moated earthworks of the castle of Alice (Dryby) Mallory, died 1412.

2. Tomb of Sir Thomas Andrews, died 1563/4, and his wives, Charwelton church, Northamptonshire. His first wife was Katherine Cave, descendant of Sir Thomas Malory of Newbold Revel.

3. (*above*) Arms of Sir Thomas Andrews, died 1590, at Charwelton, Northamptonshire.

4. (*right*) Tomb of Sir Ralph Green, died 1417, and effigy of his wife, Katherine Mallory, at Lowick church, Northamptonshire.

5. Tudor facade of the Mallory manor house at Papworth St Agnes, Cambridgeshire.

6. (*above*) Achievement of arms of Mallory of Papworth St Agnes, Cambridgeshire, found as a whitewashed plaster ceiling in the manor house. *c.* 1586-1600.

7. (*above right*) Corbel (lamp bracket) in the manor house at Papworth St Agnes.

8. (*right*) Arms of a descendant of Elena (Malory) Bernard, in Isleham, Cambridgeshire.

9. Medieval stained glass portraits of Sir Thomas Peyton, died 1484, and his wife Margaret Bernard, in Long Melford church, Suffolk.

10. Memorial to Susan (Mallory) Boundy, died 1669, in Shelton, Bedfordshire.

11. Venetian stained glass panel depicting the arms of Sir William Ingilby, died 1578, and his wife Ann Malory of Studley Royal. The panel is found in Ripley Castle, Yorkshire.

12. (*above*) Ruins of Fountains Abbey, Yorkshire. (Mallorie family of Studley Royal.)

13. (*below*) The front of Fountains Hall.

16. Memorial to Sir John Mallorie of Studley Royal, died 1655/6, and his son William, in Ripon Cathedral, Yorkshire.

17. Portrait of Daniel Mallory, Mayor of Warwick in 1834 and 1835.

herald in the Mallory family was Christopher Cahill, Esq., Norroy, who died in 1510 and can no longer advise us (*see* footnote, page 81).

The Visitations of Cambridgeshire in 1575 and 1619 record the arms of the Peyton family, descendants of the Bernards at Isleham. In the list of quarterings, the tenth is given as 'Gules a lion rampant Or collared Azure'. This lion, in the church, has no collar, but carries an azure crescent on its shoulder, the cadency mark for a second son. The Visitations say that these are the arms of 'Mallory'. (Could it be the Kirkby Mallory lion 'differenced', having a single tail and with the colours reversed?) There are other lions of various colours on various fields, on other Peyton tombs in the church, in particular one in the 21st quarter of the shield of Sir John Peyton (died 1620), which is 'Or a lion rampant Gules'. There are other possibilities, however. In addition to the arms on the tombs, the shields of the early benefactors of the church are ranged round the nave and in the aisles. In the north aisle, the second shield is ascribed in the church guide book to Margaret Bernard, the daughter and heir of Sir John and Elena Bernard, and her husband, Thomas Peyton. The first arms, which occupy half the shield (impaling), are those of the Peyton family, 'Sable a cross engrailed Or in the first quarter a molet of the second' (A black shield charged with a crinkly golden cross and a golden object resembling a five-pointed star.)

Next are two 'eighths' depicting the arms of Sir John Bernard. He was the son of Robert Bernard and Elizabeth Lylling, daughter of Sir Nicholas and Mary Lylling of East Lilling. The Bernard arms are 'Argent a bear rampant Sable collared and muzzled Or'. (A silver shield charged with a black rampant bear wearing a golden collar and muzzle.) The Lylling arms, which are below those of Bernard, are 'Gules three fishes naiant in pale Argent a bordure engrailed of the second'. (A red shield with a silver border, charged with three little silver fishes swimming neatly in echelon.) These impale a further two 'eighths', ascribed to Elena Mallory. The entire field of this area is silver. In the top 'eighth' there is a 'Demi-lion rampant couped Gules'. (A rampant red lion with a single tail, cut off at the waist.)

There is a bell still in the belfry, dated 1484, which was cast for Thomas Peyton, who died in 1484. It also commemorates his wife and her parents, all of whom were benefactors of the church. It carries two shields. One bears the arms of Sir John Bernard and Elena Mallory: 'Quarterly Bernard and Lylling' impaling the 'Mallory' demi-lion. The other shield, for Thomas Peyton and Margaret Bernard, is exactly similar to the second shield in the north aisle, described above.

The couped demi-lion (rampant) is regarded as unusual when appearing as a coat-of-arms and it is more often used as a crest (Brooke-Little). It is in any case an extreme 'difference' from the Kirkby Mallory arms. *The Genealogy of the Peyton Family,* by Hayden (first published 1891) gives the usual Kirkby Mallory arms for Elena. It has been amended to the 'demi-lion' in the corrections of 1959. This lion is present elsewhere in the church.

In *A Tudor Book of Arms*, Harl. MS. 2169 (not necessarily a book of Tudor arms) by J. Foster, the following note appears: 'B. Mallory. Argent a demi-lyon rampant Gules'. This is unidentified and not dated. Who was 'B. Mallory'? The only male 'B. Mallory' known to the writer occurs as the first name on the pedigree of Mallory of Holwell (Beds.); Bertram Mallory, who lived *circa* 1150 (*see* Bedfordshire notes).

It may be that these are the arms of Bertram of Holwell that descended to Elena Bernard. The only other 'demi-lion' with a single tail appearing in a Mallory coat-of-arms is that ascribed to Irish Mallorys in 1625 and having traditional Mallory tinctures. There is one instance of a two-tailed 'demi-lion' quoted by Foster for a 'William Maulare' in the reign of Henry III (1216–72). Only the colour of the lion is given: red. It is from the St George's Roll. Humphery-Smith in 1973 gives these arms on a gold shield. They are possibly the arms of Mallorys of Welton (*see* Northants.), also in the inheritance of this branch. (No William is recorded at Welton before 1272.)

The *V.C.H. Bedfordshire* gives the usual Kirkby Mallory arms in the illustration of the arms of the Holwell Mallorys and so does the Bedfordshire historian Khulicke, but the lion has a single tail in his illustration. In neither case are these arms ascribed to a particular individual at Holwell. The Cambridgeshire Visitations list, but do not identify, the Isleham 'demi-lion'.

The next shield in the north aisle, ascribed in the church guide book to Thomas Peyton, the grandson of Elena Mallory, also has controversial charges. The second and fourth quarters should be the arms of both his (heiress) grandmothers. Grace Burgoyne's arms are charged with a wonderful medieval shaggy dog (the guide book more properly calls it a lion), and not the handsome hound (Talbot) of the Burgoynes. The 'Mallory' quarter is 'Argent three boars' heads couped Sable tusked of the first'. (A silver shield with three black boars' heads with silver tusks.) Miscellaneous boars' heads appear with stubborn frequency as the arms of Mallorys in the literature, although no record has been found of the first Mallory to whom such arms were granted. Dugdale describes arms charged with boars' heads as those of a Warwickshire Mallory, John Mallory of Winwick (v 1363). These arms were possibly inherited by his branch of the family from their ancient holdings at Swinford (*see* Newbold Revell notes). Furthermore, Baker, in the history of the Mallory manor at Welton (Northants.), describes a deed of 1366 relating to the manor of Lichborough (also owned by the Warwickshre branch) which was sealed with a pendant shield showing 'a cross' and 'a fess between 3 boars' heads'. (*see also* the arms at Charwelton, (Northants.).

There are further complications. The guide book ascribes the Isleham boars' heads to Elena's first husband, whose name was Swynnerton of Whilton, near Ipswich (Suffolk). But Burke (1976 edn.) gives no arms charged with boars' heads to either Swynnerton or Swinnerton. Their arms are, in the main, variations on 'Argent a cross flory Sable'. (A silver shield charged with a black cross having a petal-shape to the ends of its arms.) The Visitations ascribe these to Hasleden. Burke gives 'Hasleday Co. Cambridge' and 'Hasledon Co. Beds.', in addition to Swynnerton. These arms are also present in Isleham church, but they have, in addition, a silver molet at the centre of the cross and may be the arms of Frances Hasledon, wife of Sir Robert Peyton (died 1550).

It seems that besides the possible inaccuracy in respect of the Burgoyne arms, a further double error affects Thomas Peyton's shield. Not only is no Mallory lion present, but the arms of another family (other than Swynnerton) whose name could be associated with swine, have been substituted. The Swinford connection may be valid, but it is more likely to be an extraordinary coincidence, as in the fact that the husband of Thomas Peyton's great aunt was Sir Robert Swynburn (Swynborne) of Little Horkesley in Essex. (Banks gives Swinburne and different arms.) The brass of Sir Thomas Swynborne of 1412, at Little Horkesley, indicates that the family were Lancastrians. One coat-of-arms for Swinborne is 'Gules 3 boars' heads couped Argent'. It is, however, remarkable that a shield which appears to have mistakes in two of its 'quarters' should have been acceptable to the donor and have passed the heralds' inspections in later years.

Combining information given by Baker, Nichols, and Gibbons, the following interesting facts emerge. The wife of Sir Anketil Mallory of Kirkby Mallory, Alice née Dryby, the Lady of Bytham, called Alice Basset in her will which was proved in Sleaford, Lincs., in 1412 (see Kirkby Mallory), bequeathed a missal to the church at Weston Colville in Cambridgeshire. The village is south of Isleham. The missal was decorated with the arms of the Colvile family.

The pedigree of the Colvile family, states that Roger, Baron Colvile, who died in 1287, had three children. His first daughter married Ralph Basset of Sapcote, circa 1292, and their son, Ralph Basset of Sapcote, married Alice Dryby. After he died in 1378 she married Sir Anketil Mallory. The second daughter of the first Ralph Basset married into the family of Gernon and their son, Sir John Gernon of Derby, and Ralph Basset, inherited Bytham together, circa 1336. They also inherited Abington (Northants.) which passed to the Bernard family in 1419 via the Lylling family. Sir John Gernon's daughter, Mary, married Sir John Peyton (died 1393). Their great-grandson was Thomas Peyton, who married Margaret Bernard (see below). There were, therefore, early connections between all these families and the Mallorys of Kirkby Mallory, long before the marriage of Elena Mallory and Sir John Bernard. The arms of the Colvile family and the Gernon arms are quartered in Isleham church. Bytham eventually became the property of a Sir Robert Swynburne (spelling from the footnotes to the transcript of the will by Gibbons). The Northamptonshire notes augment and clarify these relationships. Further research will be required to confirm which arms belong to Elena and whether her forebears descended directly from Kirkby Mallory. Did Bertram of Holwell pass on a demi-lion as the arms of his branch? The evidence on the bell appears to support this.

The Warwickshire Mallorys were Lancastrian supporters, while Griffith suggests a Yorkshire adherence for Papworth Mallorys. Since the Bernards were Lancastrians, it seems reasonable to assume that Elena's parents were too.

Of interest is the fact that in Dugdale's day, the Peyton cross (Sable a cross engrailed Or, etc.), was present in the window of Billesley church in Warwickshire. (In the same 'hundred' as Botley: Billesley, which never recovered from the depopulation caused by the Black Death in 1361, is not identified on the modern map. The rebuilt church is described by Arthur Mee.)

The Lady Elena (Mallory) Bernard died in 1440, leaving a son, Thomas, and daughters Mary, Margaret and Catherine. Thomas died before his father. Sir John remarried, but died in 1451 leaving no male heir. His widow was Elizabeth Sakevyle, who died in 1464. He was succeeded by Elena's eldest daughter, Margaret Bernard, who inherited all the joint properties of Isleham, Holwell, Welton and Wold. Between 1464 and 1466 she married Thomas Peyton (Payton) of Peyton, son of John Peyton of Suffolk and Grace Burgoyne of Drayton in Cambridgeshire (settlement C. Close, 5 Edw. IV, m.12). Thomas Peyton was born at Drayton in 1416. He was High Sheriff for Cambs. and Hunts. in 1443 and 1453. Margaret (Bernard) Peyton predeceased her husband and he married another Margaret; Margaret Francis of Wickambrook. He died in 1484, the year before *Le Morte d'Arthur* was published. His eldest son, Thomas, died without issue in 1490, and was succeeded by Sir Crystofer Peyton, Margaret Francis's son, for a short while, probably during the minority of his nephew, Robert, the grandson of Margaret Bernard. Robert succeeded to Isleham in 1490 and was knighted two years later. From him descended a long line of distinguished men one of whom, Sir John Peyton of Isleham, was honoured by James I with a baronetcy in 1611 (N.D.B.). The Peyton family enjoyed other favours of King James and must have frequently encountered the Papworth Mallorys at court. Many members of the family emigrated to Virginia and the New World. The Yorkshire and Cheshire Mallorys also provided founder members of the colony of Virginia.

There are a few additional small coincidences to note. In the reign of Elizabeth I, a male descendant of Sir John Bernard's brother married a lady of the Cave family. A few years previously the Newbold Revel heiress sisters also married into the Cave family.

A Yorkshire Mallory held Sutton-on-Derwent, near York, in 1284. Part of this property was inherited by a Catherine Peyton in 1711. The connection between this Yorkshire Mallory and those at Studley Royal has so far not been established.

Immediately after the death of his father in 1484, young Thomas Peyton sold Welton and Wold, but their holding at Holwell was retained until 1564, when another Thomas Peyton aleined it to Robert Ivory (F. of F. Div. Cos. Hill, 4 Eliz., *V.C.H. Bedford*).

Oliver Cromwell's shadow fell on the Peyton family as well as on the Mallorys, and was responsible for them leaving Isleham. The English branch of the Peytons retained the title of lord of Isleham manor until the present day. The Peytons hold a family reunion every seven years at Isleham, many coming from America, Canada and Australia. They have enthusiastically maintained their lovely church which is the pride of the village. St Andrews, much larger than might be expected from the present size of the community it serves, is full of treasures, from the enormous sanctuary handle on the south door, to the huge bedstead tomb of the first baronet. There is also a truly magnificent angel roof, the gift of Crystofer Peyton. Ten of the original starry host of 60 remain.

One brass memorial, of which there are several, is to Sir John Bernard, who fought at Agincourt, and his wife, Elena Mallory. He wears the Lancastrian collar of 'SS', his lady's little dog wears a collar of bells. The inscription reads:

Hic jacit Johes Bernard miles qui obit xxiiii die march. Ano dom. MCCCCLI.
Et Dona Elena Swynton. Uxoris petci Johes Bernard milites. filie et heres
Johes Mallory millites. De Com Nohant. qui obit XIII die mens Octrobris.
Ano Dom MCCCCXL. et Dona Elizabeth Sakevyle. secunde uxoris petci
Johnis Bernard Miles. qui obit x die Mens Julie. Ano Dom MCCCCLXIII
[and a prayer]

Fig. 7. Sir John Bernard and his wife Elena Mallory, died 1440, Isleham church, Cambridgeshire.

Fig. 8. Sir Thomas Peyton, died 1484, and his wives. The first, Margaret Bernard (daughter of Elena Mallory) is shown in a brocade gown. From Isleham church, Cambridgeshire.

There is a contraction sign above 'Swynton', indicating the omission of another syllable, viz.: 'Swynnerton'.

If the Mallorys of Papworth St Agnes were Yorkist before the time of Thomas, they may not have fraternised with Elena's Lancastrian husband. No evidence of these two Cambridgeshire families having been acquainted has so far been discovered, in spite of the ubiquity of Alice Dryby.

By the high altar, a tomb chest bears another large and exquisite brass. It shows Thomas Peyton with both his Margarets. Margaret Bernard wears a gorgeous gown worthy of her mercer relatives. Both ladies have identical necklaces, the Peyton jewels perhaps. At Margaret Bernard's feet is a poppy seed-head. A plant which could be a poppy with four seed-heads is between the knight's feet. They may be a reference to their offspring and fertility, or may be they were to invoke the care of Morpheus. Poor Lady Francis is rather plain. The inscription, which is difficult to decipher, reads roughly as follows:

> Orate pro anima Thome Peyton Armiger. et Margarete et Margarete. uxores,
> qui quidem Thomas obit XXX die mentis juli. Ano Domini. Millimo
> CCCCLXXXIIII [and a prayer]

These two brasses are the only memorials in the church which have immediate connections with the Mallorys, but there are others of the Peyton family which, taken all together, present a fascinating sequence of armour, costume and style.

The manor house, which was sold by the Peytons in the 19th century, lies to the west of the church, built on the site of Elena's home, the medieval 'Bernard's Hall'.

In the church of the Holy Trinity at Long Melford in Suffolk, there is a beautiful contemporary stained glass window with portraits of Margaret Bernard and Sir Thomas Peyton. Her livery is Peyton impaling Bernard and Lylling.

Much of the information in this chapter was incidental to reading in respect of Mallory branches in other counties. The more significant sources are given in the text, but the collection of material in the Cambridge Public Library was particularly useful for all Cambridgeshire enquiries. The handbook provided by the church at Isleham contains a valuable description of the contents and history of the church and the history of the Peyton family. Part of their pedigree is also given by Banks. The writer is indebted to the vicar of Isleham who, in an exceptional summer, nobly ascended the tower on the hottest day of the year to sketch the all-important bell.

Note: Christopher Cahill, Esq.

There is some confusion in the records of this herald and his wife. Christopher Cahill held several offices in the College of Arms, being at one time, Norroy King of Arms and in 1493, Carlisle Herald. The Revd. Mark Noble in *The History of the College of Arms* (1805) states that another writer 'mistakes his (Cahill's) baptismal and gives the name of this Office for that of his family one. The best writers are extremely confused'. Noble also supplies the epitaph from Cahill's tomb in Brentford church: 'Here lyeth the body of Christopher Cahill, alias Norroy King of Arms. Who died — 1510'. Noble says 'he left no issue by his wife Eleanor, daughter of — Mallory. Some pedigrees make this person his mother instead of his wife'. However, *The Collectannae Topographica et Genealogica* (1835), vol. 5, says that in the sepulchral inscriptions which existed in the church of the Grey Friars in London in the time of Henry VIII, there was the following (related to

Christopher Cahill, alias Norroy, obit. 1510): 'In Capella Se Maria (F.277), Alicia, Carlett, alias Norroy, 2a filia Thome Malore armiger de com. Cantuarij. Obit 13 Aug. 157 (sic qu — 507)'.

Do we read Thomas of Canterbury (Cantuaria), or Alice of Canterbury? If the former, we have another Thomas who might have written *Le Morte*. It seems that Alicia, and not Eleanor, was indeed Cahill's wife. Thomas Mallory of Papworth St Agnes, Cambridgeshire (Canatabrigia), names three daughters in his will, dated 1469. The first (i.e., not '2a') was Alice. The second was Ellen (Elena), the third Elizabeth.

The fact that Thomas of Papworth's will is registered under the P.C.C. may not have any significance relative to the above. The Cambridge County Archivist, M. Farrar, states that 'The more wealthy and pretentious tended to use this court even in cases where inferior courts would have had jurisdiction'. (*Genealogical Sources in Cambridgeshire*.) Matthews may have been hasty in dismissing 'the man of Kent'.

No reference in the *V.C.H.*; Isleham is about 15 miles N.E. of Cambridge;
Long Melford is about 23 miles S.E. of Cambridge.

Chapter Five

SUSSEX

THIS CHAPTER is an extension of 'Cambridgeshire', for which references have been given above. The information has been collected mainly from the Appendices to 'The Duppa-Isham Correspondence', edited by Gyles Isham, Bt. (published by the Northamptonshire Record Society), *The Civil War in Sussex,* by Sir Charles Thomas-Stanford, the guidebook to Preston Manor (1965 edn.), Nichols's *Leicestershire,* and the *D.N.B.* (Sir Gyles Isham and the *D.N.B.* also refer to the Thurloe State Papers, vol. 7, and the Clarendon State Papers, vol. 15.) In 1980 two families surnamed Mallory reside in Sussex.

Preston and East Hoathly

The Cambridgeshire branch of the Mallory family is connected to the Shirley family of Preston, Sussex, by marriage and by one of the more tragic enterprises of the Civil War. Burton says the Shirleys were descended from an ancient and eminent Saxon family, the first of whom is named as Sewalus, lord of Staunton Harold, Leics., in 1085. The surname of Shirley (Sherley) had evolved by 1317. The family intermarried with the same prominent Norman families as the Mallorys, including the family of Basset.

In the reign of Henry VIII, a second son of the Staunton Harold line founded a branch at Wistenton (now called Wiston) in Sussex. The Tudor manor still stands, near Chanctonbury Ring. By 1575 the family were also lords of Preston, eight miles to the east, in the person of Sir Anthony Shirley, the second son of William Shirley of Wiston. Sir Anthony married Barbara, daughter of Sir Thomas Walsingham of Kent. Their eldest daughter, Judith Shirley, married Sir Henry Mallory of Papworth St Agnes, Cambridgeshire. They lived at Papworth St Agnes, where at least three son and six daughters were born. Sir Henry was knighted in 1605. Sometime between 1635 and 1637 he sold his Cambridgeshire properties and there is no further record of Mallorys in the county after that time. The family also owned property in Bedfordshire, but does not appear to have removed there. They were connected with the court of King Charles I, and one son, Anthony, was buried at Richmond in 1640. There was another son, William, whose history has not been traced, and a third son, Captain 'Henery' Mallory, who inherited Anthony's property. All these brothers were direct descendants of the Thomas of Papworth St Agnes who might have written *Le Morte d'Arthur.*

When Charles II was in exile his supporters in Britain were busy organising a widespread rising intended to overthrow Cromwell. One of the chief instigators was

Sir Henry Slingsby of Yorkshire, a staunch Royalist and a friend of the Yorkshire Mallorys. Several counties were involved and the gentry of Sussex joined the conspiracy under the leadership of John Mordaunt, second son of the Earl of Peterborough.

Cromwell issued an edict early in March 1658, ordering all those who had fought for the Crown to remain within five miles of their homes. In spite of this restriction and the consequently increased vigilance on the part of the Commonwealth troops, it seems that Captain Henery Mallory made his way by secret Sussex combes to his mother's family home at Preston Manor. There he joined Sir Anthony Shirley (grandson of the first Anthony of Preston) and other Shirley relatives, all of whom were committed to the conspiracy.

However, the plot had already been betrayed to Thurloe, Cromwell's Secretary of State. When the plans of the Royalists were almost ripe, all the conspirators were arrested countrywide. Thurloe boasted that every Cavalier had been taken. Captain Henery was arrested at the beginning of April and 'persuaded' to implicate Mordaunt who was to answer a charge of treason, with its terrible penalties.

Henery Mallory, emulating an earlier Mallory goalbreaker, contrived to escape on the very eve of Mordaunt's trial (1 June), with the consequence that the prosecution, lacking its principal witness, was obliged to acquit Mordaunt, who was released. Lady Mordaunt played some part in arranging Henery's escape. He stayed hidden for at least a week. When Mordaunt was safe, Mallory could possibly have taken advantage of the Royalist underground network and slipped away to France. Instead, either to satisfy the code of honour of the times, or because of treachery, he was rearrested. He stood trial and was condemned, but the curious Fates that govern Mallory destinies produced a reprieve and he suffered the lesser horror of imprisonment in the Tower; there he was incarcerated for at least a year until the Restoration set him free.

Many very gallant men suffered dreadfully, and it seems in restrospect unnecessarily, as a result of this unfortunate conspiracy. Three months after, Oliver Cromwell was dead of natural causes and his son and successor, Richard Cromwell, abdicated only a year later. Within another 12 months Charles II was king of England.

Sir Anthony Shirley was created a baronet in 1665. His portrait still hangs in Preston Manor. After his release, Captain Henery returned to Sussex and lived for a time at East Hoathly, near Lewes, but there is no record of him marrying or dying there. The parish records are incomplete for the years 1642–63. He inherited a small fortune and may have gone to London, for he was the residual legatee of Bishop Duppa's wife.

Bishop Brian Duppa was tutor to Charles II and married Jane Killingtree who was the granddaughter of Sir William Mallory of Papworth St Agnes. Sir William was also the great-grandfather of Captain Henery Mallory. (She was the daughter of Nicholas Killingtree and Jane Mallory, daughter of Sir William Mallory. Sir William's brother was Lord Mayor of London.) Although this was a rather extended connection, Captain Henery was a favourite of the Duppas. The bishop left him a legacy, and his 'Aunt' Jane after bequests to two of his sisters and two other Mallorys (John and Richard), left most of her money to Henery in 1665. (He did not inherit the Duppa house.) Both the Duppas are buried in Westminster Abbey. (The Duppa connection suggests that Mallorys could have met Van Dyck, see Yorkshire portrait, below.)

The manor of Preston was a place of great delight half a century ago. On sunny days its doors stood wide to admit the perfume of roses, lavender and heliotrope, which mingled on the hour with the tinkles, chimes and bells of a family of clocks, so large that the announcements of one hour, retreating into the depths of the house, overtook the beginning of the next. Today it is a pleasant refuge from the busy streets and teeming holiday beaches. It contains a museum devoted to beautiful antique furniture and the collections of the last private owners of the manor, Sir Charles and Lady Thomas-Stanford. The house, gardens and park now belong to the Borough of Brighton and are open to visitors.

Preston 100; East Hoathly is 15 miles N.W. of Brighton; *V.C.H. Sussex*, Vol. 7, p. 268.

Chapter Six

BEDFORDSHIRE

THE MALLORY MANORS in Bedfordshire are connected directly with the two families in Cambridgeshire. The main sources of information were *The History and Antiquities of the County of Northamptonshire,* by George Baker (1882), *The History and Antiquities of the County of Leicestershire,* by J. Nichols (1810), *A Bedfordshire Armorial,* by F. W. Kuhlicke, and material gathered in reading for the history of other branches of the Mallory family. Correspondence with Professor Lester Mallory and Mr. Don Mallory clarified the pedigree of the Mallorys of Shelton. In 1980 two families surnamed Mallory remain in Bedfordshire.

Holwell: Mallory property prior to 1154 until 1421

The manor of Holwell was owned by the branch of the Mallory family who were also lords of Welton and Old (alias Wold), in Northamptonshire. Their coat-of-arms is not described with certainty by any authority, but it is discussed in the chapter on Cambridgeshire, under the manor of Isleham. The first name to appear in the Mallory history of Holwell is Bertram Mallore. His wife, Egaline, made a gift of part of a mill to the Abbey of Lavendon in Buckinghamshire. The mill, one of several in the village of Hanslope, also in Bucks., was the joint gift of Egaline and John de Bidun. He was the founder of the abbey, and in 1154 was the Sheriff of Buckingham. This provides a date for Bertram Mallory of either late in the reign of King Stephen or in the reign of Henry II, and it seems that he could have been another son of the Richard Mallory (spelled Maulare in Welton Survey) who held at Swinford and at Welton (and was probably the father of Geoffrey Mallory, lord of Kirkby Mallory), since Welton eventually became a property 'in the manor' of Kirkby Mallory.

The foundation grants were all confirmed in 1227, including Hanslope Mill (Dugdale, *Monasticon,* and Chart. R. 11, Henry III, No. 38). It is of interest to note here that the Abbey of Biddlesdon, Bucks., founded in 1147, had among its early patrons two people whose families married members of the Mallory family; Sir Richard Corbet and Lord Zouche. In 1241 a Henry Mallory was Abbot of Biddlesdon (*see also* Charwelton, Northants.).

Bertram and Egaline had two sons, Sir Simon and Robert. Robert's son, also Simon, died without issue, and a grant of land, which Sir Simon had made to his nephew Simon, was claimed by the nephew's widow, Alice Mallory, in 1228. (F. of F. Beds., 12 Hen III).

One of these Simons served on a Bedfordshire jury in 1202. This was in the transition period that led to the demise of the old Norman system of justice. Men could now have their disputes decided on the evidence of 12 men, chosen to support their claims (not for impartiality as in the present day), summoned by knights who represented each party. (Churchill, *Birth of Britain*.) It was an alternative to trial by ordeal or by combat under surveillance of referees. A landowner could provide himself with a champion, but in the event of the opposition putting up a 'Harry Gow', it may have been more prudent to choose the jury system.

Sir Simon's son, Robert, alive in 1241, was the next lord of Holwell (Harl. Chart. 51D, 14). He was also lord of Welton (Testa Neville) (*see* the Northants. notes). The descent of the Holwell Mallorys from Bertram was proved by Robert's eldest son, John Mallory, who succeeded as lord of Holwell, Welton and Wold (F. of F., Edw. I, 1285/6). John's wife was 'Joan'. Kuhlicke says that he (or more probably his son, John) was ordered to raise a company of men-at-arms and take them to swell the army gathering at Portsmouth for Edward III's campaign in France. The date quoted for this is 1316, which is too early for Edward III, and too early for the Hundred Years War. The war began in 1338 to enforce Edward's claim to the French throne. It seems that 1316 was a misprint and that John Mallory and the men from Holwell were among the valiant longbowmen and dismounted cavalry who defeated the French at Crècy in 1346. A Sir John Mallory held Welton and other property 'of' Sir Anketil of Kirkby Mallory during the reign of Edward III (*see* Northants.).

Robert Mallory's second son was Richard, whose son, William (married to Amy), died in 1360 and may have inherited Sudborough (Northants.). There is no further news of them at Holwell, but they have been suggested very tentatively (Griffith) as one possible pair of ancestors for the Mallorys of Papworth St Agnes in Cambridge- shire. From the relevant notes it will be seen that there is also a possibility that the Papworth Mallorys held a direct descent from Kirkby Mallory and that Sudborough William may have been some relative other than the father, of Anketil (father of Ala).

Robert had a third son, Segwyn, whose son was called Simon. The branch of Mallorys which held Woodford in Northants. in the 16th century used the name Simon frequently and may have been descended from this last Holwell Simon, although the arms (*see* Isleham) suggest otherwise and there are other possibilities (*see* Pedigree M). However, the Holwell arms aside, such a descent would also link Holwell to the manors of Saddington and Welton in Leicestershire and so back to Kirkby Mallory. The arms of the Woodford Mallory family are similar to arms of Kirkby Mallory; in the arms of the Walton family the lion has a single tail (*see* Welton, Northants. arms). The Holwell arms may have been a demi-lion rampant with a single tail.

The name John Mallory appears as lord of Holwell in an inquisition in 1359 in respect of a Simon Frances who held land 'of John Mallory', and again in 1421, when Sir John Mallory 'lord of Holwell and Welton', died. He was also 'lord of Wold'. His daughter and heir was Elena Mallory who took Welton and Holwell, and later Wold, to her marriage with Sir John Bernard of Isleham, Cambs. Details of this, their subsequent history and coats-of-arms, are given under Isleham. Their daughter, Margaret Bernard, inherited all their joint properties and they passed to her husband,

Thomas Peyton, who became lord of Isleham by the marriage. In 1484 he sold Welton and Wold, but the Peyton family retained Holwell until 1564, when another Thomas Peyton sold the manor to Robert Ivory (F. of F., 6 Eliz.).

The Mallory house is no longer recognisable, but two possible sites remain. An ancient barn and parts of stone walls to the west of the village are given in the *V.C.H.*, Holwellbury Farm to the north, has been suggested as another by the Bedfordshire archivist. Holwell has migrated between Bedfordshire and Hertfordshire as county boundaries altered from time to time. It was finally transferred to Bedfordshire in 1831.

The church, which has no Mallory memorials, is dedicated to St Peter.

Clifton 100; *V.C.H. Beds.*, V.2, p. 286 (*also Bucks.*, V.1); Sir Walter Scott, *The Fair Maid of Perth*; 35 miles from Isleham; 5 miles N.W. of Hitchin, 20 miles S.W. of Cambridge.

Shelton (and Dean): Mallory property 1387 to 1714

The manor of Shelton has the distinction of being the last manorial property to be relinquished by any member of the Mallory family. Yet its long history does not provide much of interest to add to that of the Mallorys of Papworth St Agnes (Cambs.), who were its principal owners. There is, however, an extensive pedigree which augments the Cambridgeshire records. The parish records, bishops' transcripts and Visitations for the manors of Shelton and neighbouring Dean, and for Papworth St Agnes and Papworth Everard should be studied together. The arms of this branch, given in the 1634 Visitation, are 'Or A lion rampant queue fourche Gules within a bordure Gules. A Crest A Nag's head couped Gules. Charged with a Fleur de Lys', indicating perhaps the arms of a sixth son.

The Mallorys owned no manor at Dean (Beds. archivist), but they married into a Dean family and may have acquired land in that village, which adjoins Shelton farmland.

Some of the children born at Papworth were baptized at Shelton church where the Mallorys still held part of the advowson as late as 1706. It seems likely that Shelton was the home of some members of this branch of the family before they owned Papworth St Agnes and their ties with it were those of affection.

In 1387 Shelton Manor was quit-claimed to John de la Warre, Anketin Mallory and William Palmer. (F. of F. 10, Rich. II, 76). The Palmer family were connected by marriage to the Mallorys of Papworth St Agnes. Shelton once supported two manors, one of which belonged to the Wake family for over 200 years. They had a connection with the Mallorys of Studley Royal (Yorks.) and 'The wife of John Wakys' benefitted under a Papworth will.

If Anketin was the Sir Anketil Mallory who sold Kirkby Mallory in 1377, it is to be expected that he would have resided mainly at his wife's home, Castle Bytham.

The next confirmation of Shelton as Mallory property came in 1398, when it was quit-claimed to a syndicate consisting in part of a 'Sir William Mallory of Papworth' (F. of F. 21, Rich. II, 135), according to the *V.C.H.* The reference goes on to say 'Sir William Papworth is here read as Sir William Mallory of Papworth'. From the

Cambridgeshire records it is known that William Papworth of Papworth St Agnes was still alive (*see* his will, 1415). He left Papworth to a William Mallory, son of Anketil Mallory. What the significance of these facts are is not clear, but the William Mallory who seems to have inherited the Papworth properties would have been only 12 years old in 1398. Certainly a Sir William Mallory of Papworth St Agnes died seised of Shelton in 1445 (I.P.M. 23, H.6, 10).

The 1634 Visitation (Harl., vol. 19) omits one generation and attributes the children of Sir William Mallory of Papworth (obit. 1585) to his father, Anthony (*see* wills).

The records for Bedfordshire are incomplete for the years following. Shelton was one of the homes of the Mallorys for another two centuries. Sir William Mallory, the builder of the Papworth house which stands today, had a large family. A John Malory 'of Papworth' had a son, Matthew 'of Shelton'. One of Sir William's sons, Peter Mallory, married Frances Estrey of Wood End (Beds.). They had five children of whom one, Ralph, was lord of Shelton in 1635 (Rec. R. Beds. 11, Chas. I, 7). It has been suggested that Ralph's cousin at Papworth, Sir Henry Mallory, who appears to have sold Papworth prior to 1637, may have done so in order to pay his 'ship money' to King Charles I. Ralph of Shelton had to subscribe to this levy, and there is a sorry tale of complaint by the villagers that Mr. Ralph had eased his portion by increasing their expected contributions. An interesting comment on the times, if the village could criticise the lord of the manor in this way, even though he was the grand-nephew of a Lord Mayor of London.

He married Grace Neal, who belonged to the Neals of Lower (Nether) Dean. The Neals were from Yeldon in Bedfordshire and acquired their Dean property after Henry VIII's redistribution of the assets of Huntingdon Priory. They lived at Dean until 1682.

Ralph and Grace Mallory's eldest son, Peter, was born in May 1607 (Harl. Soc. xix, 22). His wife was, perhaps, Susan Weedon of Chesham (Bucks.), who married a Peter Mallory. In 1667 he conveyed the manor to William Busby, whose family seem to have enjoyed possession of it for about four decades. (It is possible that the Mallorys lived in the house during this time.) Peter Mallory was buried at Dean in September 1688. His son was William, born in 1639, and his daughter, Susanna, was two years older. Susanna married the rector of Shelton, Thomas Boundy. Her memorial may still be seen in the church. Perhaps they all lived in the rectory until Boundy remarried.

In 1705 a Francis Mallory began legal proceedings to have the manor returned to the family, but it proved to be a long wrangle, for it was not until 1714 that a William Busby (presumably a descendant of the first) admitted defeat. (Rec. R. Beds., 13 Anne, Rot. 76). It must have cost more than it was worth, for Francis immediately sold the manor to a Theophilus Dillingham for £520. (F. of F. Beds. 1, Geo. I.) Who this Francis Mallory was, is still to be discovered. He may have been Francis, the second son of Ralph, a very old gentleman in 1714, or perhaps he was Francis who lived at Milford Haven in 1666 (*see* Ch. IX, State Papers).

The village of Shelton is a pleasant rural community today. Shelton Hall, which is considered by the county archivist to be the site of the Mallory manor, was once a large rectangular moated complex, with house walls over four feet in thickness. Now only the west wing remains. There are still parts of the great medieval walls incorporated in the building: one bedroom and the staircase are of the time of Mallory occupation. The present lady of the manor can find no Mallory artefact similar to those at Papworth St Agnes.

The charming church is dedicated to St Mary. On the west wall, near the altar, is a memorial tablet to Susanna Mallory and two of her sons. It also commemorates Thomas Boundy's second wife who was a Neal. It is decorated with gloomy little death's heads and breaks out into such flamboyant Latin that the message is almost incomprehensible. A near translation is as follows' 'Susanna and Grace, wives, Thomas and Joseph sons, of Thomas Boundy Rector. Here lie nearby, hoping for The Resurrection, Susan daughter of Peter Malory of this town, Gentleman which wife leaves five sons. Peter, Thomas, John, Joseph, Jacob and one daughter Mary. She died, aged 33+, in the year of our lord 1669. Grace daughter of Paul Neal of Dean, died in the year of our lord 1691 aged 64. Thomas died 1664. Joseph died 1660'.

A bell in the church at Dean was made by Tobie Norris in 1671, perhaps the son of Thomas Norris who made the Papworth St Agnes bell.

Stodden 100; *V.C.H. Beds.*, V.3, p. 161; 10 miles N. of Bedford; 15 miles N.W. of Papworth
St Agnes; 25 miles N. of Holwell.

Chapter Seven

YORKSHIRE

MUCH VALUABLE INFORMATION about the Yorkshire Mallorys and their descendants came from correspondence, in addition to the books and papers listed below. A brief bibliography of the main works consulted is given.

V.C.H. Yorkshire; public records in London and Yorkshire; H.M.S.O. publications; *The Ill-framed Knight,* Prof. W. Matthews, 1966; 'Thomas Malory: The Hutton Documents', P. J. C. Field, *Medium Aevum,* 1979; Yorkshire archaeological and topographical journals (courtesy of the Haddon Library); *Yorkshire—East Riding,* G. Wright, 1976; *The Genealogy of the Mallorys of Virginia,* Henry R. Mallory, U.S.A., 1955; the works of J. Walbran (the Studley historian *par excellence*); in particular, his Appendix No. XI to *Memorials of the Abbey of St Mary of Fountains,* vol. 2 (1), entitled 'A Genealogical and Biographical Memoir of the lords of Studley in Yorkshire' (*Surtees Society,* vol. LXVII), 1876-78; the guide books to Fountains Hall and Ripon cathedral; extract from *The History of Harewood,* J. Jones, 1859 (kindly supplied by Harewood Estate Office). Other literature is mentioned in the text. Correspondence, which is gratefully acknowledged, with Mrs B. Sharp, Mr. C. Watson, Mr. J. Portess and the Studley Estate Office, Mrs. Mary Hey, Mrs. C. Mallorie, Mr. Henry Vyner, Miss C. Ayre, Skipton Castle, Ltd., and Mrs. Joan Mallory Reeve of the U.S.A., also Dr. Mae Guild Barrett of Seattle, U.S.A. The collection of Mallory/ Mallorie papers known as 'The Vyner Papers', once housed at Studley Royal, are divided between Leeds City Archives and Leeds University. A catalogue has been published. The writer is indebted to Sir Thomas Ingilby, Bt., for kind permission to take and to publish the photograph of the Ingilby/Mallory arms in Ripley Castle and to the estate staff for their help. J. Dawson confirmed the extant arms at Hutton Conyers.

Members of Parliament for the County include Sir William Mallory of Studley, for York in 1585 (also High Sheriff 1592) and Sir John Mallory of Studley in 1601 for Thirsk. Sir John Mallory of Studley in 1603, for Ripon; William Mallory, Esq., 1614-39, for Ripon (six occasions); Sir John Mallorie, in 1640, for Ripon; and John Aislabie, in 1702, for Ripon (also Chancellor of the Exchequer). Today rather more than a dozen Mallory (Mallorie) families reside in the county.

The Mallorys of Yorkshire are best represented by the family which lived for centuries at Hutton Conyers and Studley Royal, although they were preceded by less famous Mallory knights in other parts of the county. The Mallorys of Cheshire and many now resident in the United States of America are directly descended from the Studley family. It is probably true to say that the majority of living Mallorys may trace their ancestry first to Yorkshire. Spelling the name 'Mallorie' seems to have greatest popularity in the families connected with Studley Royal, but not consistently so.

Walbran, working at Studley around 1878, gives invaluable details extracted from the family papers, to augment the several Visitations, which are rather short on dates, but provide the pedigrees on which most researchers rely. Others continue to discover corrections in wills and deeds.

Scholars researching Studley's Thomas Mallory (*circa* 1450) have found sufficient material relative to only two generations of the family to fill their books. The mine is by no means exhausted. The history of the later Yorkshire Mallorys suffers from a surfeit of information that, paradoxically, raises as many questions as answers. It will therefore be appreciated that only a selection can be included in one chapter suitable for this book, although Yorkshire may generate more interest than other counties among 20th-century Mallorys. Fuller details of the origins of the earliest Anketils may never be discovered, but the lives and descendants of the younger sons of Studley Royal remain to be researched in the escheats, fines, inquisitions, wills and many series of rolls, bishops' transcripts, parish records, and the census returns.

Dr. Mae Guild Barrett suggests that the Mallorys probably understood the Celtic languages and so would have been invaluable ambassadors in Wales and Scotland, on behalf of the kings of both England and Scotland. Matilda was supported by her uncle, David I (*see* Origins below); William the Lion and David, Earl of Huntingdon, supported 'Young King Henry' (*see* above); Yorkshire Mallorys were connected with the court of Queen Margaret, wife of Alexander III. These few instances appear to support Dr. Barrett's theory. *See also* Mallorys in Ireland, below.

Octon (Oketon): Mallory property 1229, then female descent
Sutton-on-Derwent: Mallory property in 1284
Kilham: settled by Mallory family 1629 to 1970+

As in other counties, the earliest Mallory records in Yorkshire commence with the familiar proliferation of Anketils and Anketyns, easily confused and written of by some authorities as one individual, who was, therefore, as hale and hearty in 1381 as he had been in 1229.

The first of these was Sir Anketil Mallory, who in 1229 married a child bride, Sarah, the daughter and heir of the great Yorkshire baron, William de Mulethorpe (Mowthorpe). (Clo. Rolls.) For reasons given below, it appears that Sir Anketil was a son (or close relative), of Sir Richard of Kirkby Mallory. The Kirkby Mallory family were in favour in royal circles at that time and it is no surprise to find Henry III feeling well-disposed towards members of the northern branch. He spent the Christmas following Anketil's marriage, at York. During the visit he kindly allowed Sir Anketil a year's grace in which to discharge the debts Baron Mowthorpe had incurred with the famous money-lender, Aaron the Jew. What Aaron thought of this generosity is not recorded. In 1230 Henry also pardoned Mallory for falling behind with the scutage due for the knight's fee on Mowthorpe's property. (Clo. Rolls.) Henry's benevolence extended to making Anketil a marriage settlement in 1231 of the manor of Octon, which he held by the service of providing 'one archer for the defence of

York castle' and 'a serjeant to lead the King's treasure through the country'. (Fees, ii, f. 1354.) In this note, Anketil is referred to as 'Anketin'. Twenty years later Anketil had sub-let his Octon lands in five tenancies.

Henry went further. In 1234 he gave Anketil the timber to build his manor house at Terrington (? Tyverington) in Bulmer Wapentake, where he also held the demesne lands at Mowthorpe and other property at Wiggenthorpe and Huntingdon. The gift was of 'six oaks from his forest of Galtres' (*V.C.H.*). In 1384 there was still an Anketil (Anketin) Mallory at Huntingdon (Chancery I.P.M.7, Rich. II, No. 59), who docs not appear to have been a direct descendant of Octon Anketil. It is interesting to note that in 1859 the property was inherited by Lady Mary Vyner, who had connections with the Studley Royal Mallories.

From inquisitions and other records, it is known that Sir Anketil's children were (at least) two sons and four daughters. The eldest son, Anketil (or Anketin) seems to have died before his father and to have left no offspring (but posthumous children were often ignored, as the Studley records prove).

An Anketil Malore (spelt 'Anketin' and 'Anketille') was sent 'on the King's business' to the brilliant court of the young Scots king Alexander III, the husband of King Henry's daughter, Margaret. Alexander, who was crowned on the stone of Scone when only seven years of age, moved his court about the country, but most frequently settled at grey Stirling, secure on its mighty crag above the town. The elder Anketil is less likely to have been despatched on such a mission and there is none other of the name at that time except his son. The reaffirmation of the 'letters of protection' in 1252, may still be read in 'The Calendar of Documents Relating to Scotland'.

In 1253 King Henry desired his return. The affairs of the distaff side of his household were under the supervision of the queen of England. Henry sent a memorandum to Queen Alienora in July of that year, requesting her to arrange for 'Anketille Malore' to be recalled from Queen Margaret's service. (Cal. Pat.) For a brief instant, they glow into life, then history disobligingly turns a page and they are gone.

Sir Anketil's will is not preserved. He died before his second son, Nicholas, who died without issue in 1274; his sisters, Margery, Sarah, Alice (Avis) and Nicholaa were his joint heirs. (Cal. I.P.M. V.2, Edw. I, H.M.S.O. pub.) In addition to the properties listed above, they inherited North Dalton, which they held 'of the King', and property at Clifford.

Margery married Ralph Salvain. They received the demesne lands of Mowthorpe, which in 1299 were held by Sir William Mallory, lord of Walton, in custody for their son, Anketin Salvain (FF.F.Y., 27 Edw. I, No. 12) (*see also* Walton). Their daughters were Nicholaa and Katherine Salvain. Anketin Salvain received a grant of Free Warren at Mowthorpe in 1309 and in 1317; Sir Anketin obtained the release of the property of his sisters. He married Iseult, who presented him with Nicholas and Ellen. Sir Anketin died in 1351. His aunt Sarah also had a son, Henry de Grimstone, who proved his age at York on 'Thursday the morrow of St Giles 16, Edw. I' (H.M.S.O. pub.).

Margery Salvain's great-great-great-grandson, John Lane, had a daughter, Agnes Lane, who became the mother of Sir Christopher Danby of Thorpe Perrow. He was the father of Mary Danby who married Sir Christopher Mallory (obit. 1555) of Studley Royal.

After Anketil of Octon and his son, two further Anketils are recorded in Yorkshire. The first was Anketil Mallory who held the lordship of Sutton-on-Derwent in 1284, under Peter de Malo Lacu, who held it 'of the King' (Cal. Clo.; *Feud Aids*, V.6). Did he have Mallory heirs? Part of the property came to Catherine Peyton in 1711 (*see* Isleham, Cambridge).

A hundred or so years later, in 1381, there was a mandate to the mayor and bailiffs of York to 'Implement the law in regard to unlawful assembly'. Anketil Mallory, knight, was included. He was also commissioned to assemble in Lincolnshire to resist insurgents and two years later was told off to go and see to the floods affecting the Lincolnshire lands of Joan, Princess of Wales. In 1385 he was putting up 'Bekyns' and assembling archers and other armed men against a possible French invasion (Cal. Pat. Rich II). The only Anketil Mallory in the pedigrees at that time was the over-worked Sir Anketil, husband of Alice Dryby, of Kirkby Mallory, etc. The lady had some interests in Yorkshire, one being the Colville manor of Thornton Steward (FF. Yorks. 8, Rich. II, No. 40).

There is another reference to an Anketil Mallory, who also appears to be Alice Dryby's husband. The Archbishop of York, William Zouche, who died in 1352, remarked that his 'young kinsman Anketil Mallory' was *'armiger literatus'*. Apart from the intriguing inference that he was a man of unusual accomplishments in the way of Latin and the art of writing, it provides no definite identification. (*The Nobility of Later Medieval England*, McFarlane.)

The manor of Octon lies less than an hour's walk away from the village of Kilham where Mallorys are recorded in an unbroken line from 1629 to the 1970s. Anketil's line appears to have died out and we see no more Mallorys in the region in between. This would appear to be another case of 'springing out'.

The records commence in 1622. The first Mallory mentioned is George 'Mallorie', who baptized his first short-lived child, Ursula, in 1629. His second little daughter was also christened Ursula in 1631 (bishops' transcripts). A William 'aged 22 in 1663' (parish regs.), and therefore born in 1641, must have been a son of George, possibly George of Studley Royal, b. 1591.

It is considered to be bad genealogy to make deductions based upon names, although it seems reasonable to suppose that a Prissick Mallory and a Gibson Mallory, born further afield in the East Riding, could surely have been related to Elizabeth Gibson and Mary Prissick, who were both wives of Kilham Mallorys. The relevant generations at Studley Royal, including George, born 1591, had famous relatives: Sir William and Dame Ursula, who were in George's case, his grandparents. Besides 'Ursula' (which occurs thrice at Studley, and only once more in all the Mallory pedigrees: at Lichborough in 1550), the names 'William' or 'George' were given to the two eldest sons in many succeeding generations. The surname, after several aberrations, became 'Mallory' in 1700.

William, born 1641, died in 1688. In the probate of his will (Deanery Pec. Mar. 1688) his son, also a George, is styled 'Gent.'. Gentleman George calls himself 'yeoman' in his own will, written in 1698 by himself. The will and inventory (probate Oct. 1700) confirm that he was wealthy enough. He died 'from a fall of a horfe' (parish reg.). He owned a self-sufficient farm comprising 169 acres of growing corn (measured in oxgangs); wheat, malt and barley (measured in quarters) from 240 acres, already harvested. He also owned two woods and grazing for 180 sheep, three swine, 50 pigs, five horses, six oxen, four cows, 12 heifers; and seven beehives. His house was commodious for the times and comfortably furnished. Two servants' beds and bedding 'in ye litle chamber', indicate inside servants. In addition to outhouses, there was a big barn. Together with the ready cash mentioned in his will, he was probably worth in the region of £1,000.

He and the other early Mallorys of Kilham were educated, could read and write, and had some Latin; William was a churchwarden. Kilham held important regional markets for the sale of livestock. A civic office of swineherd was created to supervise the arrangements for the thousands of pigs brought for sale in those days. William Mallory, 'a farmer', who died in 1747, seems to have held this post. He was probably one of the last. Although Kilham was a thriving business township and agricultural centre from the earliest times, in the 18th century a rapid decline occurred, perhaps due to plague or drought. (The Driffield canal which impoverished much of the area was not built until later.) The population of Kilham was reduced to a third and many farms and houses stood empty, the garths (fields) going to waste. To alleviate the hardship of the remaining villagers, Lord D'arcy fostered brickmaking and its attendant trades, for the clay was to be found on his land nearby. This was after 1743. No doubt there was a good market for the product as a lining for the canal when it came.

In common with their peers the Gibsons, Lamploughs, Reads, Agars, and most of their neighbours, Mallorys were reduced to artisan status; a phase of 'indigent circumstances' had set in again.

In the 19th century, industrial expansion and the advent of the splendid steam locomotive, offered a living to the hardworking and intelligent. From bricks to steam, Kilham Mallorys progressed. By the 20th century they were dispersed far from Yorkshire (*see* introduction). In modern times they have emulated their medieval kinsmen; fighting in two world wars, holding commissions in the armed forces, serving in Her Majesty's Life Guard, becoming members of a London City Livery Company (the Scriveners), and holding responsible civil positions in authority. (It is not intended that living members of the family should be embarrassed by close identification.) The census returns augment the information of the transcripts and parish registers.

Dickering Wappentake

Octon (Thwing)

Six miles north of Great Driffield, some 30 miles east of Ripon. The pre-18th-century village has vanished, together with the chapel.

Kilham

Three miles north of Great Driffield. A friendly village in pleasant rural surroundings. Church: All Saints.

Harthill Wappentake

Sutton-on-Derwent

Eighteen miles south-west of Great Driffield, five miles south-east of York. Church: St Michael. *V.C.H.* (East Riding).

Huttons Conyers: Mallory property before 1347 to C17.
Studley Royal: Mallory property, circa *1438 to 1674 (then descendants)*
Fountains Hall: acquired by Mallory descendants 1768 until 1974

The family known as 'the Mallories of Studley Royal', first appear at Hutton Conyers, another property near Ripon. The Visitations (Harl. Soc.) of 1563, 1584 and 1612, all give an unidentified Sir Thomas Mallory 'married a daughter of the Lord Zouche', as the father of the first Mallory lord of Hutton Conyers, a Sir Christopher Mallory, who died in 1374. Sir Thomas was therefore alive at the beginning of the century and Lord Zouche was probably William Lord Zouch of Harryngworth (Northants.), or his son. There are two recorded Thomases who may qualify. Both belonged to the Kirkby Mallory family, but for reasons given under Kirkby Mallory, it seems that Sir Thomas, son of Sir William Mallory of Tachebrook Mallory and Walton, v 1293, was the father of Sir Christopher. A later William Lord Zouche married Margaret Greene, daughter of Sir Henry Greene whose family also had connections with the Mallory family (*see* Leics. and Northants.).

The Zouches, descended from the counts and earls of Brittany, established themselves in many counties in England, especially in Leicestershire, Northamptonshire and the West Country. William (son of Eudo and grandson of Sir Alan, Constable of the Tower) was the first Baron Zouche of Harryngworth. He was summoned to parliament in 1308. The arms of Zouche of Harryngworth were 'Gules 10 bezants (4. 3. 2. 1)'. The arms of Mallory impaling Zouche given in the 1563/4 Visitation to Yorkshire (Harl. Pub. Soc. 16, 1881) are: 'Or a lion rampant with two tails Gules collared Pearl (silver)', Mallory: impaling 'Gules 15 bezants (5. 4. 3. 2. 1) a canton Ermine', Zouche.

These are the arms of the earlier Zouche family of Somerset and Wiltshire. Since these ancient families extended to all parts, local associations are not necessarily to be expected, although Harryngworth is the more likely.

Sir Christopher Mallory, known as 'of Hutton' in 1347 (deed Burton, Mon. Ebor.), and spelled 'Cristoforo Maillore', in documents dated 1351–69, married Joan Conyers in 1336 (FF. York 29, Edw. III, 11). His wife, heiress to Robert Conyers the last of his line, was a descendant of an ancient and great Norman family, Constables of Durham since the time of the Conqueror. Their falchion, symbol of their fealty to the Prince-Bishops, may still be seen in Durham cathedral. These mighty swords appear to be almost too enormous to lift, but medieval English knights were adept in the art of fighting with them. Such a weapon would have been very handy when doughty Sir John 'Coniers' slew the 'monstrus and poysonus wyvern, aske or worme' of family tradition. Joan was confirmed as inheriting Hutton in 1347. Hutton became known as Hutton Conyers; another of their properties, Norton, now a charming Jacobean house, known as Norton Conyers, lies three and a half miles north of Ripon and may be viewed. By the 19th century, the Conyers' fortunes had faded. The very last Sir Thomas was found breaking stones in a workhouse.

Sir Christopher and Joan were followed by three sons: Christopher; a Sir John, whose son, William, married Jane, and died in 1423; and Sir William, who succeeded to Hutton. Sir Christopher is variously reported as dying in 1374 and 1378. Sir William, lord of Hutton before 1398, married another heiress, Katherine Nunewick of Nunewick. He died in 1412. Their daughter, Isabella, married a Sir John Saville, and their son, William, who succeeded, married Joan, daughter of Sir William Plumpton (executed for his part in Scrope's rebellion against Henry IV) and Alice Gisbourne. (Shall Mallorys admit kinship with the wicked Sir Guy?) Their heir, not recorded by Walbran but noted in the *V.C.H.*, was a Christopher Mallory who died in 1427 or thereabouts. His widow, Isabel, married Sir William Vincent in 1434, who claimed half the manor (De Banco Roll. FF. Yorks 16, Hen. VI, 18). Matthews questions this placing of Christopher in the pedigree. Christopher's heir began the story of the Mallorys at Studley by marrying the heiress to the property.

Dionysia Tempest, a daughter of Sir William Tempest of Studley, traced her ancestry through her mother back to Duncan King of Scots, who was murdered in 1040 by Macbeth. The family also gave us the earls of Huntingdon, Robert the Bruce, and, indeed, the Zouche family, all of whom had other Mallory connections. Mallorys who find themselves descended from Dionysia and who delight in fairy tales, may care to contemplate the possibility that via Margaret, sister of Edgar the Atheling and wife of Duncan's son, the line goes back to Charlemagne himself (*The Washington Ancestry,* T. Page, 1932.)

Centuries later, descendants of Dionysia were to be early colonisers of the state of Virginia. The descendants of her great-great-great-uncle John Washington (v. 1260), were to be the parents of General George Washington, first President of the United States of America in 1732. Dionysia's grandfather, William Washington, inherited Washington Old Hall (Tyne and Wear). Also part of Dionysia's inheritance, it remained in the family until 1613. Her father's family was descended from Richard le Aleman, lord of Studley in 1180. When Sir William Tempest died in 1444, Dionysia and her sister, Isobel, were his coheirs. Isobel Tempest inherited the manor of Norton Conyers and married Richard Norton. Their son, Sir John Norton, was Dionysia's heir in the Tempest line. A great many properties of no great importance to this history are described by Walbran, Matthews and others.

William Mallory is recorded as lord of Hutton in 1438. (Dep. Keepers Rep., xliv, 514). He married Dionysia before 1451; Field indicates a child marriage. She was described as the wife of William Mallory and was 36 years of age in October 1451, when her father's inheritance was legally distributed between Dionysia and others, following her sister's death (I.P.M.). William is styled 'Esquiyer' in the 1452 documents, 'armiger' in his will, probated 1475 (Reg. Test. Ebor. iv, 125), and 'Knight' in the York escheats of 1476. In 1451 Dionysia inherited a property at Foston, near the earlier Mallory manor at Octon. Their chantry, first allowed in 1458, became the Studley chapel, dedicated to the Blessed Virgin Mary.

If Mallory stories are sparse in Yorkshire between 1300 and 1415, the next four or five generations more than compensate. Sir William and Dionysia produced at least twelve children, and subsequent heirs were not behind in following their example. From this time, the manors of Hutton Conyers and Studley may be read as one for all practical purposes until the time of the Civil War. The houses will be described separately at the end of this section. All known children in each generation appear in the pedigree, but not all have been researched in sufficient depth to yield their histories or descendants. The order of the births of some children varies from one source to another. The best option is applied in the pedigree below.

William Mallory, described as 'the eldest son' by Walbran and as 'son and heir' in documents relating to the manor of Washington (Surtees), but placed second in the Visitations, fought at Edgecote in 1469, together with his kinsmen, Sir James 'Coniers' and his son, James 'Coniers'. A footnote to Baker's *Northamptonshire* refers to a 'Thomas Wake, son of William Mallory' who also rallied to the Conyers. Who could he be? (Matthews' report of this entry separates Wake from Mallory.)

Two younger sons of Sir William and Dionysia were soon to be riding out from Studley to do battle. Sir Thomas Mallory, alive in 1430, by tradition fought in the wars on the Continent. Matthews sought to show that he may have been taken prisoner-of-war, with access during captivity to inspiring literature and sufficient leisure (as a gentleman prisoner) to have written *Le Morte*. Sir William himself appears to have been a bibliophile (*see* Lichboro', Northants.), although Sloane 706 is a 'Treatif a Urines' and may suggest a sportsman's interest in its contents. There can be little doubt that such a wealthy and eminent family would have enjoyed some measure of culture. There is, too, the fascinating and probably misleading discovery of a manuscript copy of *Le Suite du Merlin* on which a 16th-century scribe had written *'Ci commence le livre que Sir Thomas Malori chevalier reduce in Engloys et fuist emprente par William Caxton'.* This is in Cambridge University Library and was part of a collection of papers going back to the 12th century found in exciting circumstances and an old trunk at Ribstone Hall, Wetherby, Yorks. (*see also* Kelliher).

Field has written attacking Matthews' theory and nearly succeeds in demolishing Thomas as well. The article contains much useful argument and supplementary information. (*Medium Aevum, 48, 1979.*)

Probably because of the troubled times, Christopher (usually described as 'armiger') was allowed to marry Isobel Matthews in Ripon, 'without banns' in January 1485 (Test. Ebor iii, 350). In August he fought on Bosworth Field. From Harl. MSS. 542. Burton quotes the following:

> Kynge Richard smyled and swore . . . Part of theyr names yow here that come to Kynge Richard . . . Duke of Norfolk, Earl of Surrey, Earl of Kent, Earl of Shrowsberry, Earl of Northumberland, Earl of Westmorland . . . Scrope of Bolton . . . Sir William Conyers, Sir Christofer de Mallery . . . [etc.] . . . All these sware King Richard shall wear the Crowne.

Sir William's eldest son (not first in all records) was Sir John Mallory (alive in 1422) who predeceased his father; possibly killed at Towton. He was dead by 1470. He had time to found a chantry to St Wilfrid in Ripon cathedral (Valor. Eccl. Henry VIII, v 252) and seems to have been granted Studley by his mother, while the family continued to regard Hutton as their main seat. Walbran notes that John's wife,

Elizabeth, founded another chantry at Ripon, to St John, in 1487 (Ripon Chapter Acts, 282), but Matthews, giving the same reference, says it was at Hutton. Sir John's eldest son, William, succeeded grandfather William to the family estates in 1475. Sir William's other sons, George, 'armiger', still alive in 1506, Richard, 'Gent', who died in 1506, and Henry, all may have had offspring. Son Robert died without issue.

The marriage of the next Sir William of 'Studley and Hutton', brought even greater wealth into the Mallory coffers and added to the lustre of their name. His wife, Joan, daughter of Sir John Constable of Halsham, inherited a marriage portion of 500 marks (will, 1473). This lady, on her mother Lora's side, was descended from William Lord Fitzhugh (died 1452), who traced his ancestry back to Lord Marmion, who was himself descended from a granddaughter of Henry II and Fair Rosamund. Joan Constable's grandmother, wife of Lord Fitzhugh, was descended from a bevy of earls and the fifth Baron Willoughby (the earls of Arundel [1326], Oxford [1296], Surrey [1305], Pembroke [1219], the first Earl of Leicester, and King Henry I of France: Mormon Registers, courtesy D. Mallory). As a result of the improved financial climate, Sir William was able to 'Main Prize' in Chancery to help his friend, Sir John Scrope of Bolton, to the tune of £2,000 in 1488 (Cal. Pat.).

Sir William and Joan produced a son, John, and possibly a son, William, who Walbran discovered in the papers referring to Washington. William does not appear in the Visitations and it may be that Walbran confused him with another, later, William (see below). Sir William, knighted by the Earl of Northumberland in 1482, accompanied him when he rode to greet Henry VII four years later:

> In Barnesdale, a little beyond the Robin Hudde Stone, Therle of Northumberland with a right great and noble Company mete and gave attendance upon the Kyng with 38 knyghts besides Esquiers and Yeomen. Part of thes knyghts names are ensuen . . . Sir Robert Constable Sir John Pickering Sir Robert Plumpton Sir Chris Warde Sir William Malary Sir Thomas Malyvera . . . [etc.] and Sir William Ingleby. (Leland, Col., iv, 185).

Sir William died in 1498, succeeded by Sir John Mallory of Studley and Hutton, knight.

By the time he died in 1527, Sir John had married four times. Whether this testifies to the desirability of a Mallory match, his tenacity or his charm, the records do not tell us. Only one of these ladies produced children whose descendants continued beyond two generations. A sad loss to the Mallory family, since at one time, two sons and a grandson promised well for the continuance of the family name. The will of his last wife's son, George Mallory of Tickhill Castle, who died 1580, mentions a 'Cozen' Anthony Mallory of whom there is no other record. (Reg. Test. Ebor, xxii. 5). Sir John's heir, who outlived them all, was the son of his first wife, Margaret Thwaytes. He was Sir William, who succeeded in 1527, 'aged 30'.

From *The History of Harewood* it seems that Sir John had another son, not listed in the Visitations: 'Peter Mallorie, a younger son of Sir John Mallorie, settled in the village'. The village was Dunkeswick, the date, 1562. Peter's will, written in 1562, is in the Borthwick Institute. His sons were William and Octus (Dunkeswick, 18 miles south of Studley) (see Pedigrees).

Sir William married Jane Norton (Johanna in his will), who was the daughter of one of Isobel Tempest's descendant at Norton Conyers. Nine children followed. Sir William was prominent in all the main events that took place in Yorkshire during the tempestuous reign of Henry VIII.

Although Henry .VIII was a Catholic, his cavalier proceedings in both government and religion occasioned the Catholics of the North so much conern that they staged a protest, known as 'The Pilgrimage of Grace', which foundered dismally and was regarded as a rebellion. Sir William Mallory had been present at all their meetings. The Duke of Norfolk devised a macabre trial of the unfortunate 'rebels'. To afford the king a little pleasant diversion, he arranged that the men summoned to serve on the jury should each be either a relative or good friend of the accused. Sir William served on this jury, but was able at least to assist the deposed Abbot Thirsk; he rode to London and obtained a pension for him. (Baga de Secrets, Kings Bench.) He also served on a jury with an even more frightful duty before it, the one that tried the unhappy Catherine Howard. (*The Stapletons of Wighill,* H. Chetwynd-Stapleton, 1884, and *The Stapletons of Yorkshire,* 1897).

Sir William's daughters all made interesting marriages; Margaret to another member of the Conyers family, John of Eaton-on-Usk; Catherine married Sir George Radcliffe, lord of Derwentwater and Warden of the East Marches towards Scotland; Anne married Sir William Ingleby (Ingilby), of Ripley Castle, near Harrogate. Their third son, Francis, was a Jesuit and suffered a barbarous martyr's death for his faith, at Elizabeth I's direction. He hid for some years in a priest hole behind the panelling in the Knights' Chamber at Ripley. It may still be seen today. Sir William Ingleby's portrait and one of Francis are hung there. The Mallory arms appear in a beautiful Venetian stained glass window in the stair-well of the castle, which is still the home of the Ingilby family. It is open to the public daily. The tomb of the next Sir William, Anne's eldest son, is in the church. Elizabeth married Sir Robert Stapleton, and after, her cousin, Marmaduke Slingsby of Scriven.

Dorothy was contracted when only seven, to Sir George Bowes, who married her when he was 14 years of age (*D.N.B.*). They founded the ancestral Mallory/Bowes line of the Bowes-Lyon family and of Elizabeth II, Queen of England. (Sir George's mother, Elizabeth Aske, left her family to become a disciple of John Knox.) Sir George was to become famous for his gentlemanly custody of Mary Queen of Scots on her journey to Bolton. Bowes was Marshal North of the Trent and during the rebellion of the Northern Earls he held Barnard Castle which, ill-equipped, was under siege by his enemies for 11 days in 1569. Queen Elizabeth I treated him shamefully in later life. He accompanied Sir William Mallory in a variety of events. Leland leaves us the following report of one of the grandest, Henry VIII's visit to Yorkshire in 1541:

> A company of Gentlemen in velvet and 4000 armed Yeomen, all mounted; the King on his courser, in cloth of gold trimmed with Ermine. (Drake: Ebor, p. 127.)

There were two more daughters and two sons. Sir Christopher Mallory, the heir, aged 22 when his father died in 1547 (the same year as Henry VIII), only lived to be thirty. His young wife, Mary, daughter of Sir Christopher Danby (died 1571) of Thorpe Perrow, and of Elizabeth, daughter of Lord Latimer of Danby (confusing coincidence of names), bore Sir Christopher Mallory's son after his death in 1555 (Ch. I.P.M. Ser. 2, cv 47). This child, John Mallory, was ousted from his rightful inheritance by the early demise of his father, for Sir William's second son, William, named as his brother's heir (Ch. I.P.M. Ser. 2, cii, 59), stepped into his place by virtue of the inquisition post mortem. In 1578, by a writ of *amoveus manus* (Fine R., 20 Eliz., No. 30), John Mallory claimed a third part of the manors of Studley and Nunewick 'by right of his father Christopher'. Whether his claim succeeded and whether he had descendants, is still to be discovered.

The Mallorys who founded Mallorytown in Ontario, Canada, the founders of the Mallory Shipping Line and the Mallory Battery Company, are descended from a Peter Mallory whose antecedents are elusive. His date of birth is not known, but he signed the Planters' Covenant in New Haven in 1644. One untried theory is that he might have been John's son, 'paid off' by his uncle, Sir William. Other circumstantial evidence seems to connect him with either Yorkshire or Cheshire. This is not the place to discuss this intriguing puzzle at length (*see* below).

Through all the grevious persecutions and wars that religion brought in the 16th and 17th centuries, the Mallorys followed their own consciences as often as they took a prudent view and conformed. At Studley Royal the family had, in the main, been devoted Catholics. 'It is said of old Sir William that he stood at the door of his church for several days resisting the officers sent to put down the Catholic service.' (*Troubles of our Catholic Forefathers,* Rev. J. Morris.) The new Sir William changed all that, and became one of the most energetic anti-Papists of his day. Born in 1530, he lived through the reigns of four monarchs and Lady Jane Grey. William was 17 when Henry VIII died, he married Ursula, daughter of George Gale of York, who was Master of the Mint at York. (Apropos the 'guitter bole' referred to under Woodford, Northants., Ursula's mother in her will dated 1557 and contemporary with Dorothy Mallory, left jewellery described as 'a flowre of golde wythe the stone in yt and wythe a lytle chyne of golde'. Gold could not be mistaken for any other word. York Reg.)

In 1569 the Earls of Northumberland and Westmorland raised a rebellion in the North to protest at the imprisonment of Mary Queen of Scots and to show their hatred of the Protestant prayer book. This rising was put down, a foretaste of the unsuccessful plots by Mary's supporters, and the beginning of her long captivity. The Earl of Sussex commended Sir William Mallory to Queen Elizabeth for his part in the affair: 'truly serving the Queen from the first suspicion of the rebellion'. William was speedily appointed High Steward of Ripon. (*Cal. State Papers.*) Walbran describes him as 'an exceedingly active and able person'. His portrait reveals a determined mouth beneath the whiskers, a direct gaze and a strong aquiline nose. Dedicated to furthering the advance of the Protestant faith, he was nevertheless listed by Sir Thomas Gargrave in 1574 as one of the 'less evyll protestants'. (*Chaps. of Yorks. Hist.,* J. J. Cartwright.) This assessment may have been reversed in 1579 when Sir William captured Dobson and Mudde. In 1585 he was M.P. for Yorkshire and served as High Sheriff in 1592.

His nine sons had varied careers. The heir was Sir John, described below. The second, William, died childless, and is incorrectly identified by Walbran who confuses him with a son of his brother Thomas. Thomas, a Bachelor of Divinity, became Dean of Chester and founded the line of Mallorys of Cheshire. Assuming the lofty role of the virtuous son, he told tales to his father of his brother, Robert, who went 'to the dogs' in his own way. Robert, entered as a student at Lincolns Inn, was always absent from his studies. A letter exists written in 1594 by the sorrowing father to Lord Burleigh, requesting his lordship to apprehend his undutiful offspring and give him his lordship's personal attention. Fortunately for Robert, he seems to have been safe from the rack, already 'become a papist beyond the seas'. (Lansdown MS. 77.)

Christopher was not a lucky name in the Mallory family. Sir William's third son of this name died young, and the fifth, also Christopher, was murdered when riding home from Ireland. He would have been no more than 20 years old. A letter written by Queen Elizabeth I about this tragic event is in the Catalogue Hist. MSS., vi, 450. He was buried in Ripon Minster in 1598. In the same year, Sir William sat on the committee which drew up a set of rules, still extant, to reform the business concerns in the town of Ripon (York. Arch. and Top. Journals). Son George, also buried in the Minster, did not distinguish himself. (George died 1615.)

Chetwynd-Stapleton, in the pedigree of his family, includes a marriage in the time of King Stephen (1135-54) between Sir John Stapleton, Comptroller of the King's Household, and a Jane Mallory. In 1584, Sir Robert Stapleton was the first husband of Elizabeth, daughter of Sir William Mallory, who died in 1547. Stapleton writes of much to interest Mallorys. He describes one escapade in which one of his ancestors and a Francis Mallory, probably the ninth son of Sir William Mallory and Ursula Gale, played a trick on Edwin Sandys, Archbishop of York, when they were all staying at *The Bull* in Doncaster in 1582. Happily, Sandys did not insist on taking his revenge. There was a son, Peter, baptized at Ripon in 1576, about whom nothing further is known. Walbran doubtfully suggests another 'son', Phillip. He is not in the Visitation, nor in the Mormons' Register. He was a son of Sir William's son, Dean Thomas. Phillip, born 1617, B.A. in 1637, was rector of Norton (near Stockton-on-Tees). Ejected by the Parliamentarians in 1644, he is believed to have sailed with Prince Rupert for the West Indies. He lived in Virginia, but returned to England to die in 1661. Henry R. Mallory suggests that there is a small Mallory mystery to solve relative to the Reverend Phillip.

John, George, Thomas, Christopher, Robert and Francis were all named in Sir William's will. Daughters Anne, Dorothie, Julian and Elizabeth (the second Elizabeth and youngest child) received legacies. Joan (Jane in the Visitations) and Eleanor (who did not die until 1623) were omitted. (Reg. Test. Ebor, xxix, 3). The will was written in 1586, probated in 1603—the year Queen Elizabeth I died. Sir William was buried at Ripon a year earlier. His heir was his eldest son, Sir John Mallory of Studley and Hutton, knight, born about 1554.

After the North's attempt to put Mary Queen of Scots on Elizabeth's throne had failed, Catholics paid heavy penalties, none more so than those who had the misfortune to be judged by Stephen Proctor, owner of Fountains Hall and Sir John's neighbour. Although a Protestant himself, Sir John was a tolerant man, and he became so incensed by the harsh sentences imposed by the J.P. that he tried to have him assassinated. More than one assault was made in the dark avenues of the park, to no avail. Proctor returned the compliment by seeking to lure Sir John to the Mallory house (called 'Hugans', in the Strand) in London, with the express design that he should catch 'the Plague' then rife in that quarter of the City. (Possibly the virulent smallpox: Queen Elizabeth I almost died in that epidemic.)

The end of Elizabeth's reign witnessed the beginning of the decline in Mallory finances. The estate provided for a great many dependant, or partially dependant relatives. In addition to the elderly, Sir John and his father had 34 young people in their care. King James had been on the throne for 10 years, however, when it became necessary for the family to realise the assets of their Washington manors and estates.

This Sir John was a Member of the Council for the North in 1599 and M.P. for Thirsk in 1601 and 1603. During his lifetime, the first colonists went to Virginia. Sir John was one of the gentlemen in 1606 who held shares in the Company which founded the colony. His relatives in Cheshire (below) were among the early emigrants.

His wife, Anne, daughter of Lord Eure of Witton Castle in Durham, presented him with 18 children before she died in 1627 (Walbran's date). The Visitations (last 1612) all insist on one wife, Walbran gives two. The second lady he describes as Troth, daughter of Sir William Tyrwhitt of Scotter, Lincs., and the widow of Sir Geoffrey Foljambe of Aldwark, who died in 1585. It is curious to note that her will, written in 1616 and probated in 1617, seems to preclude the possibility of her being Sir John Mallory's wife, although in it she is styled 'Dame Troth Mallorye of Aldwark'. (Reg. Test. Ebor, xxxiv, 442). However, 'Collectanae Topographica et Genealogia': particulars of the family of Foljambe (vol. 2, p. 73), state that 'Sir Geoffrey died 28 Eliz. and married Troth Tirwhitt, who afterwards married Sir William Mallory of Studley'. Sir Geoffrey's monument is at Chesterfield. It seems that Sir William (who died without issue), brother of Sir John, may have been the correct spouse. In 1604, her sister bequeathed her a diamond ring; she is twice styled 'the Lady Mallorie' in this will.

Lady Anne's last three children were born after 1596. No will or inquisition at the time of her death is given. The discrepancies are increased by the existence of Sir John's third daughter, also named Troth, born before 1582. (Perhaps Dame Troth was her godmother, however.) Dame Troth (Tyrwhitt) Mallory left a considerable amount of silver (none of it to Mallorys), including 'my little silver kann parcel gwilt'. various silver 'bowells' and the diamond ring. (Reg. Test. Ebor, xxxiv, 422). One daughter was christened with the then fashionable name of Triphena, the twins Jane and Olive sounding surprisingly modern by comparison.

Nine sons, and they Mallorys, might be expected to provide some excitement. They do not disappoint us. The heir, William 'Esq.' (born 1578) as might be expected became steadily more financially embarrassed. (His support of Charles I was a heavy burden on the estate.) A regular Harold Skimpole, he kept the use of his eldest sister's portion until he was near death himself and washed his hands of all his responsibilities, laying the onus on honouring all his legacies and considerable debts on his son, John. (Will. Reg. Test. Ebor, xlviii, 161. Walbran.)

Of Sir John's other sons, one was a Catholic and lived for the most part in Flanders. Stephen Proctor, already dead by 1620, could not have been behind the plot that resulted in Christopher being imprisoned the moment he stepped ashore at Tower Wharf on a visit to his family. A pause to read the notices at the landing stage gave their enemies time to have him arrested on the fantastic charge that he had played the part of the Devil in a masque in Yorkshire, which ended in Mephistopheles carrying King James off to Hell and damning all Protestants. The scandalised tones in which he protested his innocence ring down the years: 'I am but lately come from the Archduchess' country, for my health'.

Sir Edward Mallory, probably the eighth son, was sent to the Tower on another trumped-up charge, six years previously. The popular opinion that he was unjustly convicted resulted in an extraordinary demonstration, many persons demanding to be imprisoned with him.

Another son, Ralph Mallory, continued the family's mercer traditions and became a draper and citizen of London.

The Mallorys inspired the lugubrious Master of Ripon School to compose verses on many suitable and unsuitable occasions. He wrote poems to Sir John to celebrate the latter's recovery from an illness and to lament his death and another when Sir John's grandsons joined the school, opening with the following lines:

> See here the map of human miserie,
> The Labyrinth that you are entering to.

William Mallory, 'Esq', eager to serve his countrymen and popular withal, was elected to parliament six times between the years 1614 and 1639. He was J.P. for the West Riding in 1622. He married Alice, daughter of Sir James Bellingham, in 1599. According to Burke, he was knighted at Oxford in 1642 and granted the arms of 'Or a lion rampant Gules Collared Argent', and crest: 'A nag's head couped Gules Collared Argent'. This seems to have been confused with the knighting of Captain William Mallory (see Ormerod, 'Cheshire' and 'The Knights of England', below. See also his will, below, in which he is styled 'Esquire'). Their first son, William (born 1603), married Mary Palmes. She was the daughter of Sir Guy Palmes of Lindley; another Royalist family. She is styled 'Mary Mallory of Hutton Conyers' in her will. (Reg. Test. Ebor, xliv, 257). William died in 1636. Walbran attributes John, baptised June 1626, buried one year later at Ripon, to them.

(Sir) William, 'Esq', died in 1645 leaving a will that was not probated until 1652. Alice predeceased him in 1611. Their second son, christened Thomas, only survived a year. The third son, John, baptized in 1610 but described as one year old in 1612 (Visitation), became heir to his father and to his father's problems. He was to be the last Mallory knight of Studley Royal. He was born only a few years before King Charles I, and, like the Henry Mallorys of Papworth St Agnes, was to become caught up in the fateful years of the Civil War in England. Sir John married Mary Moseley, who was to prove an admirable and worthy companion in his all-too-short life. Their elegant portrait, still in the care of the estate, was given to the people of Ripon by Commander Clare Vyner, the last private owner of Fountains Hall, in 1966. It is discussed below. In 1641 the king knighted him at Whitehall. (Some records give 1646, but see 'Knights of England' and List of M.P.s below.)

Sir John's father was colonel of the train-band foot regiments of the West Riding. Sir John, M.P. for Ripon in 1640, was a fighting colonel of those regiments and of a regiment of dragoons. His greatest adversary in the Civil War was Sir Thomas Mauleverer, a neighbour whose ancestors have been offered as those of the Mallory family (*see* Chapter IX). Sir Thomas and his forces occupied Ripon, treating the townsfolk and their property to abuse and injury. Sir John Mallory, as governor of Skipton Castle, was in command of the valiant garrison, defending it against Colonel Thorneton. He contrived to lead a troop of horse from the castle and ride to the rescue of Ripon, some ten or so miles away by road. They successfully routed Mauleverer and his men after a skirmish through the streets and in the market place, where the Ripon watchman, in tricorne and gaiters, still nightly blows his ancient horn and announces that 'All is well'.

The siege of Skipton lasted three years. Cromwell regarded the castle as the most troublesome in Yorkshire, but the gallant band remaining when Sir John was finally forced to surrender, had earned the respect of the enemy. The articles of the surrender are still at Skipton, telling of the brave sight the defenders made as they marched out, in (permitted) full battle array, bullets between their teeth, matches lit 'at both ends', colours flying and a safe conduct for all. Skipton, its massive walls defying time as well as man, is now open to the public. Long the home of the Earls of Cumberland, it was restored in 1650 by Lady Anne Clifford, last of the line.

The Royalist gentlemen of Yorkshire were obliged to pay small fortunes to the Parliamentarian government. Sir John's 'fine' was over £2,000—in 1645 no inconsiderable part of the family's wealth. The Mallory house at Hutton Conyers, in the absence of its owners, was attacked by the Parliamentarians. Their cannon balls still come to light on the site of the house.

Mary Moseley, who lived until 1701, bore seven recorded children. Alice, the eldest, was baptised at Ripon in 1639; then followed Mary, born in 1640. She married George Aislabie of York and was the last Mallory bearing the name to inherit the Studley estates. The third daughter, Elizabeth, was born in 1642 according to Walbran, but was 'aged 23' in 1675 in Paver's Marriage Lics. In 1656 she was a pawn of the witch-hunting zealots. Said to have been put under a spell of demoniac possession by a poor woman named Mary Wade, she spewed out a stream of objects which included the customary ridiculous paraphernalia of pins and feathers. Her age at the time of the trial is given in Surtees as 14 years. Although the 'Evidence' seems to support this, perhaps it should read four years? Baby Anne, who was born at Skipton in 1643, only survived a few months. The next child, placed at number five by Walbran, was Jane, who lacks a baptismal date. She married Arthur Ingram of Barraby, a brother of Viscount Irwin. Ingram was father-in-law to George Carey, brother of Lord Falkland. Jane was buried at Whitkirk in 1693. Her tomb still exists, but neither the published parish registers nor her memorial can provide her date of birth. (Correspondence with Rev. M. Hunter of Whitkirk.) Paver's Marriage Lics. say 'aged 21' in 1674, which implies that she was born in 1653. The only known son, William 'Mallorie', was baptized in 1647. If he is the subject of the Studley portrait (below), he appears to have been a frail child.

Sir John was disabled in the war. When he died in 1655 it was in the expectation that his son would carry on his name (now fashionably styled 'Mallorie') and the family tradition. But it was not to be. William died, aged 20, of an unknown cause, in 1666. Mary, as his oldest surviving sister, succeeded to the estates which thus became the property of her husband, George Aislabie, an ardent Royalist with his own grant of arms (Harl. MS. 1172–3), who died in a duel, entirely of his own making. It came about in this way. Mr. Johnathan Jennings, a beau of Mary Mallory's sister, escorting the lady home after a party, found that her brother-in-law had locked her out. To avoid compromising her, he took her to while away the rest of the night at his own married sister's home. Although Miss Mallory's honour was untarnished, Jennings complained vehemently next day to Aislabie and the result was the duel and the sudden demise of George, who was buried in York Minster in 1674. Mary followed him in 1682. Jennings obtained a pardon from the king and was later knighted. (Depositions from York Castle, Surtees Soc. Pub. for 1861, vol. 2, CXCVI, p. 210.) After a fire in the Minster in 1829 the east wall of the choir fell, causing much damage. All that remains on view of their memorials now is a blue stone in the choir inscribed:

> 'Hic jacet Georgius Aislabie de civitate Ebor. Armiger
> Principalis Archiepatus Ebor Registrarius: Qui obit
> dee imo die januarij   Anno Domino 1674'

Walbran describes Mrs. Aislabie's memorial, also a blue stone, inscribed:

> 'Hic jacet Maria filia Domini Johannis Mallory nuper
> de Studley militis, defuncti. ac nuper uxor Georgii
> Aislabie de civitate Ebor; armigeri, principalis
> archiepiscopi Ebor registrarii, et jam defuncti, quae
> obitt XIX die Januarii anno Domini 1682'

At one time a wooden funeral hatchment hung over the memorials, bearing a lozenge escutcheon of their arms: 'Gules 3 lozenges in fess Argent inter as many lions' heads erased Or (Aislabie) impaling Or a Lyon rampant double queue Gules collared Argent (Mallory)'. There were also two inscribed brass plates. All these were either burned, stolen, or perhaps turned face downwards when the floor was relaid.

Mary bore 12 children: five were sons, one of whom, christened Mallory, shot himself. The second, George, was also buried in the Minster in February 1675, aged about 10 years. The fourth son, John Aislabie, born 1670, was M.P. and Mayor of Ripon. At the time of the South Sea Bubble (1718-20: during the reign of George I), he was Chancellor of the Exchequer. His precipitate retirement from office, which does not appear to have had an adverse effect on his finances, was directly responsible for the birth of one of the loveliest pleasure grounds in England. John lived a further 20 years or so. In that time he rebuilt Studley Royal (in 1742) and with the service of his gardener, William Fisher, laid out the Water gardens; harnessing the river Skell to form a lake, pools, cascades and canals, which were further enhanced when his son, William, purchased the rest of the valley and Fountains Hall in 1768. William continued his father's vision. Fountains Abbey ruins formed a spectacular feature of the scheme. One great cedar which he planted in the cloister, has just achieved its full majesty.

William's wife was the daughter of the Earl of Essex. Their line failed; the estates passed to distant relatives connected through Vyner marriages, first to Viscount Goderich, Rt. Hon. Frederick Robinson, 1st Earl of Ripon, and his family. His grandson, Frederick Robinson, 2nd Marquis of Ripon, died childless in 1923. The properties returned to more direct descendants of Mary Mallory's daughter, Mary Aislabie, who had married Sir William Robinson, Bt., over 200 years previously. Since so many male Studley Mallories survived, it is sad that the estates were entailed away from the immediate family's descendants.

In Queen Victoria's reign, Lady Mary Gertrude Robinson, niece of Lord Grantham, married Captain Henry Vyner; their son, Robert, was succeeded by daughters. Daughter Mary Vyner married Lord Alwyne Compton, son of the Marquis of Northampton, and their second son, Clare George Compton, assumed the name and arms of Vyner in 1912 by royal licence. He married a daughter of the Duke of Richmond in 1923, and Studley and Fountains became their home. Their two eldest children, Elizabeth and Charles de Grey Vyner, gave their young lives in the Second World War. A thought-provoking memorial to them and to all those lost in the conflict, is in the entrance to Fountains Hall. Their third child, Henry, and his family made their home there until recent times.

In 1966 the West Riding County Council purchased all but Fountains Hall for the nation. This included the Studley Royal Estate, Fountains Abbey ruins, and the Deer Park. In 1969 the Council bought Fountains Hall, but the Vyner family continued to live there. In 1974 the counties of England were rearranged and the North Riding authorities received control of the estates. The Vyner family removed to their Scottish home, generously leaving the contents of Fountains Hall to delight the visitor. The last tenuous link with the Mallory family had ended.

In the early 1980s, administrative difficulties deprived us of much that was once enjoyed. Studley Royal was sold as a private residence and Fountains Hall emptied and closed. It is very satisfying to note that in 1983, the National Trust has acquired the parks, the abbey ruins and the Hall, and that these are once again available to the public.

The house at Hutton Conyers, once an extensive mansion on an earlier moated site set in an extensive park, gradually fell into decay. The Mallory manor farm house is extant. Walbran describes a richly ornamented ceiling in a neglected apartment in the farm house. Part of the decoration is 'the Mallory's arms displayed in compartments, but without a shield and without an impalement. The lion, perhaps through ignorance of the artist, is represented rather salient than rampant' (*see* Papworth St Agnes). In the 16th and 17th centuries it seems to have also been occupied by some 'cousins' of the Studley family who were yeomen farmers. Walbran records a 'George Mallorye of Hutton Conyers, yoman' buried at Ripon in 1585, another of the same name and station buried at Ripon in 1638, and sundry other Mallorys, all related (*see* next section). But Walbran also says, 'The mansion is shaded by a goodly row of giant sycamores, which give it a pleasing air of solemnity, and seem still to assert its claims to a rank above that of an ordinary farm-hold'. That was in 1841. The mansion no longer exists, although 'in a field now called the Hall Garth, the foundations show themselves in every direction' (letter, North Yorks. Archivist).

Studley Royal, of which nothing now remains except the converted stable block, was the victim of at least three major conflagrations. The old Mallory house was burnt as a result of William Aislabie's hospitable fires and feasting provided for a houseful of guests on Christmas Day, 1716. The second fire was in the time of the second Marquis of Ripon in the autumn of 1885. During the Second World War, Studley Royal, in common with most of Britain's stately homes, did its 'war work' and became the refuge of a 'bombed-out' girls' school. After the end of hostilities in 1945, while being refurbished, the house was completely gutted, although some of the contents were saved by willing helpers from the estate and surrounding countryside.

John Aislabie had built an imposing stone mansion in his new garden and deer park. The remaining stables give only a hint of its grand style. Even so, they constitute a pleasant and impressive residence surrounding a vast cobbled courtyard in the centre of which the ancient well, ringed by 'Rosemary for Remembrance', gives constant promise of cool refreshment. An atmosphere of enduring peace, rare today, pervades the house.

The Studley portrait is by tradition of Sir John Mallorie, his wife, Mary Mosely, and their daughter, Jane. The writer, on first viewing it, was seized by the impression that the child was a boy, but further investigation only served to uncover another Mallory mystery. Photography was difficult since the canvas is obscured by layers of damp-fogged varnish. The best details are reproduced in this book. The workmanship is of high quality, reminiscent of Van Dyck. It appeared to the writer, that with four or more daughters, it was not reasonable to suppose that the parents would have selected Jane, who was not the eldest, to feature in such an important painting, which is life-size and was probably painted for posterity. Further more, given a son and heir, to have a daughter in the place of honour seems even more unlikely. Known dates do not assist the identification however. Jane was born, at the earliest, ten months after 1643, William in 1646. Neither of them would have been five years of age, the probable age of the child in the portrait, in 1635.

Lady Mallorie's costume was high fashion in 1635. (*Costumes for Births, Marriages and Deaths,* Cunningham and Lucas.) The crossed bow at her bosom is typical of the year and the layered lace-trimmed cuffs and heavy sleeves are all in keeping (*also see* list below). Perhaps a lady in Yorkshire may have been a little behind the latest London modes, although the Mallorys were no strangers to London society. Perhaps their finances dictated extreme economy, although her pearls, apparently the size of walnuts, belie this assumption.

A photograph was sent to the Victoria and Albert Museum in 1979, where Miss Avril Hart of the Textile and Dress Department was able to confirm that in her view, the child was a boy, unbreeched. The customary age for taking a boy out of petticoats was about five years. Sir John's elder brother, William, died in 1636. He married Mary Palmes of Lindley, near Harrogate. One child, John, who was born in 1626 but died a year later, is attributed by Walbran to them. They may have had other sons and this family could be the subject of the portrait.

The Studley Estate Office further pointed out that the child seemed to be painted on a panel which could have been stitched into an earlier picture. The charming use of the leading-strings may have been a clever device to disguise the joins. Perhaps the Mallorys, blessed at last with a son, had the portrait (either the whole, or piecemeal) painted just before William was breeched. The portrait is now in the hands of restorers, and the cleaned surface is eagerly awaited. It may tell us who the artist was, what the dim view in the background represents, the date of the work and whether tradition or speculation is correct. If the child is a boy and the date near 1635, we must seek another son, perhaps born away from Studley (in London?) and unrecorded in the Ripon records.

Ripon Minster was the scene of many glad and sad events in the lives of the Mallory/Mallorie family, century after century. Leland's characteristic phrases tell us that in Tudor times there was 'A Tumbe of one of the Malories in the Southe Parte of the Cross of the Chapel and without, as I herd, lyeth dyvers of them under slate stones'.

The cathedral suffered great damage at the hands of the Puritans and later major collapses. In 1979 the 'slate stones' were not sought, but one or two wall plaques commemorating the Mallorys and their descendants were photographed inside. In the south transept, known as 'the Mallorie Chapel', the most significant memorial is that of the last Sir John. The photograph, speaks for itself. At the apex of the design are the arms of Sir John impaling those of Mary Moseley. All is very dim, but it can be seen that they are 'Or a lion rampant double queued Gules collared Argent' (Mallory) impaling' 'Azure a fess Or between three trefoils slipped Erminois' (Moseley).

The arms of the Studley Mallorys were derived from those of Kirkby Mallory. One grant describes a 'lion rampant Gules gorged with a ducal coronet Argent'. ('Honour of Kirkby Malzeard, Studley and Gowland', T. Gowland), possibly a personal 'difference' for the gentleman whose services to his sovereign may also have occasioned the change of name from Studley to Studley Royal. A herald, travelling in 1718, wrote enthusiastically about the beauties of Studley, which he referred to as 'Stoodley'. (Lansdowne MSS. 911: 'Journal of John Warburton, Somerset Herald.) Today the word is pronounced 'Studd-ley'. 'Studley' indicates a connection with horses; 'Royal' may have the meaning of splendid or excellent.

The Visitations of Yorkshire (1584/5 and 1612) say that Mallory quartered the arms of Conyers of Hutton (1), Nunwick of Nunwick (2), Tempest of Studley (3), and Washington (4):

(1) 'Azure a maunche Ermine'.
(2) 'Sable an eagle displayed Or'.
(3) 'Argent a bend engrailed between 6 martlets Sable'.
(4) 'Azure 2 bars and in chief 3 mullets pierced Argent'.
Crest: 'On a torce Or and Gules a horse's head couped Gules'.

Metcalfe ascribes quarterings (1), (3) and (4) and 'Or a lion rampant double queued gorged Argent', to Sir William Mallory, knighted 20 Edw. IV (1481/2). The *Virginia Magazine of History and Biography* (1905/7) gives the Mallory arms impaling Zouche. The crest is the same as that of the Mallorys of Cambridgeshire and of Woodford, Northants. In 1644 the arms of Aislabie were also quartered (5). 'Gules 3 Loz. conjoined in fess Argent between 3 lions heads erased Or'. The Visitation of 1480/1500 (Surtees Soc. Pub.) has the Mallory lion with one tail and a collar, and a double tail with no collar, as examples for Yorkshire.

Minor properties owned by the family include Nunwick, Brompton, Northallerton, Aldfield, Winkesley, Grantley, Woodhouse, Coppedhewick, Lynton-in-Craven, West Gate (Ripon), Hylton Floghen (Westmorland), Trafford (Durham), and very early coal mines in the Dales.

The village for Studley Royal is called Studley Roger. The parish church with its tall spire was built at the end of a vista in the park by the Marchioness Henrietta Vyner to commemorate her brother, Frederick Vyner, who came to an untimely end at the hands of Greek bandits in 1871. It is dedicated, like Dionysia's Chantry, to St Mary. A 14th-century silver bowl and cover from Studley Royal church is in the collection of silver at the Victoria and Albert Museum.

> Allerton Wappentake: North Riding; Hutton Conyers: one mile N. of Ripon; Studley and Fountains: 1½ miles S. of Ripon; Ripon: some 15 miles N.W. or York.

> *V.C.H.: North Riding*, vol. I; Charles Dickens, *Bleak House*; William Shakespeare, *Hamlet*.

Note (1): An unidentified William Mallory, Esq., was chaplain on an inquisition which sat on a vacancy in the chantry of St Cuthbert's Chapel at Norton Conyers in 1446 (*Arch. and Topogr. Jo.*).

Note (2): Copt Hewick Hall, now owned by the Earl and Countess of Ronaldshay, has beautiful gardens which are sometimes opened to the public. It is only a short distance from Fountains.

Note (3): Costumes in Studley Royal portrait: *see A History of English Costume*, Iris Brooke; *Handbook of English Costume in the 17th century*, C. Willet Cunnington and Phillis Cunnington; *Children's Costume in England, 1300 to 1930*, Phillis Cunnington and Anne Buck. Portrait of children of Charles I, by Van Dyck in 1635: Charles II, aged four years. Costume almost identical to that of Studley child. Mary, small girl dressed as a lady, no cap. James II, an infant in long full skirts and cap. (In Galleria Sabauda, Turin.) Portrait of the same children a year later, also by Van Dyck. Shows Charles II breeched and Mary now has a pearl necklace and ringlets. (Coll. H.M. Queen.)

Chapter Eight

CHESHIRE

THE MAIN BRANCH of the Mallory family in Cheshire spans eight generations whose home was at Mobberley. Although their pedigree is well documented, there were six sons (in addition to those who 'died young') whose careers are not recorded after the entry of their births. There is also a lack of information about their daily lives in the account given by G. Omerod in his *History of Cheshire,* written in 1832, which was the chief source consulted for this chapter. Consequently, the family appears to have been composed of a Trollopian succession of smug ecclesiastics, addicted to 15-foot high marble tombstones and interminable Latin memorials. But this does them no justice, for the early members of the family had a lively time of it during the Civil War. The 18th-century rectors no doubt shared the alarms at the threatened French invasion and enjoyed pleasures similar to those described by Parson Woodforde of Norfolk, whose engaging diaries probably serve as a model for life at Mobberley as much as his own, from undergraduate days at Oxford to the end of his days at Weston Longeville.

Correspondence with Mrs. A. V. Longridge and her son, Dr. R. G. M. Longridge and Mrs. Barbara Newton Dunn, all descendants of the Rev. George Leigh, provided further enlightment and the writer is indebted to Messrs. E. and J. Bailie for details of the interior of the church, and other family matters. Mr. Patrick Mallory provided what is given about the Mallorys of Maynooth, near Dublin. There are three Mallory families resident near Mobberley today, two of whom are descended from an entirely different sub-branch of the Yorkshire Mallories.

Mobberley (also Davenham and Northenden): Mallory incumbents 1621 to 1832

The Mallorys of Mobberley were descended from Sir William Mallory of Studley Royal, who died in 1602. His wife was Ursula Gale (*see* Yorkshire). Sir William's seventh son, Thomas, born 1566, was parson of Davenham for over forty years. Later he became rector of Mobberley and dean of Chester. He married Elizabeth, daughter of his bishop, Richard Vaughan. In old age, his Royalist sympathies caused him to take refuge in the deanery of Chester cathedral for two years. There, on 3 April 1644, as Ormerod puts it, 'Which day being Wednesday, he died'. He is buried in the choir of the cathedral.

Dean Thomas was blessed with eight sons and five daughters. The pedigree given by Ormerod does not agree with the biographies given by the *D.N.B.* In the pedigree, there are two children baptized 'Thomas', the second son baptized 29 August 1605, who died 'without issue' (? an infant) and the fourth son, whose date of birth is not given, who became rector of Northenden and fathered a large family. The *D.N.B.* combines these two Thomases. Ormerod's pedigree was derived from several sources: 'Sir P. Leycester's Tabley', Visitation of 1663, correspondence with members of the family alive in 1882, Parish Registers and monuments. Possibly the discrepancy is another instance of the unreliability of verbal evidence.

There are diverging paths to follow in the histories of the descendants of the dean. The first will take the reader through the years and events which concern the family at Mobberley, a return being made to the first generation to tell the history of the descendants of the other children, in turn.

Parson Woodforde, disappointed in love early in his life, remained a bachelor. Mallory rectories, however, were frequently astir with Mama's confinement. The eldest son, Richard, has no date recorded for his birth. He married Lucy Holland. Four of their descendants were incumbents at Mobberley. Like his cousin, Sir John, at Studley Royal, Richard was 'fined' a considerable sum by the Parliamentarians at the end of the Civil War. His eldest son, Thomas, was born in 1635. When 21 years of age, Thomas married Mary Burgess of Macclesfield and died eight years later. He lies in the chancel at Mobberley. Their eldest son, also a Thomas, born in 1657, became another rector of Mobberley. Elected in 1684, at the beginning of the reign of James II, he was deprived of his living six years later. Queen Mary and Dutch William were now on the throne and James in exile in Ireland. In 1689 six bishops and several hundred clergymen refused to swear allegiance to the new king and queen. They were all deprived of their beneficies; Ormerod does not tell us whether Thomas of Mobberley was dismissed for the same offence. He died a bachelor in 1713, a year before the accession of George I. He was a freeholder of 'Mobberley Old Hall', the Mallory manor, and held the advowson of the church in 1672.

The property and the advowson passed to his third sister, Alicia, who married her cousin, George Mallory, at Mobberley in 1691. George was vicar of Laraughbrian (now Maynooth), County Kildare (*see* George Mallory, v 1632, below). Alicia had five other sisters. Her son, George Mallory, M.A., was patron of Mobberley church. He married Sarah Plumb, died in 1732 and was buried at Mobberley. His son, Thomas Mallory, LL.B., born 1727 (the first year of the reign of George II) was rector of Mobberley and vicar of Huyton in Lancashire, where he died in 1786, three years after the end of the American War of Independence. His wife was Barbara Farington from Lancashire, and they produced three sons and one daughter. The first two sons, George and Thomas, and their daughter, all died young, leaving the last son, John Holdsworth Mallory, M.A., who became the next rector of Mobberley in 1795. His wife was Julia Crowder. Their only recorded child was Julia, born at Mobberley in 1805. And here is the point in Mobberley history where confusion (which still persists) began. The year in which John Holdsworth Mallory died, Julia married his curate, George Leigh, M.A. He became rector of Mobberley and assumed the name of Mallory, and occupied the Old Hall. He also acquired a grant of Mallory arms, suitably 'differenced' (derived from those of Sir William of Studley Royal): 'Or a lion rampant Gules collared Argent a Canton Azure'. The lion has a single tail. The crest:

'On a wreath a horse's head couped Gules'. In 1885, his descendants occupied Newton Hall (Crockford's *Directory*).

Julia's children were George Mallory, B.A., a deacon, who was born in 1833, and Harriet, born in 1834. George died a bachelor in 1864. Harriet married the Revd. Robert Lloyd, rector of Blo'Norton in Norfolk. Thus ended the line of the Mallorys of Mobberley. Julia died in 1835. George (Leigh) Mallory married again in 1836. His wife, Henrietta Trafford, produced seven fine sons and five daughters, all surnamed 'Leigh Mallory'. However, as Dr. Longridge points out, most of them felt uncomfortable with that name and preferred to return to their true patronymic of 'Leigh'; other branches and their descendants retained the double surname.

It is sad that the Mallorys with their past reputation for valour, must emulate the honesty of the Leighs and so may not claim one of the world's most famous Mallorys as their own—George Leigh Mallory, who vanished with his comrade, Irvine, about 600 feet from the top 'going well for the summit' on Mount Everest, in 1925. (George's father, Herbert Leigh, adopted the name Mallory in 1907, so George's generation were Leigh Leigh Mallory.) However, Mallorys and Leighs alike may wish to visit the memorial court built in his honour by Magdalene College in Cambridge.

In addition to Thomas, Richard and Lucy also had two other sons, Richard and William, both alive in 1667, about whom no more is known, and two daughters (*see* pedigree).

The third son of the dean (Ormerod's Ped.) was a captain in Charles I's army. William Mallory, born 1606, did not marry and died without issue. Omerod says 'knighted 1642': there seems to be a confusion with (Sir) William of Studley Royal, but *see* 'The Knights of England', Appendix I, p. 132.

The next son (fifth, according to Ormerod, but fourth according to Earwaker), Thomas, appears in the *D.N.B.,* as baptized at Davenham in 1605. He read for his degree at New College, Oxford (Foster, 'Alumnii', 3, 936). He held the living at Easington for two years, and in 1634, his brother, Richard, and William Forster, Gent. (son of William Forster, D.D., the Bishop of Sodor and Mann, of Gilbertian fame, who had just died) presented him to the living at Northenden. This presentation met with some opposition, and in August 1635, the king (the patron *hac vice*) re-presented him; this time there was no difficulty (Earwaker, *History of East Cheshire,* vol. I).

The bishop had bequeathed the advowson of Northenden church and the rectory to Thomas Mallory. His son, Francis Mallory, was left a legacy by the good bishop. At the outbreak of the Civil War, Thomas Mallory rode immediately to join Robert Tatton and the small band who were holding the mansion of Wythenshaw. This house was besieged by Fairfax and Duckenfield for two years, surrendering after the last long winter, in February 1643. It seems that Mallory was taken prisoner with the rest of the garrison.

> Upon Sonday the xxv of ffebruary 1643, mr Tatton of Wythenshawe Howse, being garrisoned by the Kings side, was taken by storme . . . wherein were mr Tatton, some few gent and not many souldyers, w'ch had quarter gyven them. The number of the pr'soners being but few.

The list of the defending force begins with 'Thomas Mallory, clerke (the ejected Rector of Northenden)'. The inventory taken by Duckenfield at the house, includes 'one p'r of Harpsicalls' valued at seven pounds. He notes that 'The ammuniton was but little'.

Robert Tatton compounded for his estates; Thomas Mallory's property and living were sequestrated. In May 1660 he petitioned Parliament for a return of the income of his properties (Hist. Comm. 7th Rep. Part I). A month later, Charles II having been restored to the throne, Thomas was reinstated and made a canon of Chester. In December he was created a doctor of divinity, and is henceforth identified in the records as 'Thomas Mallory the Divine'. In 1662 he was appointed rector of Eccleston and Brindle in Lancashire, where he died in 1671. In his will, proved at Chester in May 1674, he asked to be buried in the chancel at Eccleston.

He married twice; some authorities have mistakenly assumed that he had a third wife, Mary. Mary Mallory appears to have been his daughter, possibly taking her mother's place after the latter's decease. His first wife, Jane, died in February 1638 after producing six children, none of whom are to be found in the Northenden parish registers. They are all mentioned in their father's will, however. In the will, he refers to 'my dear wife Frances'.

During the Civil War it seems that the family, bereft of their father and mother, were allowed to live on at Northenden and to receive sufficient money from the bishop's legacy to eke out an existence in the rectory. In the receipts of the church, ministered by a Mr. Rootes during the absence of the rector, is a small sum given to 'Mrs. Mary Mallory to buy provisions for the Scotch Army'. It raises thoughts of troops being billeted in the house. Mary Mallory is called 'Mary Ford' in her father's will. The other children named in the will are, 'son John, drugster in London', 'Thomas and Roger in Virginia', and daughter 'Jane Stampe', and 'Susanna'. The *D.N.B.* ascribes to the 'second wife', called 'Mary', a 'sone and heir Francis', and a 'daughter Elizabeth' who died in 1655 and is buried at Northenden. Susanna may have also been a child of his second wife, Frances (v 1671).

Since Francis was alive in 1634, he must have been Jane's son. John, the drugster, was probably the father of another John, a merchant in London, who mentions other relatives living in Virginia, America, in his will (1747). Sons Thomas and Roger were in Virginia at the time of their father's death. Thomas, aged 40 in 1676, is identified by Henry R. Mallory as the ancestor of the Mallorys of Prince George and Brunswick. Roger Mallory held the rank of captain and was the ancestor of the influential and prosperous line to which Henry R. Mallory himself belonged (*see* Yorkshire). Other Mobberley Mallorys also sailed to start a new life in Virginia: *The Genealogist,* vol. XV, N.S., Pedigree Batte, says that Martha, daughter of Thomas Mallory, doctor in divinity and dean of Chester, married John Batte of Oakwell Hall, near Birstall. He was a Royalist captain who fought at the battle of Aldwalton and surrendered to Fairfax in 1646. He, too, 'compounded' for his estates. (J. W. Clay, 'The Yorkshire Gentry at the time of the Civil War'.) The Battes went to Virginia and so did Mrs. Batte's brother, Phillip, ninth son of the dean, born 1617, and graduate of Oxford University (*see* Yorkshire notes). Some of the plantation slaves of the Virginia Mallorys were given their master's surname, which their descendants retain.

The dean's fifth son was George Mallory, curate of Mobberley under his father in 1632. He married Alice Streathill. They had 'many children' and settled in Ireland. The parish registers perished in the fire at the Dublin Record Office in 1922. They appear to have had a son, Thomas, who was the minister of Laraughbrian (now called Maynooth) in Kildare. His son, Cyriac, was apprentice silversmith in 1692 and freed in 1699. He lived in Dublin. Another George Mallory was vicar of Maynooth (v 1691) above.

There were four more sons born to the dean who are recorded with the minimum of information in Ormerod's pedigree: John, bapt. 1612; Avery; Everard; and Francis, bapt. 1622.

His daughter, Elizabeth, married Thomas Glover, and the youngest daughter, Mary, who died in 1664, was the wife of Edward Wyrley, who seems to have followed the dean as rector of Mobberley. Edward Wyrley, M.A., was a younger brother of Sir John Wyrley of Hampstead Hall in Staffordshire. Royalists, they, too, were sequestered in the years of the Commonwealth. Readers are directed to Henry R. Mallory's book for the ensuing history of the Mallorys in the United States of America.

Mobberley rectory survives today; Pevsner describes Mobberley Old Hall as a fine Jacobean house. There are many memorials to the Mallory rectors in the church and a quantity of stained glass. The most magnificent is the window dedicated to the memory of the climber, George Leigh Mallory. There are other memorials to distinguished members of the Leigh (Leigh Mallory) family. One stained glass window depicts the arms of the Mallory family, bearing the collared rampant lion. Ormerod describes a 'singular' parchment stretched on a frame and hung in the vestry. It was surely the artist's drawing for a vast marble tomb now erected in the church. It bears the inscription:

S. Ma.

> Thomae Mallory AM., hujus eclesice rectoris, vivi proseipia ac prietate aeque celebris ex arbaro d'no Gulielmo Mallory de Studley in agro Eboracensi baronetto, a proavo Thoma Mallory, d'ni Gulielmi filio, S.T.P. necon ecclesiae Cestraensis venerabili decano, ex avo Ricardi Mallory de Mobberley, decani Cestaensis filio natu maximo a partre Thomae Mallory, et Maria filia, Gulielmi Burgess de Macclesfield, generosi Oriundi, qui ob jura mente difficiliora a cliemo (?) imposita anno Dni. 1688, (quasi exul altari) vitam privatum egit, donec cum sacris ministrare in hac aede viventi interdictum erat, huit sacrario quod una cum cencella propis sumptibus extruxit, mortuus redit 24 die Aprilis anno D'ni 1713 aeat 55. Et hic spei gloriosae ressurectionis pace quiescit Monumentum hoc mater superstes. M.D.Q.P.

(The term 'baronetto' should not be allowed to give rise to delusions of grandeur amongst 20th-century Mallorys, but *see* Introduction above.)

There are other tombs with inscriptions, including those of George (Leigh) Mallory, M.A. (died 1885) and his wife Julia Holdsworth Mallory (died 1835), aged only 29 years. The church is dedicated to St Wilfrid.

Bucklow 100; Mobberley: 8 miles N.W. of Macclesfield; Davenham: 12 miles W. of Macclesfield; Northenden: 7 miles S. of Manchester City Centre; Wythenshaw Hall: at Northenden. Home of Tatton family for over 500 years. It is now the home of the Manchester City Art Galleries and a collection of beautiful furniture and objets d'art. It is open from April to September for public viewing.

Brindle and Eccleston: near Chorley, Lancs. (Chorley: 8 miles S. of Preston); Maynooth: 15 miles W. of Dublin, Ireland

Note: A portrait once existed of Thomas the Divine, a photograph of which appears in Henry R. Mallory's book. In it, Thomas appears to have been a dark-eyed, full-lipped man in bands and a dark wig, with Grandfather Sir William's nose. The portrait, by tradition a Kneller, was on its way to America in 1932, when it was destroyed in a dockside fire. In view of the paucity of original Mallory material in Britain, this was a tragedy of major proportions.

Chapter Nine

WEST COUNTRY AND MISCELLANEOUS MALLORYS IN OTHER COUNTIES – ORIGINS

West Country

Dorset

WHAT MAY BE the earliest reference is in Dorset Domesday. Geoffrey Maloret held the manors of Steeple Iwerne (not Iwerne Minster, nor Iwerne Courtney) and Todeberia (Todber), north of Blandford Forum, in 1086. These were extensive holdings at that time. They do not appear to have increased since then. The acknowledged authority on the evolution of names, P. H. Reaney, suggests that Maloret developed phonetically into Mallory (*Origins of English Surnames*, 1962, *see* 'Origins' below).

Sir Peter Mallory of Winwick (died 1311), held Dodmerton (Merton) and Melcombe, still extant to the south of Shaftesbury. Since his wife was the widow of a Constable of Corfe Castle, it is unlikely that these holdings had any previous Mallory significance (*see* Northants.).

A Thomas Mallory, either of Newbold Revel or perhaps of Papworth, was M.P. for Wareham, north of Swanage, in 1445 (*see* arguments in 'Sir Thomas Malory M.P.', by P. J. C. Field, which favour Newbold Revel Thomas).

Wiltshire

The same Thomas Mallory was also M.P. for Bedwin, south-east of Marlborough, a joint representation with Wareham, above. The descendants of Sir Thomas of Newbold Revel inherited other manors in Wiltshire that came to them by a female connection and furnish no suggestion of previous Mallory ownership. This inheritance does, however, supply the identity of the wife of the last Mallory lord of Newbold Revel, Nicholas Mallory, who died in 1513, and provides a link with the families of several of his female descendants.

The properties were the manors of Little Corsley (Corsley Kingston) and Sutton Veny (Little Sutton), near Warminster. John de Kingston held these properties of Baron Mohun of Dunster Castle (Somerset). Corsley, inherited by Margery Boughton of Cawston (Warwcs.) in 1539, was sold by her son, Edward Boughton, in 1579. Sutton Very eventually went to four cousins: William Gorffyn of Reading, Margery Cope of Cannons Ashby (Northants.), Katherine Andrews of Charwelton (Northants.), and Margery Boughton. These ladies were all descendants of Nicholas of Newbold Revel. The pedigrees given below display the relationships.

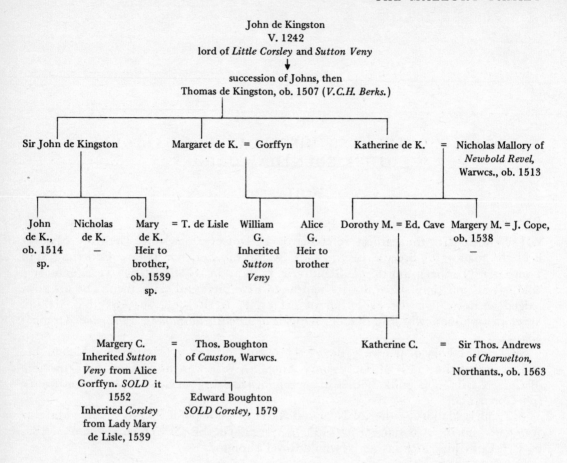

John de Kingston
V. 1242
lord of *Little Corsley* and *Sutton Veny*
↓
succession of Johns, then
Thomas de Kingston, ob. 1507 (*V.C.H. Berks.*)

Sir John de Kingston   Margaret de K. = Gorffyn   Katherine de K.   =   Nicholas Mallory of
                                                                                           Newbold Revel,
                                                                                           Warwcs., ob. 1513

John   Nicholas   Mary   = T. de Lisle   William   Alice   Dorothy M. = Ed. Cave   Margery M. = J. Cope,
de K.,   de K.   de K.   G.   G.   ob. 1538
ob. 1514   –   Heir to   Inherited Heir to   –
sp.   brother,   *Sutton   brother
                           ob. 1539   Veny*
                           sp.

                Margery C.   =   Thos. Boughton   Katherine C.   =   Sir Thos. Andrews
                Inherited *Sutton*   of *Causton*, Warwcs.   of *Charwelton*,
                Veny from Alice   Northants., ob. 1563
                Gorffyn. *SOLD* it
                1552   Edward Boughton
                Inherited *Corsley*   *SOLD Corsley*, 1579
                from Lady Mary
                de Lisle, 1539

The pedigree is based on the succession to the property given in the *V.C.H.* for Wiltshire, but prior knowledge of the family of Newbold Revel Mallorys has enabled identifications and some corrections to be made here. Margery Boughton was the granddaughter of Katherine Mallory, not daughter, as the *V.C.H.* has it. For more details *see* Warwickshire and Northamptonshire.

Devon and Somerset

The Zouche family, one of whom was the female ancestor of the Yorkshire Mallorys (*see* Studley Royal) and which had other connections by marriage with members of the Mallory family (above), owned properties in the West Country from the earliest times. The branch of the Zouche family whose particular arms have been quoted as those impaling Mallory of Studley Royal, held at North Malton in Devon, Tong Castle in Shropshire, Market Lavington and Pyrton in Wiltshire and properties in Somerset and Cambridgeshire, in addition to the seat of the main branch at Ashby de la Zouche in Leicestershire. The manor of Clare at Pyrton came to Joan, daughter-in-law of the first

Baron Zouche of Harryngworth in 1321. She married Sir William Moton of Peckleton. Mallorys also married into the Moton family.

Oxfordshire

Alvescot

It has not been possible to trace the origins of a family of Mallorys who were connected with Alvescot, near Witney. A delightful family group is represented in

Fig. 9. Alice Malorye, died 1579, and family, from Alvescot church, Oxon.

the church of St Peter there. No Christian name is given for father Mallory, the only inscription remaining being his wife's memorial. This inscription is totally enclosed in a decorative border and has the appearance of being complete. However, the brass and inscription (which is separate) are nailed to the wall, having obviously been rescued from their original site, so part may be lost. The family consists of the parents, their son and daughter. They are well dressed in sober gowns; the little girl, with her net cap and ruff is particularly appealing. The boy's costume and hair style are reminiscent of those of scholars at the Blue Coat School. The inscription reads: 'Alice Malorye deceaffed the xi daye of Februarii in ye yere of o Lorde God 1579'.

Walbran notes a Mallory gentleman, contemporary with Alice. He was John Mallory, scholar of Christ's College, M.A., 1527 (Cooper's Ath. Cantab. i, 61). He adopted Protestant principles and 'made himself obnoxious to the Bishops, who in December 1536 sent him to Oxford to recant'. Walbran goes on to stay that 'he bore his faggot at St Mary's and Dr. Smythe, the Reader in Divinity, proceeded to preach on the occasion, the church being crowded in every part'. Apparently, John's friends attempted to create a diversion, possibly with the intention of allowing him to escape, for someone raised a fire alarm. Unfortunately the mêlée which ensued, caused many injuries and some deaths among the congregation. 'Mallory finished his penance at St Frideswide's on the follow-ing day.' This tantalising little cameo does not tell us what part the faggot played, although it sounds ominous, nor whether 'finished his penance' indicates that he did recant and so lived another day.

Several Studley and Mobberley sons went up to Oxford University, but no suitable John is recorded in their pedigree at that time.

An Adair Mallory, Kt., was recorded at Oxford in 1642. He is not in the Studley Royal although his arms and crest are the same.

Middlesex

There were other Mallorys who chose to think for themselves and follow the dictates of their own consciences in religious matters, notably Andrew Mallory who appears on the list of recusants in Tottenham in 1592. There were less than a hundred of these independent thinkers, led by Lord Vaux of Harrowden (*V.C.H. Middlesex,* Edmonton hundred). He was perhaps 'Andrew Mallory Armiger' who subscribed money to build the fleet to fight the Spanish Armada in 1588 (Noble's 'Armada List', 1886).

Hertfordshire

In 1337 a John Mallore was Member of Parliament for Herts. (*V.C.H.*). An Andrew Mallory (obit. 1573) and his wife, Elizabeth, held the manor of Little Hadham (Herts.) in 1573. The house, known as 'Willian', in Broadwater hundred, came to a John Mallorye as part of his wife's inheritance (I.P.M. 7E3, Peyvre). John Mallory and his wife, Margaret, held Radwinter in 1346. Possibly Robert Mallory, alive in the reign of Henry VI, was their descendant. He and his descendants owned a manor in Hertford near Folly Bridge, known as 'Mallorys', in the 16th century. *V.C.H. Hertfordshire* says 'it is now' known as 'Lombard House' (V.3 Borough of Hertford).

Warwickshire

A pedigree published by the Harleian Society ('The Visitation of Warwickshire 1619'), which does not contain a single date of reference, cites a Simon Mallory and descendants who cannot be placed. They are in the pedigree of 'Sutton and Peytot', entitled 'Sutton and Mallory' (*see* 19th-century emigrants, Chapter X). Margaret Sutton, daughter of Henrie Sutton and Margaret Peytot, married Simon Mallorie. Their son, Robert Mallorie, had sons Robert, Johannes and William. These sons are a sad loss to the general Mallory pedigree.

Also, Isabella Eboral, daughter and heir of 'Johis Mallory de Balshall', v 1520 (Visitation 1682/3). There are later Mallorys in Warwick.

Ireland

Many Mallorys in Ireland will be descendants of George Mallory of Mobberley, v 1632 (*see* Mobberley, above). It has proved very difficult to obtain more than the briefest information about this family. Dugdale (Lists of Sumonses to Parl.) notes a Peter de Malure, holder of lands in Ireland, who was summoned to attend Parliament in 1362: 'to attend the Great Council to deliberate upon the affairs of that Kingdom' (35 Edw. III). He is thought to have been a Mallory. (Sir Peter of Winwick, Judge in Ireland, died in 1311.) (*See.* 'T. C. Banks' in the Introduction.) The Funeral Entries of Ulster note '1625, Richard Mallory, son of Anthony Mallory, Co. Cork. Arms 'Or a demi-lion rampant Gules a mullet Sable.' These arms ('differenced') are similar to those of Elena Mallory of Isleham (*see* Cambridgeshire). Richard was also entered in the register of students who graduated from Trinity College, Dublin. (Correspondence with Office of Arms, Dublin Castle and Burke's 'General Armory'.)

H.M.S.O. Published Rolls

The calendars of the many series of Rolls (and the *V.C.H.*) will no doubt provide further brief instances of Mallory history. It is not possible to make an exhaustive list in this book. A selection of random notes of interest are examples of the material available:

Cal. Charter Rolls (references are dated):

1233. Woodstock. Gift to Anketill Malore and heirs, of manor of Erdele co. Staffs. (? Staffordshire arms—below).
1245. Windsor. Anketil Malore, witness.

Cal. Curia Regis Rolls:

1196. Mention of Simoni Malure.
1200. Warwick. Case between Henricum Malleore and Hen. de Clinton.
1201. Northants. Simoni Mallery and Willelimo Malesoures (obviously not regarded as the same name).

Cal. Patent Rolls:

1568. Henry Mallory admitted Freeman of 'The Mistery of le Tylers and Bricklayers of London'. (of Fenton, Hunts. will 1587.)

1571. William Mallery, Esq., and Citizens of Lincoln to enquire into 'Heresies in Lincoln and Peterborough'.

1572. Andrew Malorye noted in connection with the manors of Liston Overhall, Essex. (There are other stray Mallorys noted in Essex records.)

1572. Robert Mallerye relinquished his lifehold on a position .as gunner at the Tower of London (Pat. 6 Eliz.).

1460+. 'Edward Mallory. Member of the King's household.' (Matthews. No refs.).

Cal. Fine Rolls:

1498. George Mallory, Collector of Customs at Kingston upon Hull.

Cal. State Papers:

1666. Frances Mallory, Collector of Customs at Milfordhaven. These include a collection of enthralling letters from Mallory to the Sec. of State and the Clerk to the Letter Office. Accounts of French smugglers, pirates and British prize-taking, and insurrections in Ireland. Much concern about His Majesty's mails. Described as 'a stranger to these parts'. (P. 267, No. 25.)

Artists

Many modern Mallorys and their descendants are accomplished artists. The talent appears to have been inherited:

(1) Merchant Taylors:

'The Pictures of the Merchant Taylors' Company', F. M. Fry, 1907: payment in May 1673 by the Court of Merchant Taylors for a portrait of 'Alderman Patience Ward, the last Master' to Robert Mallory in Popes Head Alley (£7 17s. 0d). (London.)

(2) Dublin National Art Gallery:

There is a portrait there painted by a Mallory, *circa* 1810.

(3) Portrait by Van Dyck painted in Antwerp:

The following coincidence may be of significance to the question of the origin of the Mallory family and, perhaps, of the Studley portrait: Knole House, Kent: portraits 'after Van Dyck', of Karel van Mallery, engraver; copy in Woburn Abbey, Beds.: 1571-*c*.1635. (Other copies in locations abroad.)

Battle Rolls: Exch. Q.R. 63/24, etc. (Courtesy Mr. B. Piercy.) Agincourt and Harfleur

Henry V's war with France commenced in August 1415 with the landing of a force of 10,000 men, the siege of Harfleur, and its capture. By October he had sent back the sick and wounded and resumed his advance upon Calais with only 1,000 knights and 4,000 archers, who were to earn undying fame by their victory in the battle of Agincourt on 25 October. The roll of those assembled at Southampton to sail to France, and the roll of those sent home after Harfleur, includes: 'Reynald Mayllar, Sagittarius; Johan Malarie, un dez serviturs de meistre Thomas Rodborne, chapellain du Roi. Under Hugo de Stafford, Dominus de Bouchier; Johannes Myllere, Saggitarius'. Also 'Ricardus Millere, Sagittarius', who was perhaps named Miller. The other men had names which were possibly scribe's variations of Mallory. (Some modern Mallorys, who spell their name in the conventional way, pronounce it 'Mellerie'.)

Others:

There are a few unconnected Mallorys to be found in the early records of some London churches. Some of these are to be found in the Noble Collection and publications of the Harleian Society also.

Mercers:

Several members of the Mallory family were mercers. From the notes given below, it will be seen that the Mercers' Company included Mallorys from more than one branch of the family. They are included in the text above. Anthony Mallory of Papworth St Agnes, Cambridge, was styled mercer in the Visitation to Bedfordshire, 1634. (He died in 1539.) The archivist to the Mercers' Company kindly supplied the following, from the company's records:

Admitted to the Company.

Richard Malore, late apprentice to Robert Leigh, admitted 1534. (Sir Richard.)

William Mallore, late apprentice to Richard Mallore, admitted 1542.

William, Richard and Andrew Mallory, sons of Sir Richard Mallory, admitted 1572. (Sir Richard, Master of the Company.)

John, son of William, by patrimony, admitted 1606. (More than one John is possible, *see* Peds.)

Apprentices. (Admittance to the Company is not recorded.)

Francis, son of Ralph Mallory of Shelton, Beds., gentleman, apprenticed to John Moore, mercer and free of the Eastland Company, on 12th May 1626 for 8 years.

Alvary, son of Thomas Malory of Chester, D.D., apprenticed to George Law, mercer, on 15th day 1629 for 9 years from 'last Christmas'. (*Note.* Presumably Avery, *see* p. 151, Ped. H.)

The writer is indebted to Mrs. M. Partington for the following interesting item (which is to be found in *Bess of Hardwick,* by D. Durant). A Richard Mallory went on an expedition to Constantinople in 1589, sent by the Countess of Shrewsbury, whose eldest son, Henry Cavendish, also made the journey. Perhaps this was a trading mission to acquire furnishings and other sumptuous goods. It is not beyond the bounds of possibility that Richard Mallory had supplied the lovely silks and threads which Bess and Mary Queen of Scots used to make their famous embroideries. Some of these may still be seen at Oxborough Hall. It seems likely that Richard was the son of Sir Richard Mallory noted above. (*See* chapter on Papworth St Agnes.) He may have been the Richard Malory who was knighted in 1586, noted by Metcalfe, below.

Wills, Probate and Inventories:

These are invaluable sources for further information; furnishing status, offspring and locations of families from the earliest times to the present. They are to be found in the Public Record Offices, Courts of Probate, local record offices, and in printed lists, e.g., will of William of Southwark, obit. 1611; Timothy, merchant of London, will 1621; Edward of High Easter, who died in London in 1495; Anthony of Richmond (Anthony of Papworth St Agnes) whose will was dated 1640, etc.

Possible Origins of the Mallory Family

'I can trace my ancestry back to a protoplasmal primordial atomic globule'—*Poo-Bah* (W. S. Gilbert)

As discussed elsewhere in the text, the most widely held opinion for many years was that the Mallory family was descended from Fulcher de Malsoures, who came over with the Conqueror and was a resident of a village of the same name in Brittany. I am indebted to M. Jean Favier, the Director General of the Archives of France, for identifying a village called La Malhoure, arr. St Brieuc, canton de Lamballe.

The identification of Fulcher was made in *The Battle Abbey Roll*, written by the Duchess of Cleveland in 1889 (vol. 2 and index). With the advantage of recent scholarship, this work has been discredited by new authorities. L. G. Pine says 'its' reliance on the anonymous work *The Norman People,* completely vitiates its claim to vindicate the Roll'. (*New Extinct Peerages.*) There are other detractors who are less gentle; perhaps without having read the introduction. Her Mallory history (V.2, p. 280) is rather garbled, however.

There is no original Battle Abbey Roll; of the three purported copies of it, Holinshed's in 1577 and Duchene's later copy, contain the name Mallory (Malory). There are no fewer than 29 names in the Duchess's Index that begin with the prefix 'Mal'. The earliest (Dorset) name of Maloret does not appear. If 'Mallory' were copied from the original roll, there would have been no need to derive it from 'Malsoures', not in the Roll. Reany derives Mallory from the old French 'Maloret', and says it means 'unlucky'. M. Favier says *Mallory constitue la forme anglicisée de l'ancien francais* maleuré *malheureux, infortuné, accablé de maux'*. The closest translation is 'weighed down with misfortunes', possibly some exceptional physical drawback--nobly borne? However, G. F. Garbutt suggests a connection with the word '*maillerie'*—a breaking mill for hemp used in the textile trade. There are several towns so named in France, notably La Mailleraye sur Seine. Holinshed says that in 'the Roll of Battel Abbeie, their names are not surnames but the names of the places where they were landowners'. Professor

John Rhys in Everyman's *Morte d'Arthur*, quotes Dr. Somer, who states that 'Malory connects itself with derived Latin, *Mailorius*'; but Latin gives us *'infelix'* for 'unlucky'.

Correspondence with M. Alain Boulbain of St Brieuc and M. R. de St Joan, Director of the Archives of the Cotes-du-Nord, produced no evidence of an ancient Mallory 'in any form' in the region. The librarian of the Institut Francais du Royaume-Uni extracted a list of similar names from the *Dictionnaire etymologique des nomes de lieux en France* (Duzet et Rostaing, 1963). The earliest entries were 'Malleret', Creuse (cant La Courtine), Malroy (Mallarey, 1128). Lat.: *melarius, pommier,* et suff. lat. coll.-etum. V. Malleloy. Other entries were Malleloy (various), including Meilleray, Seine et Marne, 1135; Haute Savoie; preceded by 'Melleray' from 'de Maleriato', 1097. A 'Mallerey' in the Jura was *'nom d'homme germ'.*

Their penchant for Christian names of Viking origin supports a Norman descent in the Medieval period. It is generally agreed among scholars that 'Mallory' should always be tri-syllabic, no matter what the spelling.

Lewis C. Lloyd in *Origins of some Anglo-Norman Families* (1951) gives: 'Malory. Tessancourt. Seine-et-Oise, arr. Versailles. Cant. Meulan. Feodary of Philip Augustus 1204-1208: Feodum Anguetini Malore de Tessancourt'. The arms of Melleret, Auvergne: 'D'Or au leon de Gules', may also be noted. These two instances are rather later than the early Mallorys in Britain. Tessancourt is in the next parish to Meulan, the 'Caput' of Robert, Comte de Meulan, the first Earl of Leicester.

It is possible that the Mallorys in England were followers of Count Robert, although 'Anguetini' lived a century later than Richard of Swinford. The first certain record of them, using the name Mallory, is in Leicestershire before 1174. The coat-of-arms of this family was a gold shield charged with a red rampant fork-tailed lion (but *see* Walton). These arms may have been derived from the arms of some of the Earls of Leicester, to whom they then owed allegiance. The arms of Simon de Montfort, Earl of Leicester (died 1265) were a red shield charged with a silver lion with a forked tail. Other Leicestershire families also adopted similar arms with 'differences' of colour, etc. (In 1975, Somerset Herald stated that 'the double-tailed lion makes his appearance in Heraldry in the late twelfth century'.)

The Earl of Leicester's banner was gold and red 'party per pale indented'; halved by an indented line. There is an uncharacteristic coat given for 'Malorye of Staffordshire', which was 'Per pale indented silver and black' (Gen. Quarterly). None of these arms resemble those of the family of Malsoures, who bore 'Parti-Azure and Gules, 3 crescents Argent., in the time of Edward II and Edward III (1307–77) (*see* introductory notes to Northamptonshire).

Another family has been put forward in an undocumented pedigree, remarkable for the fact that without exception, in each generation, every marriage is dated and followed exactly one year later by the birth of a son. It starts with Sir William de MauLiverer, born 1046, who did accompany the Conqueror. Although it becomes more familiar later, this pedigree is either correct because of the unusual detail up to 1260, or suspect for the same reason. The pedigree begins as shown at the top of the next page.

Tachebrook was divided into two parts, one known as Tachebrook Mallory and the other, which belonged to the Church, was Bishops' Tachebrook. Geoffrey Mallory

Extract from a Pedigree of Mallorie of Dunkeswick

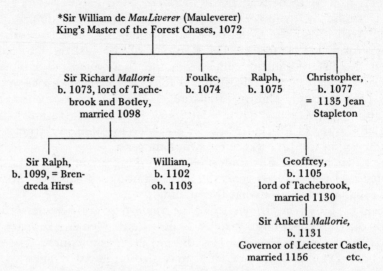

Note: Given as 'Sir Richard' in *The Roll of Battle Abbey*, by J. B. Burke, 1848.

(Courtesy Mrs. Christine Mallorie. Later entries in this pedigree are not controversial.)

of Kirkby Mallory (temp. Stephen and Henry II) appears to have been the son of Richard Mallore, who held at Swinford (temp. Stephen). Only 54 years separate them, at the most. Botley was a gift to Geoffrey from the Earl of Stafford. Tachebrook Mallory appears to have come into the family at the time of Geoffrey's son, Sir Anketil. Earlier records of Botley and Tachebrook do not suggest any Mauliverer connection. The Domesday records for Tachebrook Mallory give as holders, 'Baldwin' in 1066, and 'Roger held of Count de Meulan' in 1086. They first held in Kent and in Yorkshire: Allerton Mauleverer for 500 years and the descendants of Sir Richard Mauleverer held at (Ingleby) Arncliffe, Yorkshire, for 300 years. The name 'Mauliverer' appears in Leland's copy of *The Battle Abbey Roll,* and in Holinshed's, as 'Maleuere'. (These facts, while appearing to contradict the pedigree, may, of course, reinforce it, if 'Sir Richard, b. 1073' also held at Swinford.)

There are other discrepancies between the two versions of the Mallory pedigrees: later research may resolve these. Such an early example of the name being spelled 'Mallorie' is very unusual; the two Richard seem to have been confused with one another. Early marriages between the Conyers, the Colville and the Mauleverer families, compound the chance of error.

The Mauleverers became enemies of the Yorkshire Mallorys at the time of the Civil War. Their arms were variations on the theme of 'a red shield charged with three running silver grey-hounds wearing golden collars'. The greyhounds 'in pale'. One Mallory (of Wooderson, Yorks.), is ascribed a 'black shield charged with three silver greyhounds with golden collars'. This appears to be a 'differenced' Mauleverer coat-of-arms. Possibly a confusion in names on a list at some time in the past, or again, perhaps confirmation of the pedigree above.

A final suggested possibility, for which the writer is indebted to J. I. Bromwich, is that the family may have come with Queen Matilda's army. Their arms, assuming the first grant was of a lion with a single tail, would support this assumption and so would their sudden prominence (with no apparent previous history in England) at the end of the reign of her opponent, King Stephen, and the beginning of the reign of her son, Henry II.

Their continuing social position for several centuries, demonstrated by the burial of their ladies in the surcoat; the fact that a William Malleore kept his ready money in a purse made of cloth-of-gold (Guildhall MS. 9171/4); their emergence shortly after the time of Matilda, and certain talents and traits of character (the bad mellowed by centuries of kindlier blood), which exist in some Mallorys to this day, may indicate an early connection with the nobility of France and Norman England.

Additional coats-of-arms described for members of the Mallory family, mostly differenced grants similar to those given in this book and of their spouses' families, may be found in reference books written by the Heralds, especially in *Historic Heraldry of Britain*, and the rolls in *Aspilogia*, by Sir. A. Wagner; in Burke's (sometimes unreliable) *The General Armory*, and in *The Genealogical Quarterly*. There is not always agreement between all the authorities. Papworth's *Ordinary of Arms* should also be studied and the Surtees Soc. Pub. 1930, vol. CXLIV, p. 148 and notes. Every reader should be able to gain access to Boutell's *Heraldry*; Brooke-Little's revised edition of 1973 should be read from cover to cover for instruction and pleasure. Do not miss his remarks about lions on p. 284.

Yorkshire

Azerley; Azenby

In the words of Walbran, 'I throw together' the following notes and comments which descendants of Yorkshire Mallorys, requiring an ancestor, may find of interest. Although inconclusive, they may serve to indicate areas for further research. (The writer has not had recourse to all the original documents.) Walbran, by juxtaposing certain facts, implies that George Mallory, born 1591, a son of Sir John Mallory of Studley Royal and Anne Eure, was the same individual as George Mallory, died 1638, 'of Azerley'. However, a closer study seems to suggest a different identity for the latter.

The complications arising in this discussion in respect of similar persons and properties, are characteristic of most research into Mallory matters. Again there is a possibility of confusing two properties: only copperplate handwriting and typescript may be relied upon to distinguish between the letters 'rl' and 'nb' in Azerley and Azenby.

Sir William Mallory of Studley Royal (married Ursula Gale) held 'tythes' at Azenby. His son, George, whose will was probated in October 1615 (Reg. Test. Ebor), inherited these tithes. He married a Frances Dawson of Warsell in 1603. He was described as of 'Holling close near Ripon' in his will.

A George Mallory of Azerley, who Walbran suggests had two wives, married Frances, daughter of John Clough of Skipton Bridge par Topcliffe. (The manor of Baldersby, near Topcliffe, was owned by Edmund Clough and a widow, Francisca Jackson, in 1661. (F. of F. Yorks.) Is is also a strange coincidence that the administration of the effects of George of Azerley was granted on 6 April 1638, and George Mallory of Hutton Conyers, wrote his will in March 1638. The wife mentioned in that will was Isabell, however. His inventory was taken one year later.

George of Azerley may not have had such an immediate connection with Studley Royal as George, born 1591, who may, therefore, be available as the founder of another line. Since there were more than fifteen male Mallorys (Mallories, etc.), of Studley Royal, who may have had offspring who are not recorded in pedigrees, and possiblities of others at Hutton Conyers and at Dunkeswick, etc., there are many more avenues to explore in Yorkshire, and probably in excess of one hundred young men noted in other branches who may have had sons to follow them.

Azerley: Wapentake of Lower Claro: 4 miles N.W. of Ripon; Azenby: Wapentake of Birdforth: 6 miles N.E. of Ripon. (Also known as Ascenby and Azenbie, etc. Now known as Asenby.)

(Reference: *Place-Names of Yorkshire: North Riding; West Riding* (pt. 5), A. H. Smith, 1928.)

Chapter Ten

MALLORYS IN THE COMMONWEALTH

North America

MYSTERIES AT THE BEGINNING of the Mallory story and another at the close; it seems fitting to end this book with a Mallory puzzle of long standing. In 1644 a man calling himself Peter Mallory appeared in New Haven, America, and signed the Planters' Covenant. His first homestead was in East Haven. He joined a Protestant community and married Mary Preston, the daughter of William Preston of Giggleswick in Yorkshire. (They had emigrated in *The Truelove* in 1635.) Peter had 11 children. His sons were Peter, b. 1653, who died at Stratford in 1720; Thomas, b. 1659; Daniel, b. 1661; John, b. 1664; Joseph, b. 1666; Benjamin, b. 1668; Samuel, b. 1672/3; and William, b. 1675. These children and their descendants are all well documented in American and Canadian records. Most Canadian Mallorys are descended from these families.

Peter and Mary prospered and their descendants have been busy searching for Peter's father for many years. Since so many of the Studley Royal and Mobberley families emigrated to Virginia, it seems reasonable to look for him in their records, but without success. In no list of any known Mallorys in England does a suitable child, baptized Peter, appear.

To sign the Covenant, he must have been 'of age' (whatever that signified in 1644, in America), or at least old enough to have passed as such. He died in 1698/9. If he lived to be 95 years old, he was born no earlier than 1603. If he was aged 21 years, but not older, when he signed the Covenant, he was born in 1623. If, as tradition has it, he was 'a lad of some 14 summers' in 1637, when it is rumoured he arrived in Boston (the same year as Theophilus Eaton, who married the daughter of a bishop of Chester) this would reinforce the date of 1623. But no Peter Mallory has been discovered among the passengers of the ship (*The Hector*) that carried Eaton, nor any other arriving on those shores in 1637.

Three generations of Peter's descendants lived near New Haven, Connecticut, before going off into the wilderness. One branch left in British boats and settled in Nova Scotia (New Brunswick) in 1783. Three branches settled in Ontario and another went to Vermont. Those in Ontario founded Mallorytown. Some joined the British army under General Burgoyne. In the Revolutionary War, one of Peter's descendants, Enoch Mallory, deserted from the American army. He crossed the ice on the St Lawrence river in a hail of bullets, to join the English army drawn up on the opposite bank. There he changed his uniform in view of the enemy. After the war, he was given a grant of land in 1779, where Mallorytown was to rise. His brother, Daniel, who had been living in Vermont, settled in Mallorytown in 1784.

A descendant of Peter's son, Thomas, was Simon Mallory who joined the British army and eventually lived in the Bahamas. There are Mallorys there still, either descendants of his household or of the slaves of the Virginia Mallory plantations. (The above information came as a result of voluminous correspondence exchanged between the writer and many Mallory 'cousins', especially from Mr. Don Mallory of Vulcan, Alberta, Prof. Lester D. Mallory of California, and Commander B. Mallory, R.N., of the United Kingdom. There are detailed accounts of Peter's children and some of their descendants in a monograph written by Professor L. D. Mallory, entitled, 'Some descendants of Peter Mallory, obit 1698, revised'. 1980. It has been deposited in the Library of Congress and elsewhere. The information from Commander Mallory is contained in an undocumented extract sent to him in 1935 by R. M. bradley, a one-time resident of Mallorytown.) *See also The Mallorys of of Mystic*, J. P. Baughman, 1972.

Australia and South Africa

Although South Africa is not now a member of the Commonwealth, it is included here because of the descent of some of the Mallorys now resident there. This book is not generally concerned with later families, but Victorian Empire building, local and global wars, facilitated the spread of the Mallory family to other parts of the world. During the upper Canada Rebellion of 1838, a Norman Mallory was captured running American despatches. Condemned to death, he was sent to England from where he was deported to Australia; sentenced to join a chain-gang breaking rocks in the blazing sun, to build the road to Hobart, Tasmania. He lived to be pardoned in 1845. It is not known at the time of writing whether he stayed to found a line in Australia.

Many Australian Mallorys are descended from Daniel Mallory, twice Mayor of Warwick, who worked for the East India Co. (p. 150, Ped. N). A William Mallory was also mayor in 1805, probably Daniel's father, William. The writer is indebted to G. Davies-Smith and Mrs. Joyce Mallory Ward for their considerable assistance, and to Commander B. S. Mallory, Mr. P. Mallory, and the Warwick archivist for the information upon which the pedigree is drawn. Further research may reveal that some Warwickshire Mallorys are descended from the family recorded under 'Warwickshire' in Chapter Nine.

In South Africa, Mallorys were later on the scene. One branch of the family there is also descended from Warwick and from Daniel, Mayor of Warwick in particular. George Leigh Mallory who died on Everest (p. 153, H) has descendants in Africa and in the U.S.A. Mr. Arthur Mallory of Hull records a John Mallory (v 1820–1910) of Hoveringham, Yorks. Two of his sons, John and William, who were last heard of after 1820, emigrated to Canada. Two more of his descendants, John and Harry, alive in 1919, emigrated to Natal in South Africa.

There are also descendants of Daniel, Mayor of Warwick, and John of Hoveringham in Britain today. Many of them continue the ancient Mallory tradition of service with the armed forces or fill posts in the professions. They are well documented, but their stories lie beyond the scope of the present work.

There can be no better conclusion to this Mallory tale without end, than the words of our famous kinsman. 'And this book endeth . . . Who that woll make ony more lette hym seke out other bookis.' - 'Sir Thomas Malleorré, Knyght Presoner', *Le Morte d'Arthur,* Bk. IV. 1469. (E. Vinaver.)

APPENDIX I

Notes from *The Knights of England,* by Wm. Shaw (1906, 2 vols.).

THIS WORK CONTAINS extensive lists of knights of the British Isles, including the Orders of Chivalry and the Knights Bachelor, taken from ancient rolls and other authorities; two pages of references are given. There are nine instances of Malory/Mallory knights listed; some who appear to be identified have dates differing from those in the following pedigrees which are culled from other recognised sources. The description 'Knights of The Bath' does not refer to the (modern) Order of the Bath.

Knights of the Bath—'The names of all the knights, 267 in all, made at Whitsuntide, 34 Edw. I, on the occasion of the knighting of Edward, Prince of Wales (Edw. II), 1306 May 22nd' starts with 'Edwardus princeps Walliae' The list includes many familiar names: Wilhelmus de la Zouche, three Corbets, Radulphus Basset, Radulphus Dryby, Thomas le Grey and Thomas Malorie.

Knights dubbed by the Earl of the Earl of Northumberland on the field of Sefford (i.e., after the recovery of Berwick):

    1481, 22 August: William Malory.

Knights Bachelor:

    Dubbed by Duke of Norfolk (at Berwick).
    1560, 18 July: William Mallory.
    1564/5, 18 Feb. 'at Westminster', Richard Mallory, Lord Mayor of London. (Shaw gives an
        alternative date—1563/4, and queries this, but 1564 is correct).
    1568, Richard Malory.
    Dubbed by King James, 1603, 17 April: John Mallory of Yorkshire (spelled Mallorie in Metcalfe).
    1605, 22 May: Henry Mallory of Co. Cambridge, at Richmond.
    1641, 23 Dec., 'at Whitehall, by the King': John Mallory of York.
    1642/3, 1 Feb. (at Oxford, ?): William Mallory, Captain. (*Note*: there is confusion regarding the
        knighting of Capt. Wm., Ped. H, and Sir Wm. of Studley, Ped. E.)

    A Book of Knights, 1426–1600, by W. C. Metcalfe (1885), has some coats-of-arms as well. He also lists a Sir Richard Malory, dubbed 1586. (Richard, fifth son of Sir Richard, Lord Mayor of London, seems to be the most likely individual.)

APPENDIX II

Members called to the Parliaments of England, include:

1312 Radulphus Mallore—Leicestershire.
1337 John Mallore—Hertfordshire.
1341 John Mallore—Hertfordshire.
1350 Dom Petrus Mallore—Northamptonshire.
1362 Peter de Malure—Ireland.
1383 Egidius Mallore—Northamptonshire also served 1387/8, 1392/3, 1393/4, 1400/1, and 1402.
      (Name also Malore and Mallere.)
1413 John Malory—Warwickshire.
1419 John Mallore—Warwickshire.
1419 William Malore—Leicestershire.
1421 John Malory—Warwickshire.
1423 John Malory—Warwickshire.
1427 John Malory (armiger)—Warwickshire.
1449 Thomas Malery—Bedwin, Wiltshire.
1450 Thomas Malory—Wareham, Dorset.
1555/6 William Mallorye (armiger)—Huntingdonshire (Cambridgeshire).
1585 William Mallorie (knight)—Yorkshire.
1601 John Mallorie of Studley—Thirsk.
1603 John Mallorie of Ripon—Ripon.
1614 William Mallorie (senior)—Ripon.
1620/1 William Mallorie (knight)—Ripon.
1623/4 William Mallorie (knight)—Ripon.
1627/8 William Mallorie—Ripon.
1640 William Mallorie—Ripon.
1640 John Mallorie (knight)—Ripon. Later described as 'disabled to sit', a term that may refer to his lack of necessary financial status or the injuries he received in the Civil War.

(*See also* those mentioned in the text.)

PREFACE TO PEDIGREES

Dating

There are several dating conventions in use by professional genealogists which need to be clarified for the general reader.

1.   Calculation of age from a statement that a person was 'aged x years and more', on a given day—see note in Preface.

2.   To find date of birth from a statement that a person was 'aged (say) six years in the 10th Edward 4'—known date of accession of King Edward IV was 1461, add ten years to 1461 and subtract six years. This results in a birth date of 1465 for the individual in question.

3.   'Year' of a king—this is confusing since a king's accession to the throne may not commence in January. The boxing and coxing of the kings between the years 1422 and 1483 adds its own problems.

4.   Although there was more than enough trouble in the world already, in 1752 parliament revoked the ancient system whereby a year started on Lady Day (25 March), and instituted 1 January as New Year's Day. Consequently, for dates between 1 January and 24 March in the years before 1752, a convention known as double-dating is used. A date of 10 February 1566 is written as 10 February 1566/7, indicating that the event occurred in the historical year of 1567.

5.   In the ancient records (eg. the lists of Sheriffs) a date appearing in the form '7 Hen 2', means the seventh year of the reign of King Henry II.

Abbreviations used in Pedigrees

Temp.	alive during the reign of the king.
v.	living at that date.
b.	born.
ob., obit.	died.
m, =	married.
sp.	no issue.
sp'le.	no legal issue.
s. + h.	son and heir.
Ktd.	knighted at that date.
R.C.	Roman Catholic.
▲	end of line.
—	end of Mallory connection with property.
Kt.	noted in the records as a knight at the date in question.
+	line continues.
?	statement conjectural.

Note: The system known as double dating has been used in the pedigrees.

134

PEDIGREE OF MALLORY

A plausible Pedigree to be studied in conjunction with the Text
(See key in Preface to Pedigree)

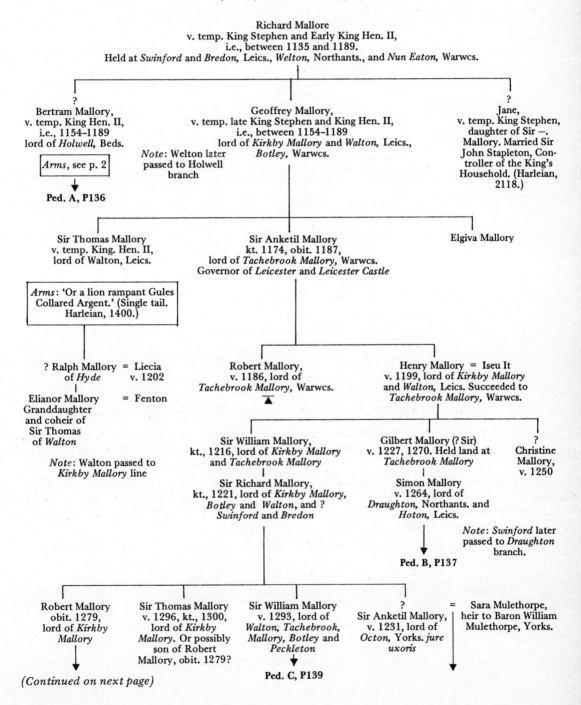

Richard Mallore
v. temp. King Stephen and Early King Hen. II,
i.e., between 1135 and 1189.
Held at *Swinford* and *Bredon*, Leics., *Welton*, Northants., and *Nun Eaton*, Warwcs.

?
Bertram Mallory,
v. temp. King Hen. II,
i.e., 1154–1189
lord of *Holwell*, Beds.

Arms, see p. 2

Ped. A, P136

Geoffrey Mallory,
v. temp. late King Stephen and King Hen. II,
i.e., between 1154–1189
lord of *Kirkby Mallory* and *Walton*, Leics.,
Botley, Warwcs.

Note: Welton later
passed to Holwell
branch

?
Jane,
v. temp. King Stephen,
daughter of Sir —.
Mallory. Married Sir
John Stapleton, Con-
troller of the King's
Household. (Harleian,
2118.)

Sir Thomas Mallory
v. temp. King. Hen. II,
lord of Walton, Leics.

Arms: 'Or a lion rampant Gules
Collared Argent.' (Single tail.
Harleian, 1400.)

Sir Anketil Mallory
kt. 1174, obit. 1187,
lord of *Tachebrook Mallory*, Warwcs.
Governor of *Leicester* and *Leicester Castle*

Elgiva Mallory

? Ralph Mallory = Liecia
of *Hyde*   v. 1202

Elianor Mallory   = Fenton
Granddaughter
and coheir of
Sir Thomas
of *Walton*

Note: Walton passed to
Kirkby Mallory line

Robert Mallory,
v. 1186, lord of
Tachebrook Mallory, Warwcs.
▲

Henry Mallory = Iseu lt
v. 1199, lord of *Kirkby Mallory*
and *Walton*, Leics. Succeeded to
Tachebrook Mallory, Warwcs.

Sir William Mallory,
kt., 1216, lord of *Kirkby Mallory*
and *Tachebrook Mallory*

Sir Richard Mallory,
kt., 1221, lord of *Kirkby Mallory*,
Botley and *Walton*, and ?
Swinford and *Bredon*

Gilbert Mallory (? Sir)
v. 1227, 1270. Held land at
Tachebrook Mallory

Simon Mallory
v. 1264, lord of
Draughton, Northants. and
Hoton, Leics.

Note: Swinford later
passed to *Draughton*
branch.

Ped. B, P137

?
Christine
Mallory,
v. 1250

Robert Mallory
obit. 1279,
lord of *Kirkby
Mallory*

Sir Thomas Mallory
v. 1296, kt., 1300,
lord of *Kirkby
Mallory*. Or possibly
son of Robert
Mallory, obit. 1279?

Sir William Mallory
v. 1293, lord of
*Walton, Tachebrook,
Mallory, Botley* and
Peckleton

Ped. C, P139

?
Sir Anketil Mallory,
v. 1231, lord of
Octon, Yorks. *jure
uxoris*

= Sara Mulethorpe,
heir to Baron William
Mulethorpe, Yorks.

(Continued on next page)

Pedigree of Mallory—*continued*

Sir Ralph Mallory = Agnes
kt. 1280   v. 1290
v. 1300   (Cal. Clo.)

Anketil Mallory
ob. s.p.

Nicholas Mallory
ob. 1275 s.p.

Ped. C, P.4.

Margery Mallory = Ralph Salvain   Avis   Nicholaa   Sarah

Anketin Salvain
v. 1309

Sir Anketyn Salvain (Salveyn), obit. 1351

Note: Sir William Mallory, v. 1293, had custody of Anketin Salvain and his lands during his minority. Yorkshire lands in *Dalton, Mulethorpe, Wiggenthorpe, Huntingdon* and *Clifford.* (Fines.)

Arms: 'Argent a chevron Gules Three boars heads Gules' (Boutell).

PEDIGREE A (continued from p. 135)

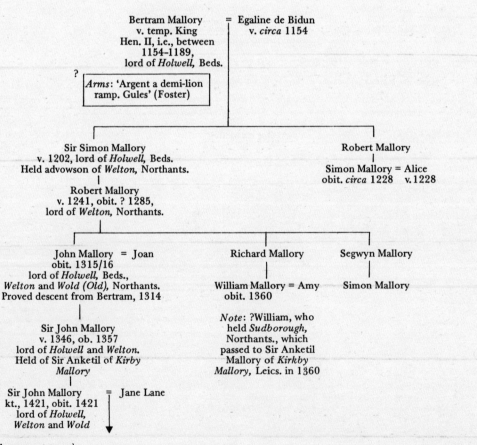

(Continued on next page)

Pedigree of Mallory—*continued*

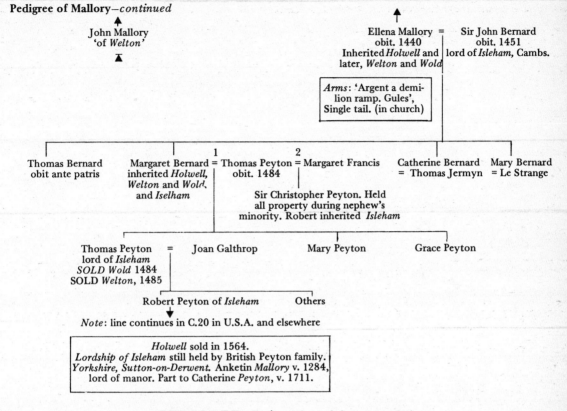

John Mallory
'of *Welton*'

Ellena Mallory = Sir John Bernard
obit. 1440   obit. 1451
Inherited *Holwell* and | lord of *Iseham*, Cambs.
later, *Welton* and *Wold*

Arms: 'Argent a demi-
lion ramp. Gules',
Single tail. (in church)

| Thomas Bernard obit ante patris | Margaret Bernard inherited *Holwell*, *Welton* and *Wold*, and *Iselham* | Thomas Peyton obit. 1484 | Margaret Francis | Catherine Bernard = Thomas Jermyn | Mary Bernard = Le Strange |

1   2

Sir Christopher Peyton. Held
all property during nephew's
minority. Robert inherited *Iseham*

| Thomas Peyton lord of *Iseham* SOLD *Wold* 1484 SOLD *Welton*, 1485 | = Joan Galthrop | Mary Peyton | Grace Peyton |

Robert Peyton of *Iseham*   Others

Note: line continues in C.20 in U.S.A. and elsewhere

Holwell sold in 1564.
Lordship of Iseham still held by British Peyton family.
Yorkshire, Sutton-on-Derwent. Anketin *Mallory* v. 1284,
lord of manor. Part to Catherine *Peyton*, v. 1711.

PEDIGREE B (continued from p. 135)

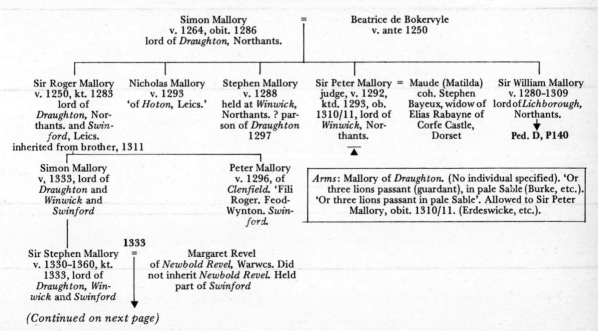

Simon Mallory   =   Beatrice de Bokervyle
v. 1264, obit. 1286   v. ante 1250
lord of *Draughton*, Northants.

| Sir Roger Mallory v. 1250, kt. 1283 lord of *Draughton*, Northants. and *Swinford*, Leics. inherited from brother, 1311 | Nicholas Mallory v. 1293 'of *Hoton*, Leics.' | Stephen Mallory v. 1288 held at *Winwick*, Northants. ? parson of *Draughton* 1297 | Sir Peter Mallory judge, v. 1292, ktd. 1293, ob. 1310/11, lord of *Winwick*, Northants. | Maude (Matilda) coh. Stephen Bayeux, widow of Elias Rabayne of Corfe Castle, Dorset | Sir William Mallory v. 1280–1309 lord of *Lichborough*, Northants. **Ped. D, P140** |

| Simon Mallory v, 1333, lord of *Draughton* and *Winwick* and *Swinford* | Peter Mallory v. 1296, of *Clenfield*. 'Fili Roger. FeodWynton. *Swinford*. |

Arms: Mallory of *Draughton*. (No individual specified). 'Or
three lions passant (guardant), in pale Sable (Burke, etc.).
'Or three lions passant in pale Sable'. Allowed to Sir Peter
Mallory, obit. 1310/11. (Erdeswicke, etc.).

1333

| Sir Stephen Mallory v. 1330–1360, kt. 1333, lord of *Draughton*, Winwick and *Swinford* | = | Margaret Revel of *Newbold Revel*, Warwcs. Did not inherit *Newbold Revel*. Held part of *Swinford* |

(Continued on next page)

Pedigree of Mallory—*continued*

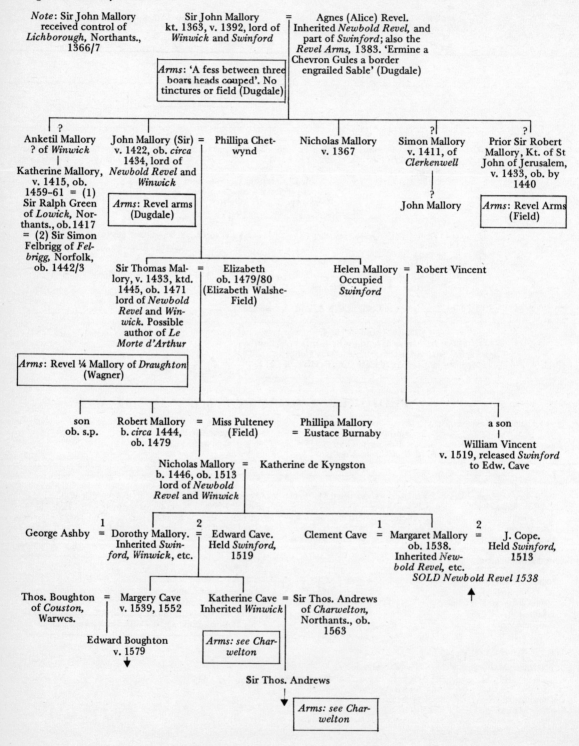

Note: Sir John Mallory received control of *Lichborough*, Northants., 1366/7

Sir John Mallory kt. 1363, v. 1392, lord of *Winwick* and *Swinford* = Agnes (Alice) Revel. Inherited *Newbold Revel*, and part of *Swinford*; also the *Revel Arms*, 1383. 'Ermine a Chevron Gules a border engrailed Sable' (Dugdale)

Arms: 'A fess between three boars heads couped'. No tinctures or field (Dugdale)

? — Anketil Mallory ? of *Winwick* | Katherine Mallory, v. 1415, ob. 1459–61 = (1) Sir Ralph Green of *Lowick*, Northants., ob. 1417 = (2) Sir Simon Felbrigg of *Felbrigg*, Norfolk, ob. 1442/3

John Mallory (Sir) v. 1422, ob. *circa* 1434, lord of *Newbold Revel* and *Winwick* = Phillipa Chetwynd

Arms: Revel arms (Dugdale)

Nicholas Mallory v. 1367

? — Simon Mallory v. 1411, of *Clerkenwell* | ? John Mallory

? — Prior Sir Robert Mallory, Kt. of St John of Jerusalem, v. 1433, ob. by 1440

Arms: Revel Arms (Field)

Sir Thomas Mallory, v. 1433, ktd. 1445, ob. 1471 lord of *Newbold Revel* and *Winwick*. Possible author of *Le Morte d'Arthur* = Elizabeth ob. 1479/80 (Elizabeth Walshe-Field)

Helen Mallory Occupied *Swinford* = Robert Vincent

Arms: Revel ¼ Mallory of *Draughton* (Wagner)

son ob. s.p.

Robert Mallory b. *circa* 1444, ob. 1479 = Miss Pulteney (Field)

Phillipa Mallory = Eustace Burnaby

a son | William Vincent v. 1519, released *Swinford* to Edw. Cave

Nicholas Mallory b. 1446, ob. 1513 lord of *Newbold Revel* and *Winwick* = Katherine de Kyngston

George Ashby =¹ Dorothy Mallory. Inherited *Swinford*, *Winwick*, etc. =² Edward Cave. Held *Swinford*, 1519

Clement Cave =¹ Margaret Mallory. ob. 1538. Inherited *Newbold Revel*, etc. *SOLD Newbold Revel 1538* =² J. Cope. Held *Swinford*, 1513

Thos. Boughton of *Couston*, Warwcs. = Margery Cave v. 1539, 1552 | Edward Boughton v. 1579

Katherine Cave Inherited *Winwick* = Sir Thos. Andrews of *Charwelton*, Northants., ob. 1563

Arms: see *Charwelton*

Sir Thos. Andrews

Arms: see *Charwelton*

PEDIGREE C (continued from p. 135)

Sir William Mallory,
kt. 1293, lord of *Walton*, Leics., *Botley, Tachebrook Mallory* and *Peckleton*, Warwcs.

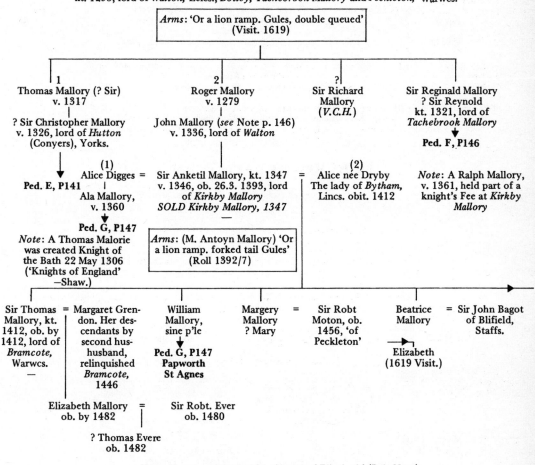

Arms: 'Or a lion ramp. Gules, double queued'
(Visit. 1619)

1
Thomas Mallory (? Sir)
v. 1317
? Sir Christopher Mallory
v. 1326, lord of *Hutton*
(Conyers), Yorks.

(1)
Alice Digges =
Ped. E, P141 |
Ala Mallory,
v. 1360
Ped. G, P147
Note: A Thomas Malorie
was created Knight of
the Bath 22 May 1306
('Knights of England'
—Shaw.)

2
Roger Mallory
v. 1279
John Mallory (*see* Note p. 146)
v. 1336, lord of *Walton*

Sir Anketil Mallory, kt. 1347
v. 1346, ob. 26.3. 1393, lord
of *Kirkby Mallory*
SOLD Kirkby Mallory, 1347
—

Arms: (M. Antoyn Mallory) 'Or
a lion ramp. forked tail Gules'
(Roll 1392/7)

?
Sir Richard
Mallory
(*V.C.H.*)

(2)
Alice née Dryby
The lady of *Bytham*,
Lincs. obit. 1412

Sir Reginald Mallory
? Sir Reynold
kt. 1321, lord of
Tachebrook Mallory
Ped. F, P146

Note: A Ralph Mallory,
v. 1361, held part of a
knight's Fee at *Kirkby
Mallory*

Sir Thomas = Margaret Gren-
Mallory, kt.   don. Her des-
1412, ob. by   cendants by
1412, lord of   second hus-
Bramcote,   band,
Warwcs.   relinquished
—   *Bramcote*,
                 1446

Elizabeth Mallory =
ob. by 1482 |

William
Mallory,
sine p'le
Ped. G, P147
**Papworth
St Agnes**

Sir Robt. Ever
ob. 1480

Margery   = Sir Robt
Mallory   Moton, ob.
? Mary   1456, 'of
                Peckleton'

Beatrice   = Sir John Bagot
Mallory   of Blifield,
             Staffs.
Elizabeth
(1619 Visit.)

? Thomas Evere
ob. 1482

Note: Her property passed to 'Aunts of Elizabeth' (P. le Neve)

Sub Pedigree E.1
Hutton Conyers
Yorkshire
Part Pedigree

Mallory of Studley Royal continued:
(ex. Walbran)
See also **Ped. E, P143**

Yeoman Farmers held farm at *Hutton Conyers*, close relatives of *Studley* family.
All baptized and buried at Ripon Coll. church, Yorks.

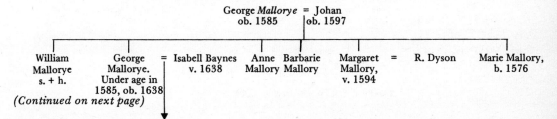

George *Mallorye* = Johan
ob. 1585   ob. 1597

William   George   = Isabell Baynes   Anne   Barbarie   Margaret   = R. Dyson   Marie Mallory,
Mallorye   Mallorye.   v. 1638   Mallory Mallory   Mallory,   b. 1576
s. + h.   Under age in   v. 1594
                1585, ob. 1638
(Continued on next page)

Pedigree of Mallory— *continued*

Note: George, b. 1620, rec'd
a sword belonging to Ralph
Mallory under father's will.
? Ralph of *Studley Royal*, v.
1590, and obit. at *Hutton
Conyers*, 1635,

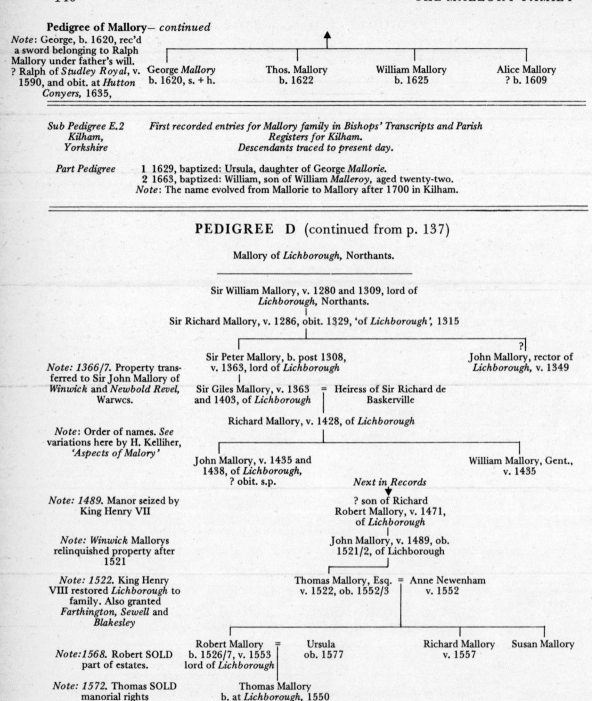

George *Mallory* b. 1620, s. + h.	Thos. Mallory b. 1622	William Mallory b. 1625	Alice Mallory ? b. 1609

---

*Sub Pedigree E.2
Kilham,
Yorkshire*

*First recorded entries for Mallory family in Bishops' Transcripts and Parish
Registers for Kilham.
Descendants traced to present day.*

Part Pedigree

1 1629, baptized: Ursula, daughter of George *Mallorie.*
2 1663, baptized: William, son of William *Malleroy,* aged twenty-two.
Note: The name evolved from Mallorie to Mallory after 1700 in Kilham.

PEDIGREE D (continued from p. 137)

Mallory of *Lichborough*, Northants.

Sir William Mallory, v. 1280 and 1309, lord of
Lichborough, Northants.

Sir Richard Mallory, v. 1286, obit. 1329, 'of *Lichborough*', 1315

Note: 1366/7. Property trans-
ferred to Sir John Mallory of
Winwick and *Newbold Revel*,
Warwcs.

Sir Peter Mallory, b. post 1308,
v. 1363, lord of *Lichborough*

John Mallory, rector of
Lichborough, v. 1349

Sir Giles Mallory, v. 1363   =   Heiress of Sir Richard de
and 1403, of *Lichborough*   Baskerville

Richard Mallory, v. 1428, of *Lichborough*

Note: Order of names. *See*
variations here by H. Kelliher,
'Aspects of Malory'

John Mallory, v. 1435 and
1438, of *Lichborough*,
? obit. s.p.

Next in Records

William Mallory, Gent.,
v. 1435

Note: 1489. Manor seized by
King Henry VII

? son of Richard
Robert Mallory, v. 1471,
of *Lichborough*

Note: Winwick Mallorys
relinquished property after
1521

John Mallory, v. 1489, ob.
1521/2, of Lichborough

Note: 1522. King Henry
VIII restored *Lichborough* to
family. Also granted
Farthington, Sewell and
Blakesley

Thomas Mallory, Esq.   =   Anne Newenham
v. 1522, ob. 1552/3   v. 1552

Note:1568. Robert SOLD
part of estates.

Robert Mallory   =   Ursula
b. 1526/7, v. 1553   ob. 1577
lord of *Lichborough*

Richard Mallory   Susan Mallory
v. 1557

Note: 1572. Thomas SOLD
manorial rights

Thomas Mallory
b. at *Lichborough*, 1550
continued in occupation

Family still at *Lichborough* in C.19

PEDIGREE E (continued from p. 139)

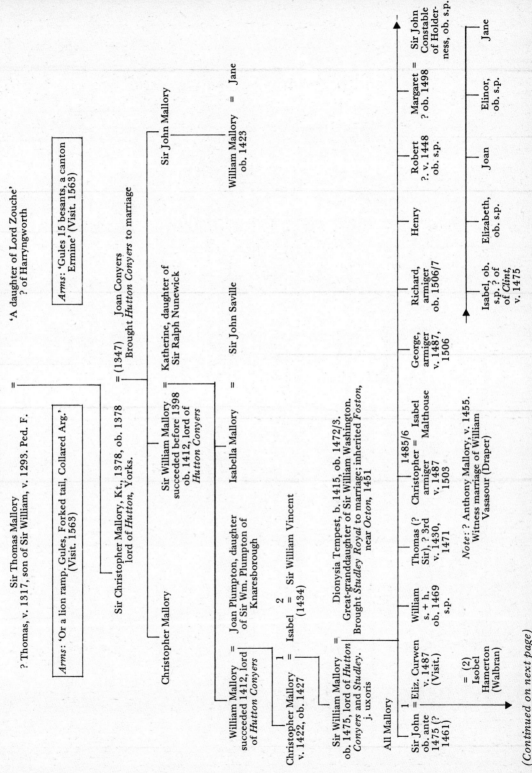

Sir Thomas Mallory
? Thomas, v. 1817, son of Sir William, v. 1293. Ped. F.

= 'A daughter of Lord Zouche' ? of Harryngworth

Arms: 'Or a lion ramp, Gules, Forked tail, Collared Arg.' (Visit. 1563)

Arms: 'Gules 15 besants, a canton Ermine' (Visit. 1563)

Sir Christopher Mallory, Kt, 1378, ob. 1378 lord of *Hutton*, Yorks.

= (1347) Joan Conyers
Brought *Hutton Conyers* to marriage

Sir William Mallory succeeded before 1398 ob. 1412, lord of *Hutton Conyers*

= Katherine, daughter of Sir Ralph Nunewick

Sir John Mallory

Christopher Mallory

Isabella Mallory

= Sir John Saville

William Mallory ob. 1423

= Jane

William Mallory succeeded 1412, lord of *Hutton Conyers*

= Joan Plumpton, daughter of Sir Wm. Plumpton of Knaresborough

Christopher Mallory v. 1422, ob. 1427

1 = Isabel
2 = Sir William Vincent (1434)

Sir William Mallory ob. 1475, lord of *Hutton Conyers* and *Studley*. j. uxoris

= Dionysia Tempest, b. 1415, ob. 1472/3. Great-granddaughter of Sir William Washington. Brought *Studley Royal* to marriage; inherited *Foston*, near *Octon*, 1451

All Mallory

Sir John = Eliz. Curwen ob. ante 1475 (? 1461)

v. 1487 (Visit.)

= (2) Isobel Hamerton (Walbran)

William s. + h. ob. 1469 s.p.

Thomas (? Sir, ? 3rd Sir), v. 1430, 1471

Christopher armiger v. 1487 1503

1485/6 = Isabel Malthouse

George, armiger v. 1487, 1506

Richard, armiger ob. 1506/7

Henry

Robert ?. v. 1448 ob. s.p.

Margaret = ?. ob. 1498

Sir John Constable of Holderness, ob. s.p.

Isabel, ob. s.p. ? of of *Clint*, v. 1475

Elizabeth, ob. s.p.

Joan

Elinor, ob. s.p.

Jane

Note: ? Anthony Mallory, v. 1455. Witness marriage of William Vasasour (Draper)

(Continued on next page)

Pedigree of Mallory—*continued*

All Mallory

Sir William, ktd. 1481/2, = Joan Constable, grand-
ob. 1498/9, lord of   daughter of Lord Fitz-
Studley and *Hutton*   hugh, daughter of Sir
Conyers. Inherited from John Constable of
Uncle William   Halsham

John   Robert   Joan
ob. s.p. ob. s.p. ob. s.p.

Note: The Visitations ascribe offspring differently from Walbran

All Mallory

Sir John, kt. 1527,   = four wives
ob. 1527/8, lord of
Studley and *Hutton*
Conyers

?
William   Agnes = Rich. Ratcliffe   Elizabeth = Sir Rich. Hamerton
(Walbran)   (Walbran)   (Walbran)

(1) Margaret Thwaytes of Lund

(2) Margaret Hastings
v. 1482, of Fenwick,
daughter of Sir Hugh

(3) Elizabeth Reade
v. 1515, of Boarstall,
co. Oxon. (? Bucks.)

(4) Anite Yorke
v. 1521, daughter of Sir
Richard Yorke

Sir William Mallory,   Peter Mallorie = Elizabeth
s. + h., ob. 1547   ob. 1562, of
Ped. E, P143   *Dunkeswick*,
                       near Hare-
                       wood. Not in
                       Visitation

Joan Mallory,
ob. 1581, = Thos.
Slingsby of Scriven

Christopher Mallory
of *Tickhill*, 2nd son.
Note: Walbran makes
him son of second wife

George Mallory,   = Elizabeth
ob. 1580, of *Tickhill Castle*,   daughter of Hugh Wyrrel of Lovershall,
                         ob. 1593

William Mallorie   Octus Mallorie

*Descendants traced to
present day*

Sampson Mallorie,
Gent., ob. 1599/1600, of
Rippon Parks =
Frances Staveley
Note: JohnMallory, Esq.,
v. 1599, in will of
Sampson Mallorie

Francis Mallory =
Thomas Wyrrel

Note: Cozen Anthony
Mallory, v. 1580, in will
of George Mallory

Arms: 'Or a lion ramp.
Gules Collared Argent'
(single tail) (Mrs. C.
Mallorie)

Crest of 'Mallory of Yorkshire'
'On a torce Or and Gules A
Horse's Head Couped Gules'
(Visits. 1584 and 1612)

PEDIGREE E (continued)

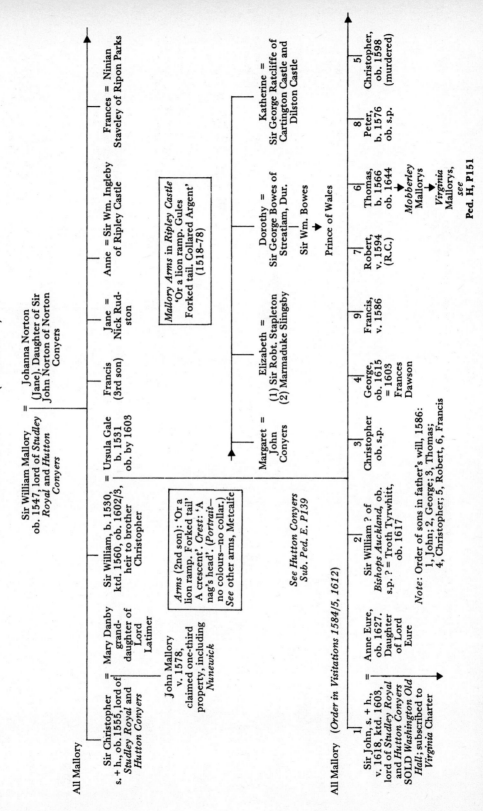

All Mallory

Sir William Mallory = Johanna Norton
ob. 1547, lord of *Studley* (Jane). Daughter of Sir
Royal and *Hutton* John Norton of Norton
Conyers Conyers

Frances = Ninian
Staveley of Ripon Parks

Anne = Sir Wm. Ingleby
of Ripley Castle

Jane =
Nick Rud-
ston

Francis
(3rd son)

Sir Christopher = Mary Danby
s. + h., ob. 1555, lord of grand-
Studley Royal and daughter of
Hutton Conyers Lord Latimer

Sir William, b. 1530, = Ursula Gale
ktd. 1560, ob. 1602/3, b. 1531
heir to brother ob. by 1603
Christopher

Mallory Arms in Ripley Castle
'Or a lion ramp. Gules
Forked tail. Collared Argent'
(1518–78)

Katherine =
Sir George Ratcliffe of
Cartington Castle and
Dilston Castle

John Mallory
v. 1578,
claimed one-third
property, including
Nunewick

Arms (2nd son): 'Or a
lion ramp. Forked tail'.
A crescent'. *Crest*: 'A
nag's head'. (*Portrait—
no colours—no collar.*)
See other arms, Metcalfe

Margaret =
John
Conyers

Elizabeth =
(1) Sir Robt. Stapleton
(2) Marmaduke Slingsby

Dorothy =
Sir George Bowes of
Streatlam, Dur.

Sir Wm. Bowes

Prince of Wales

*See Hutton Conyers
Sub. Ped. E. P139*

All Mallory *(Order in Visitations 1584/5, 1612)*

Sir John, s. + h., = Anne Eure,
v. 1618, ktd. 1603, ob. 1627.
lord of *Studley Royal* Daughter
and *Hutton Conyers* of Lord
SOLD *Washington Old* Eure
Hall; subscribed to
Virginia Charter

1

Sir William ? of
Bishops Auckland, ob.
s.p. ? = Troth Tyrwhitt,
ob. 1617

2

Note: Order of sons in father's will, 1586:
1, John; 2, George; 3, Thomas;
4, Christopher; 5, Robert, 6, Francis

Christopher
ob. s.p.

3

George,
ob. 1615
= 1603
Frances
Dawson

4

Francis,
v. 1586

9

Robert,
v. 1594
(R.C.)

7

Thomas,
b. 1566
ob. 1644

Mobberley
Mallorys
Virginia
Mallorys,
see
Ped. H, P151

6

Peter,
b. 1576
ob. s.p.

8

Christopher,
ob. 1598
(murdered)

5

(*Continued on next page*)

Pedigree of Mallory—continued

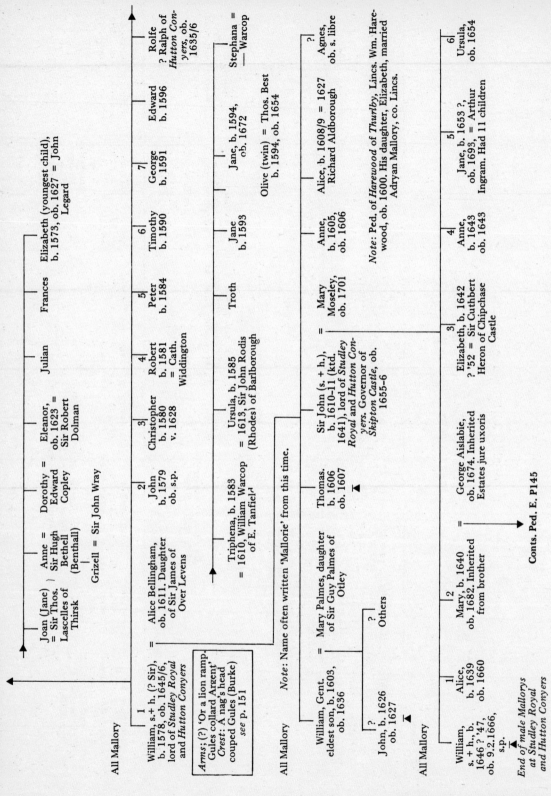

All Mallory

1
William, s.+ h. (? Sir), b. 1578, ob. 1645/6, lord of *Studley Royal* and *Hutton Conyers*

= Alice Bellingham, ob. 1611. Daughter of Sir James of Over Levens

Arms; (?) 'Or a lion ramp. Gules collard Argent' *Crest*: A nag's head couped Gules (Burke) *see p. 151*

Joan (Jane) = Sir Thos. Lascelles of Thirsk

Anne = Sir Hugh Bethell (Benthall)

Grizell = Sir John Wray

Dorothy = Edward Copley

Eleanor, ob. 1623 = Sir Robert Dolman

Julian

Frances

Elizabeth (youngest child), b. 1573, ob. 1627 = John Legard

2
John b. 1579 ob. s.p.

3
Christopher b. 1580 v. 1628

4
Robert b. 1581 = Cath. Widdington

5
Peter b. 1584

6
Timothy b. 1590

7
George b. 1591

Edward b. 1596

Rolfe ? Ralph of *Hutton Conyers*, ob. 1635/6

Triphena, b. 1583 = 1610, William Warcop of E. Tanfield

Ursula, b. 1585 = 1613, Sir John Rodis (Rhodes) of Barlborough

Troth

Jane b. 1593

Jane, b. 1594, ob. 1672

Olive (twin) = Thos. Best b. 1594, ob. 1654

Stephana = — Warcop

Note: Name often written 'Mallorie' from this time.

All Mallory

= Mary Palmes, daughter of Sir Guy Palmes of Otley

William, Gent. eldest son, b. 1603, ob. 1636

Sir John (s. + h.), b. 1610-11 (ktd. 1641), lord of *Studley Royal* and *Hutton Conyers*. Governor of *Skipton Castle*, ob. 1655-6

= Mary Moseley, ob. 1701

Thomas. b. 1606 ob. 1607

? Others

Agnes, ob. s. libre

Alice, b. 1608/9 = 1627 Richard Aldborough

Anne, b. 1605, ob. 1606

Note: Ped. of *Harewood* of *Thurlby*, Lincs. Wm. Harewood, ob. 1600. His daughter, Elizabeth, married Adryan Mallory, co. Lincs.

?
John, b. 1626 ob. 1627

All Mallory

1
Alice, b. 1639 ob. 1660

William, s. + h., b. 1646 ?. 47, ob. 9.2.1666, s.p.

2
Mary, b. 1640 ob. 1682. Inherited from brother

= George Aislabie, ob. 1674. Inherited Estates jure uxoris

3
Elizabeth, b. 1642 ?. '52 = Sir Cuthbert Heron of Chipchase Castle

4
Anne, b. 1643 ob. 1643

5
Jane, b. 1653 ?. ob. 1693, = Arthur Ingram. Had 11 children

6
Ursula, ob. 1654

End of male Mallorys at Studley Royal and Hutton Conyers

Conts. Ped. E. P145

PEDIGREE E (continued)

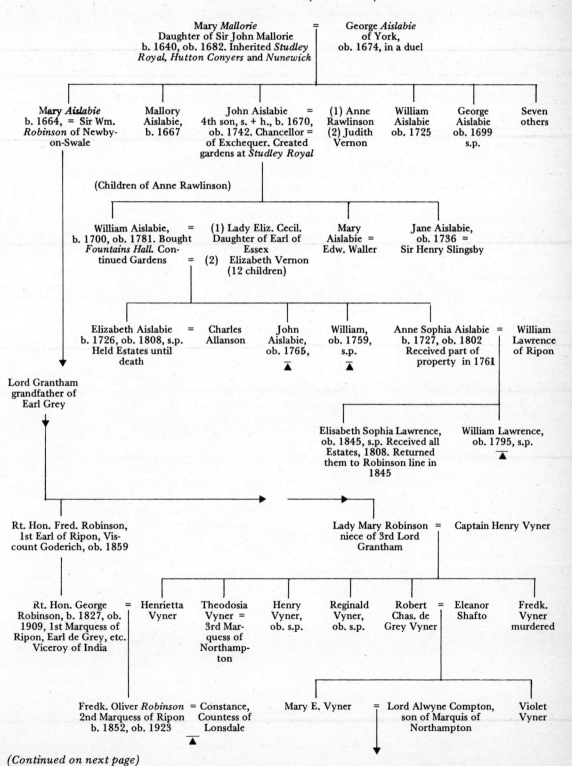

Mary *Mallorie*
Daughter of Sir John Mallorie
b. 1640, ob. 1682. Inherited *Studley
Royal, Hutton Conyers* and *Nunewick*

= George *Aislabie*
of York,
ob. 1674, in a duel

Mary *Aislabie*
b. 1664, = Sir Wm.
Robinson of Newby-
on-Swale

Mallory
Aislabie,
b. 1667

John Aislabie =
4th son, s. + h., b. 1670,
ob. 1742. Chancellor =
of Exchequer. Created
gardens at *Studley Royal*

(1) Anne
Rawlinson
(2) Judith
Vernon

William
Aislabie
ob. 1725

George
Aislabie
ob. 1699
s.p.

Seven
others

(Children of Anne Rawlinson)

William Aislabie,
b. 1700, ob. 1781. Bought
Fountains Hall. Con-
tinued Gardens

= (1) Lady Eliz. Cecil.
Daughter of Earl of
Essex
= (2) Elizabeth Vernon
(12 children)

Mary
Aislabie =
Edw. Waller

Jane Aislabie,
ob. 1736 =
Sir Henry Slingsby

Elizabeth Aislabie
b. 1726, ob. 1808, s.p.
Held Estates until
death

= Charles
Allanson

John
Aislabie,
ob. 1765,

William,
ob. 1759,
s.p.

Anne Sophia Aislabie =
b. 1727, ob. 1802
Received part of
property in 1761

William
Lawrence
of Ripon

Lord Grantham
grandfather of
Earl Grey

Elisabeth Sophia Lawrence,
ob. 1845, s.p. Received all
Estates, 1808. Returned
them to Robinson line in
1845

William Lawrence,
ob. 1795, s.p.

Rt. Hon. Fred. Robinson,
1st Earl of Ripon, Vis-
count Goderich, ob. 1859

Lady Mary Robinson =
niece of 3rd Lord
Grantham

Captain Henry Vyner

Rt. Hon. George =
Robinson, b. 1827, ob.
1909, 1st Marquess of
Ripon, Earl de Grey, etc.
Viceroy of India

Henrietta
Vyner

Theodosia
Vyner =
3rd Mar-
quess of
Northamp-
ton

Henry
Vyner,
ob. s.p.

Reginald
Vyner,
ob. s.p.

Robert =
Chas. de
Grey Vyner

Eleanor
Shafto

Fredk.
Vyner
murdered

Fredk. Oliver *Robinson* =
2nd Marquess of Ripon
b. 1852, ob. 1923

Constance,
Countess of
Lonsdale

Mary E. Vyner =

Lord Alwyne Compton,
son of Marquis of
Northampton

Violet
Vyner

(Continued on next page)

Pedigree of Mallory—*continued*

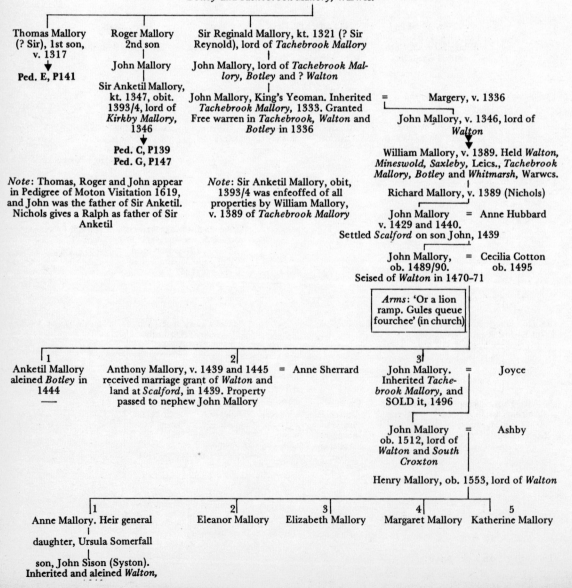

second son

Commander Clare Geo. Compton. Assumed name Vyner, = Lady Doris Gordon Lennox. Daughter
1912, by Royal licence. Received Estates 1923   of Duke of Richmond and Gordon

Elizabeth Vyner, W.R.N.S., ob. 1942,   Charles De Grey Vyner, R.N.V.R., ob.   Henry Vyner (v. 1980)
aet. 18 years   1945, aet. 19 years

Notes: 1974. Studley Royal, Fountains Hall, Abbey ruins, Estates of Studley Royal and Fountains, belonged to
West Riding C.C.
1980: Properties transferred to North Riding C.C. Studley Royal House SOLD.
1983: Fountains Hall, Abbey Ruins, Studley and Fountains, Parks, Mallory portrait, acquired by
National Trust.

PEDIGREE F (continued from p. 139)

Sir William Mallory, v. 1293, lord of *Walton-on-the-Woulds* and *Peckleton*, Leics.,
Botley and *Tachebrook Mallory*, Warwcs.

Thomas Mallory   Roger Mallory   Sir Reginald Mallory, kt. 1321 (? Sir
(? Sir), 1st son,   2nd son   Reynold), lord of *Tachebrook Mallory*
v. 1317
                        John Mallory   John Mallory, lord of *Tachebrook Mal-*
Ped. E, P141   *lory, Botley* and ? *Walton*

                        Sir Anketil Mallory,   John Mallory, King's Yeoman. Inherited   =   Margery, v. 1336
                        kt. 1347, obit.   *Tachebrook Mallory*, 1333. Granted
                        1393/4, lord of   Free warren in *Tachebrook, Walton* and   John Mallory, v. 1346, lord of
                        Kirkby Mallory,   *Botley* in 1336   *Walton*
                        1346

                        Ped. C, P139   William Mallory, v. 1389. Held *Walton,*
                        Ped. G, P147   *Mineswold, Saxleby,* Leics., *Tachebrook*
                                                                                        Mallory, Botley and *Whitmarsh,* Warwcs.

Note: Thomas, Roger and John appear   *Note*: Sir Anketil Mallory, obit,   Richard Mallory, v. 1389 (Nichols)
in Pedigree of Moton Visitation 1619,   1393/4 was enfeoffed of all
and John was the father of Sir Anketil.   properties by William Mallory,   John Mallory   =   Anne Hubbard
Nichols gives a Ralph as father of Sir   v. 1389 of *Tachebrook Mallory*   v. 1429 and 1440.
Anketil   Settled *Scalford* on son John, 1439

                                                                                    John Mallory,   =   Cecilia Cotton
                                                                                    ob. 1489/90.   ob. 1495
                                                                                    Seised of *Walton* in 1470-71

                                                                                    Arms: 'Or a lion
                                                                                    ramp. Gules queue
                                                                                    fourchee' (in church)

1   2   3
Anketil Mallory   Anthony Mallory, v. 1439 and 1445 = Anne Sherrard   John Mallory.   =   Joyce
aleined *Botley* in   received marriage grant of *Walton* and   Inherited *Tache-*
1444   land at *Scalford*, in 1439. Property   *brook Mallory*, and
———   passed to nephew John Mallory   SOLD it, 1496

                                                                              John Mallory   =   Ashby
                                                                              ob. 1512, lord of
                                                                              Walton and *South*
                                                                              Croxton

                                                                              Henry Mallory, ob. 1553, lord of *Walton*

1   2   3   4   5
Anne Mallory. Heir general   Eleanor Mallory   Elizabeth Mallory   Margaret Mallory   Katherine Mallory

daughter, Ursula Somerfall

son, John Sison (Syston).
Inherited and aleined *Walton*,

PEDIGREE G (continued from p. 146)

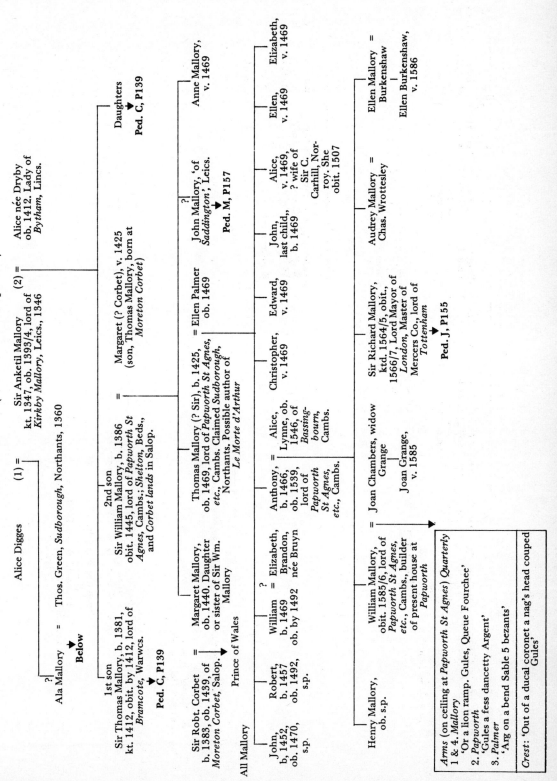

Alice Digges = (1) = **Sir Anketil Mallory** = (2) = Alice née Dryby
kt. 1347, ob. 1393/4, lord of ob. 1412, Lady of
Kirkby Mallory, Leics., 1346 *Bytham*, Lincs.

Thos. Green, *Sudborough*, Northants, 1360

? | Ala Mallory =
Below

1st son
Sir Thomas Mallory, b. 1381,
kt. 1412, obit. by 1412, lord of
Bramcote, Warwcs.

Ped. C, P139

2nd son
Sir William Mallory, b. 1386
obit. 1445, lord of *Papworth St
Agnes*, Cambs.; *Shelton*, Beds.,
and *Corbet lands* in Salop.

= Margaret (? Corbet), v. 1425
(son, Thomas Mallory, born at
Moreton Corbet)

Daughters
Ped. C, P139

Sir Robt. Corbet = Margaret Mallory,
b. 1383, ob. 1439, of   ob. 1440. Daughter
Moreton Corbet, Salop. or sister of Sir Wm.
                          Mallory

Prince of Wales

All Mallory

Thomas Mallory (? Sir), b. 1425, = Ellen Palmer   John Mallory, 'of   Anne Mallory,
ob. 1469, lord of *Papworth St Agnes*, ob. 1469   *Saddington*', Leics. v. 1469
etc., Cambs. Claimed *Sudborough*,   **Ped. M, P157**
Northants. Possible author of
Le Morte d'Arthur

John,   William   Anthony, = Alice,   Christopher, Edward,   John,   Alice,   Ellen,   Elizabeth,
b. 1452,   b. 1469   b. 1466, Lynne, ob.   v. 1469   v. 1469   last child, v. 1469,   v. 1469   v. 1469
ob. 1470,   ob. by 1492   ob. 1539, 1546, of   b. 1469   ? wife of
s.p.   s.p.   lord of *Bassing-*   Sir C.
                                 Papworth bourn,   Carhill, Nor-
Robert,   ? = Elizabeth,   *St Agnes*, Cambs.   roy. She
b. 1457   Brandon,   *etc.*, Cambs.   obit. 1507
ob. 1492,   née Bruyn
s.p.

                                 = Joan Chambers, widow   Sir Richard Mallory,   Audrey Mallory, =   Ellen Mallory =
                                   Grange   ktd. 1564/5, obit.   Chas. Wrottesley   Burkenshaw
                                                           1566/7, Lord Mayor of
                                 Joan Grange,   *London*, Master of   Ellen Burkenshaw,
                                 v. 1585   Mercers Co, lord of   v. 1586
                                                           Tottenham
William Mallory,
obit. 1585/6, lord of   **Ped. J, P155**
Papworth St Agnes,
etc., Cambs., builder
of present house at
Papworth

Henry Mallory,
ob. s.p.

Arms (on ceiling at *Papworth St Agnes*) *Quarterly*
1 & 4. *Mallory*
 'Or a lion ramp. Gules, Queue Fourchee'
2. *Papworth*
 'Gules a fess dancetty Argent'
3. *Palmer*
 'Arg on a bend Sable 5 bezants'

Crest: 'Out of a ducal coronet a nag's head couped
 Gules'

(Continued on next page)

Pedigree of Mallory—*continued*

All Mallory

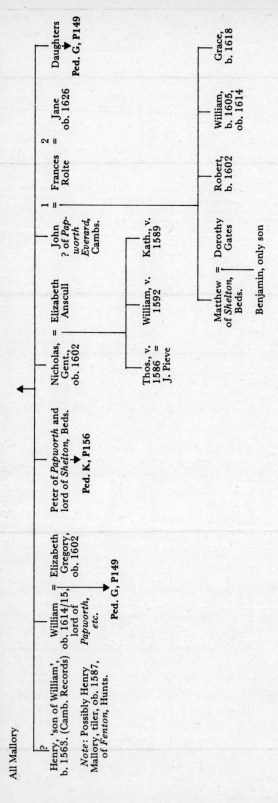

Henry, 'son of William', b. 1563. (Camb. Records)

Note: Possibly Henry Mallory, tiler, ob. 1587, of *Fenton*, Hunts.

William, ob. 1614/15, lord of *Papworth*, etc. = Elizabeth Gregory, ob. 1602

Ped. G, P149

Nicholas, Gent., ob. 1602 = Elizabeth Anscull

Thos., v. 1586 = J. Pieve

William, v. 1592

Kath., v. 1589

Matthew = Dorothy of *Shelton*, Gates Beds.

Benjamin, only son

Peter of *Papworth* and lord of *Shelton*, Beds.

Ped. K, P156

John ? of *Papworth* Everard, Cambs.

1 = Frances Rolte

2 = Jane ob. 1626

Robert, b. 1602

William, b. 1605, ob. 1614

Grace, b. 1618

Daughters

Ped. G, P149

Part Pedigree, Green of Sudborough, Northants.

Sir Anketil Mallory of *Kirkby Mallory*, ob. 1393/4

1 = Alice Digges

? =

Ala Mallory v. 1360, given *Sudborough*, Northants. by Sir Anketil Mallory

= Thomas Green of *Isham*, Northants. ? also of *Boughton* and *Greens Norton*, Northants.

John Green = Isabel

Thomas Green, v. 1469 reclaimed *Sudborough* from *Papworth Mallorys*

PEDIGREE G (continued)

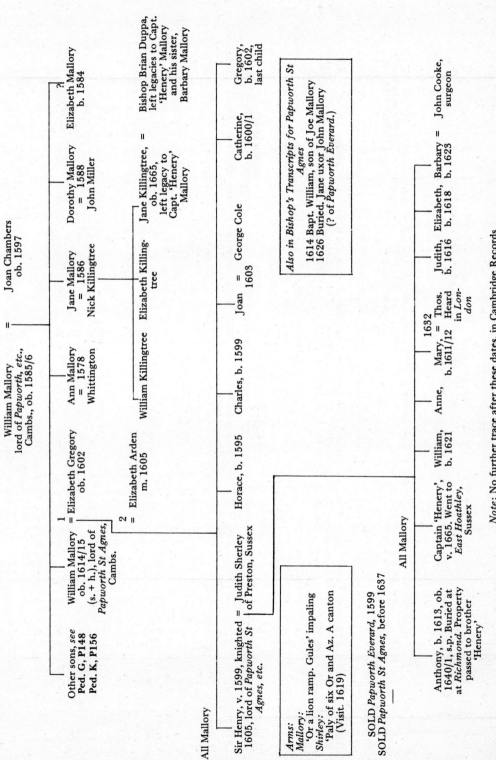

William Mallory, lord of *Papworth*, etc., Cambs., ob. 1585/6 = Joan Chambers ob. 1597

Other sons, *see* Ped. G, P148; Ped. K, P156

William Mallory ob. 1614/15 (s. + h.), lord of *Papworth St Agnes*, Cambs. — 1 = Elizabeth Gregory ob. 1602; 2 = Elizabeth Arden m. 1605

Ann Mallory = 1578 Whittington

Jane Mallory = 1586 Nick Killingtree

Dorothy Mallory = 1588 John Miller

Elizabeth Mallory b. 1584

?

Bishop Brian Duppa, left legacies to Capt. 'Henery' Mallory and his sister, Barbary Mallory

William Killingtree

Elizabeth Killingtree

Jane Killingtree, = ob. 1665, left legacy to Capt. 'Henery' Mallory

All Mallory

Sir Henry, v. 1599, knighted 1605, lord of *Papworth St Agnes*, etc. = Judith Sherley of *Preston, Sussex*

Horace, b. 1595

Charles, b. 1599

Joan = 1603 George Cole

Catherine, b. 1600/1

Gregory, b. 1602, last child

Arms:
Mallory:
'Or a lion ramp. Gules' impaling
Shirley:
'Paly of six Or and Az. A canton'
(Visit. 1619)

SOLD *Papworth Everard*, 1599
SOLD *Papworth St Agnes*, before 1637

All Mallory

Anthony, b. 1613, ob. 1640/1, s.p. Buried at at *Richmond*. Property passed to brother 'Henery'

Captain 'Henery', v. 1665. Went to *East Hoathley*, Sussex

William, b. 1621

Anne,

Mary, = 1632 Thos. Heard in *London* b. 1611/12

Judith, b. 1616

Elizabeth, b. 1618

Barbary, b. 1623 = John Cooke, surgeon

Also in Bishop's Transcripts for Papworth St Agnes
1614 Bapt. William, son of Joe Mallory
1626 Buried Jane uxor John Mallory
(? of *Papworth Everard*.)

Note: No further trace after these dates, in Cambridge Records

PEDIGREE N (Part Pedigree)

Mallory of *Warwick* and *Emigrants*

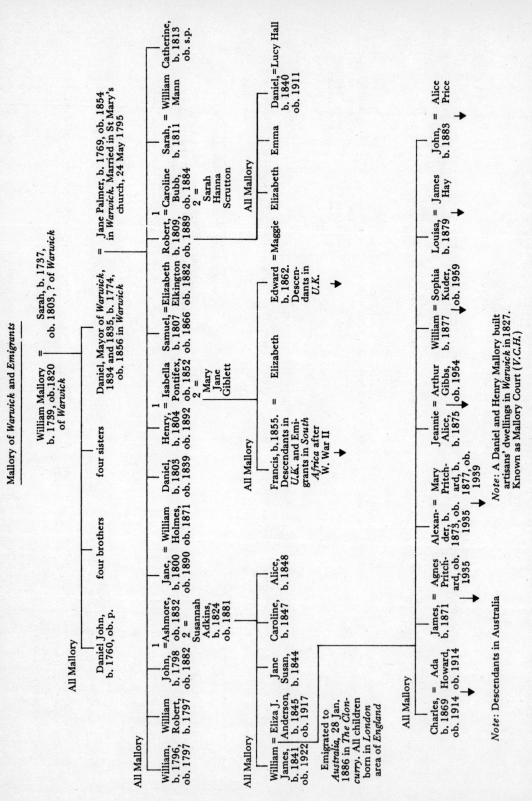

William Mallory = Sarah, b. 1737, ob. 1803, ? of *Warwick*
b. 1789, ob.1820
of *Warwick*

Daniel John, b. 1760, ob. p. — *All Mallory*

four brothers — four sisters — Daniel, Mayor of *Warwick*, 1834 and 1835, b. 1774, ob. 1856 in *Warwick* = Jane Palmer, b. 1769, ob. 1854 in *Warwick*. Married in St Mary's church, 24 May 1795

All Mallory

William, b. 1796, ob. 1797
William Robert, b. 1797
John, b. 1798, ob. 1882 = 1 Ashmore, ob. 1832; 2 = Susannah Adkins, b. 1824, ob. 1881
Jane, b. 1800, ob. 1890 = William Holmes, ob. 1871
Daniel, b. 1803, ob. 1839
Henry, b. 1804, ob. 1892 = 1 Isabella Pontifex, ob. 1852; 2 = Mary Jane Giblett
Samuel, b. 1807, ob. 1866 = Elizabeth Elkington, ob. 1882
Robert, b. 1809, ob. 1889 = 1 Caroline Bubb, b. 1811; 2 = Sarah Hanna Scrutton, ob. 1884
Sarah, b. 1811 = William Mann
Catherine, b. 1813, ob. s.p.

All Mallory

William James, b. 1841, ob. 1922 = Eliza J. Anderson, b. 1845, ob. 1917
Jane Susan, b. 1844
Caroline, b. 1847
Alice, b. 1848

Francis, b. 1855. Descendants in *U.K.* and Emigrants in *South Africa* after W. War II
Elizabeth =
Elizabeth =
Edward = Maggie, b. 1862. Descendants in *U.K.*
Emma
Daniel = Lucy Hall, b. 1840, ob. 1911

Emigrated to *Australia*, 28 Jan. 1886 in *The Cloncurry*. All children born in *London* area of *England*

All Mallory

Charles, b. 1869, ob. 1914 = Ada Howard, ob. 1914
James, b. 1871
Agnes Pritchard, ob. 1935
Alexander, b. 1873, ob. 1935 = Mary Pritchard, b. 1877, ob. 1939
Jeannie Alice, b. 1875, ob. = Arthur Gibbs, ob. 1954
William, b. 1877 = Sophia Kuder, ob. 1959
Louisa, b. 1879 = James Hay
John, b. 1883 = Alice Price

Note: Descendants in Australia

Note: A Daniel and Henry Mallory built artisans' dwellings in *Warwick* in 1827. Known as Mallory Court (*V.C.H.*).

PEDIGREE H (continued from p. 143)

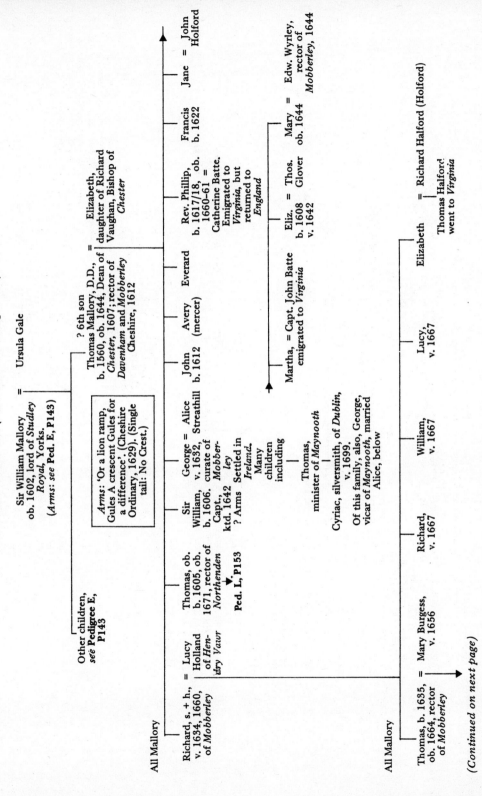

Sir William Mallory = Ursula Gale
ob. 1602, lord of *Studley
Royal*, Yorks.
(*Arms: see* **Ped. E, P143**)

Arms: 'Or a lion ramp,
Gules A crescent Gules for
a difference'. (Cheshire
Ordinary, 1629). (Single
tail: No Crest.)

? 6th son
Thomas Mallory, D.D.,
b. 1560, ob. 1644, Dean of
Chester, 1607; rector of
Davenham and *Mobberley*
Cheshire, 1612

= Elizabeth,
daughter of Richard
Vaughan, Bishop of
Chester

Other children,
see Pedigree E,
P143

All Mallory

Thomas, ob.
b. 1605, ob.
1671, rector of
Northenden
▼
Ped. L, P153

Sir
William,
b. 1606.
Capt.,
ktd. 1642
? Arms

George = Alice
v. 1632, Streathill
curate of
*Mobber-
ley*
Settled in
Ireland.
Many
children
including

John
b. 1612

Avery
(mercer)

Everard

Rev. Phillip,
b. 1617/18, ob.
1660–61 =
Catherine Batte,
Emigrated to
Virginia, but
returned to
England

Francis
b. 1622

Jane = John
Holford

Thomas,
minister of *Maynooth*

Cyriac, silversmith, of *Dublin*,
v. 1699.
Of this family, also, George,
vicar of *Maynooth*, married
Alice, below

Martha, = Capt. John Batte
emigrated to *Virginia*

Eliz. = Thos.
b. 1608 Glover
v. 1642

Mary = Edw. Wyrley,
ob. 1644 rector of
Mobberley, 1644

= Lucy
Holland
of *Hen-
bury Vawr*

Richard, s. + h.,
v. 1634, 1660,
of *Mobberley*

All Mallory

Thomas, b. 1635, = Mary Burgess,
ob. 1664, rector v. 1656
of *Mobberley*

Richard,
v. 1667

William,
v. 1667

Lucy,
v. 1667

Elizabeth = Richard Halford (Holford)

Thomas Halford
went to *Virginia*

(Continued on next page)

Pedigree of Mallory—*continued*

All Mallory

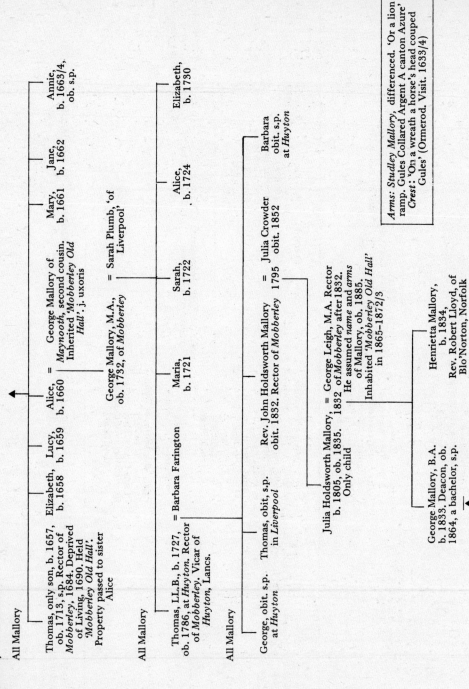

Thomas, only son, b. 1657, ob. 1713, s.p. Rector of *Mobberley*, 1684. Deprived of Living, 1690. Held *'Mobberley Old Hall'*. Property passed to sister Alice

Elizabeth, b. 1658

Lucy, b. 1659

Alice, b. 1660 = George Mallory of *Maynooth*, second cousin. Inherited *'Mobberley Old Hall'*. j. uxoris

Mary, b. 1661

Jane, b. 1662

Annie, b. 1663/4, ob. s.p.

George Mallory, M.A., ob. 1732, of *Mobberley* = Sarah Plumb, 'of Liverpool'

All Mallory

Maria, b. 1721

Sarah, b. 1722

Alice, b. 1724

Elizabeth, b. 1730

Thomas, LL.B., b. 1727, ob. 1786, at *Huyton*. Rector of *Mobberley*. Vicar of *Huyton*, Lancs. = Barbara Farington

Rev. John Holdsworth Mallory obit. 1832. Rector of *Mobberley* = Julia Crowder obit. 1852 1795

Barbara obit. s.p. at *Huyton*

All Mallory

Thomas, obit. s.p. in *Liverpool*

George, obit. s.p. at *Huyton*

Julia Holdsworth Mallory, b. 1805, ob. 1835. Only child = George Leigh, M.A. Rector 1832 of *Mobberley* after 1832. He assumed *name* and *arms* of Mallory, ob. 1885. Inhabited *'Mobberley Old Hall'* in 1865–1872/3

George Mallory, B.A. b. 1833, Deacon, ob. 1864, a bachelor, s.p. ▲

Henrietta Mallory, b. 1834, Rev. Robert Lloyd, of Blo'Norton, Norfolk

Note: George (Leigh) Mallory married again. *See* **Sub. Ped. H, P153**

Arms: Studley Mallory, differenced. 'Or a lion ramp. Gules Collared Argent A canton Azure' *Crest:* 'On a wreath a horse's head couped Gules' (Ormerod. Visit. 1633/4)

SUB-PEDIGREE H

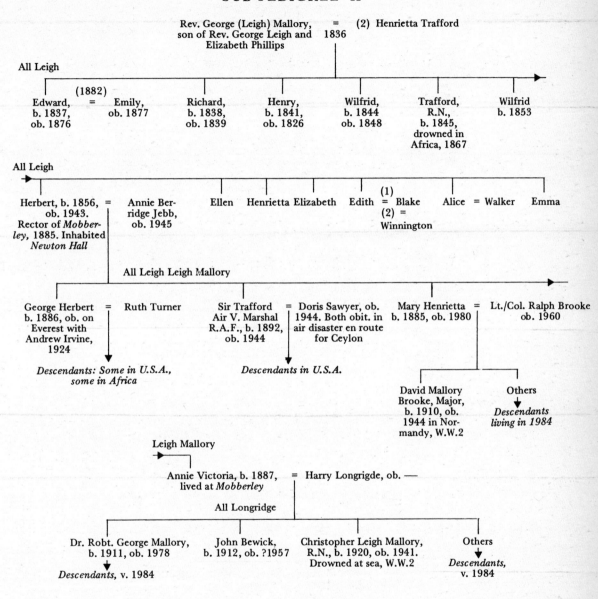

Rev. George (Leigh) Mallory,   =   (2) Henrietta Trafford
son of Rev. George Leigh and   1836
Elizabeth Phillips

All Leigh

(1882)					
Edward, b. 1837, ob. 1876 = Emily, ob. 1877	Richard, b. 1838, ob. 1839	Henry, b. 1841, ob. 1826	Wilfrid, b. 1844 ob. 1848	Trafford, R.N., b. 1845, drowned in Africa, 1867	Wilfrid b. 1853

All Leigh

Herbert, b. 1856, = Annie Ber-   Ellen   Henrietta Elizabeth   Edith   (1)   Alice = Walker   Emma
ob. 1943.   ridge Jebb,   = Blake
Rector of *Mobber-* ob. 1945   (2) =
ley, 1885. Inhabited   Winnington
Newton Hall

All Leigh Leigh Mallory

George Herbert = Ruth Turner   Sir Trafford   = Doris Sawyer, ob.   Mary Henrietta = Lt./Col. Ralph Brooke
b. 1886, ob. on   Air V. Marshal   1944. Both obit. in   b. 1885, ob. 1980   ob. 1960
Everest with   R.A.F., b. 1892, air disaster en route
Andrew Irvine,   ob. 1944   for Ceylon
1924

Descendants: Some in U.S.A.,   *Descendants in U.S.A.*
some in Africa

David Mallory   Others
Brooke, Major,   ↓
b. 1910, ob.   *Descendants*
1944 in Nor-   *living in 1984*
mandy, W.W.2

Leigh Mallory

Annie Victoria, b. 1887,   = Harry Longrigde, ob. ——
lived at *Mobberley*

All Longridge

Dr. Robt. George Mallory,   John Bewick,   Christopher Leigh Mallory,   Others
b. 1911, ob. 1978   b. 1912, ob. ?1957   R.N., b. 1920, ob. 1941.   ↓
                                                Drowned at sea, W.W.2   *Descendants,*
Descendants, v. 1984   v. 1984

PEDIGREE L

Thomas Mallory, b. 1605,   = (1) Jane, ob. 1638/9.   = (2) Frances, v. 1671
ob. 1671, son of Thomas   Had six children
Mallory, D.D. (**Ped. H**),
Rector of *Northenden,*
1634/5. Cannon of *Chester*
and D.D., 1660. Rector of
Eccleston, 1662

(Continued on next page)

Pedigree of Mallory—*continued*

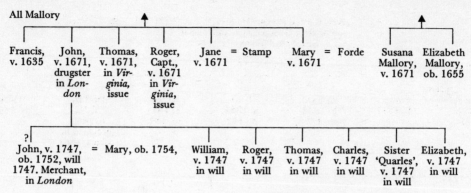

Note ? all went to *Virginia* 1668.

Notes: Genealogy of The Mallorys of Virginia., H. R. Mallory. *Descendants in U.S.A. to present day.*

1. Rev. Phillip Mallory and Katherine Batte, siblings of Thomas Mallory, ob. 1671, owned tobacco plantations in *Virginia,* America, early in 1600s.
2. Thomas Mallory, born 1636, v. 1671, lived in *Charles County* in 1676. *Descendants.*
3. Roger Mallory, Capt., v. 1671, received land grants in *Virginia* in 1660. *Descendants.*
4. Other Mallorys went to *Virginia* about the year 1668.
5. Nathaniel, sr., Nathaniel, jr., William, Elizabeth and Thomas and Roger, all appear in Land Grant to Thomas and Henry Batte. (*See* **Ped. H.**)

PEDIGREE J (continued from p. 147)
(Pedigree G continued)

Sir Richard Mallory, Lord Mayor of London
Appears as son of Anthony Mallory of *Papworth*, Cambs. in Noble's Collection, but not
in 1634 Visitation to Bedfordshire, Ped. Mallory of *Shelton*

Sir Richard Mallory,   = (1)Anne Smythe = (2)   Elizabeth, widow
Sheriff of *London,* 1557.   ob. 1560   Lane, née Pakyngton,
Master of Mercers' Company,   17 children   married Mallory by 1561/2
1557, 1562, 1565. Lord
Mayor of London, 1564.
Knighted 1564/5,   Robert Mallory   Sarah Mallory
ob. 1566/7. Lived in   b. and ob. 1562   b. 1565/6, named in
London. Lord of manor of   will, 1565/6
Tottenham

All Mallory

Daughters
1. Andrew. Inherited *Tottenham*.   1. Julyane = Richard Sharpe, mercer.
2. William.   2. Anne = Thomas —, girdler.
3. Mehezadeck (Melchisedak, v. 1575).   3. Scholastica = William Ralph, haberdasher.
4. Ffrancis.   4. Elizabeth, b. 1554.
5. Richard, b. 1551.   5. Dorothy, b. 1555.
— Clement, b. 1552.   6. Barbara.
6. Edward, b. 1557, obit. 1603.
— Thomas, b. 1560, obit. 1561.   1–6, named in will, 1565/6.

1–6, named in will. All appear to have been
under age in 1565/6.

Notes:
1. Richard Mallory = Alice Bond in 1577 at St Michael Bassishaw, Cripplegate (? Richard, b.1551).
2. Stow says, 'Sir Richard Mallory, Lord Mayor of London, obit. 1567, was a son of Anthony
   Mallory of Papworth St Agnes, obit. 1530'.
3. Francis Mallory = Ellen, v. 1575, 80, 81. Lands in Ellington (F. F. Hunts.).
4. William Mallory, son of Richard and grandson of Sir Richard, obit. 1615. (J. Pegram.)

Arms of Sir Richard Mallory

1. *Lord Mayor's Records*
   'Or a lion rampant double queued Gules within a border Gules.'

2. *Burke and Visitation to Devonshire, Pedigree Sharpe, 1620*
   'Or a lion rampant Gules collared Argent a crescent for a difference' cadency for second son.

3. *Gen. Soc. Quarterly*
   'Or a lion rampant guardant. Tail forked Gules. Collared Argent bordered Gules.'

4. *W. C. Metcalfe. A Book of Knights—1426–1600.*
   'Or a lion rampant within a border Gules. *Crest:* 'A horse's head Gules, the face and ears
   Argent. Maned and ducally gorged Or.'

PEDIGREE K (continued from p. 148)

(Pedigree G continued)

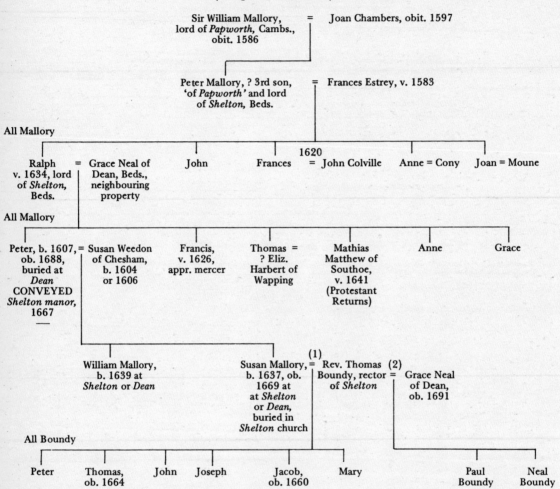

Sir William Mallory, = Joan Chambers, obit. 1597
lord of *Papworth,* Cambs.,
obit. 1586

Peter Mallory, ? 3rd son, = Frances Estrey, v. 1583
'of *Papworth'* and lord
of *Shelton,* Beds.

All Mallory

Ralph = Grace Neal of   John   Frances   1620   Anne = Cony   Joan = Moune
v. 1634, lord   Dean, Beds.,   = John Colville
of *Shelton,*   neighbouring
Beds.   property

All Mallory

Peter, b. 1607, = Susan Weedon   Francis,   Thomas =   Mathias   Anne   Grace
ob. 1688,   of Chesham,   v. 1626,   ? Eliz.   Matthew of
buried at   b. 1604   appr. mercer   Harbert of   Southoe,
Dean   or 1606   Wapping   v. 1641
CONVEYED   (Protestant
Shelton manor,   Returns)
1667

                                                          (1)
William Mallory,   Susan Mallory, = Rev. Thomas (2)
b. 1639 at   b. 1637, ob.   Boundy, rector = Grace Neal
Shelton or *Dean*   1669 at   of *Shelton*   of Dean,
                              at *Shelton*   ob. 1691
                              or *Dean,*
                              buried in
                              Shelton church

All Boundy

Peter   Thomas,   John   Joseph   Jacob,   Mary   Paul   Neal
         ob. 1664   ob. 1660   Boundy   Boundy

Note: A Francis Mallory *regained* and then SOLD *Shelton House* in 1714.

PEDIGREE M

Mallory of *Woodford-on-Nene*, Northants.
Not connected to main branch, but see Notes and Arms

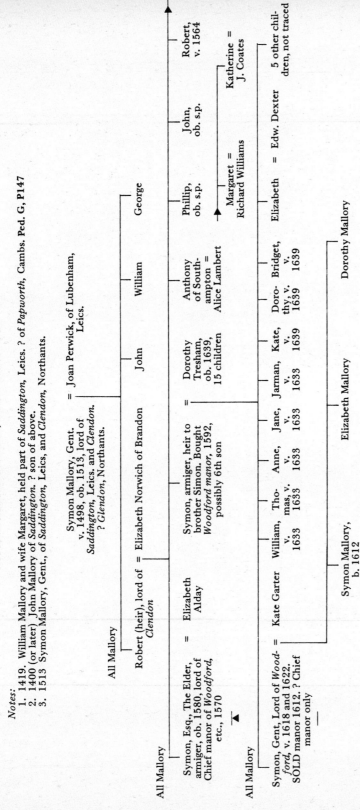

Notes:
1. 1419. William Mallory and wife Margaret, held part of *Saddington*, Leics. ? of *Papworth*, Cambs. Ped. G, **P147**
2. 1400 (or later) John Mallory of *Saddington*. ? son of above.
3. 1513 Symon Mallory, Gent., of *Saddington*, Leics, and *Clendon*, Northants.

Symon Mallory, Gent. = Joan Perwick, of Lubenham,
v. 1498, ob. 1513, lord of   Leics.
Saddington, Leics. and *Clendon*.
? *Glendon*, Northants.

All Mallory

Robert (heir), lord of = Elizabeth Norwich of Brandon
Clendon

John   William   George

All Mallory

Symon, Esq., The Elder, lord of = Elizabeth
armiger, ob. 1580, lord of   Alday
Chief manor of *Woodford*,
etc., 1570

Symon, armiger, heir to
brother Simon. Bought
Woodford manor, 1592,
possibly 6th son

Anthony of South- =
ampton =
Alice Lambert

Dorothy
Tresham,
ob. 1639,
15 children

Phillip,
ob. s.p.

John,
ob. s.p.

Robert,
v. 1564

Margaret =
Richard Williams

Katherine =
J. Coates

Elizabeth = Edw. Dexter

5 other chil-
dren, not traced

All Mallory

Symon, Gent, Lord of *Wood-* = Kate Garter
ford, v. 1618 and 1622.
SOLD manor 1612. ? Chief
manor only

William,   Tho-   Jarman,   Jane,   Anne,   Kate,   Doro-   Bridget,
v.   mas, v.   v.   v.   v.   1639   thy, v.   v.
1633   1633   1633   1633   1633   1639   1639

Symon Mallory,
b. 1612

Elizabeth Mallory

Dorothy Mallory

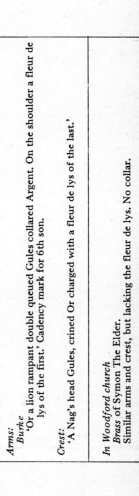

Arms:
  Burke
  'Or a lion rampant double queued Gules collared Argent. On the shoulder a fleur de
  lys of the first.' Cadency mark for 6th son.

Crest:
  'A Nag's head Gules, crined Or charged with a fleur de lys of the last.'

In Woodford church
  Brass of Symon The Elder.
  Similar arms and crest, but lacking the fleur de lys. No collar.

INDEX OF PEOPLE

Mallorys of Studley Royal, Hutton Conyers and Connected Branches

INDEX OF PEOPLE

Mallorys other than Studley Royal and Branches

160

THE MALLORY FAMILY

Sir Stephen 1333, Draughton and Winwick, m. Revel, 10, 40
Symon (gent.) 1513, Saddington and Clendon, 48
Symon (the elder) d. 1580, Woodford-on-Nene, 48, 50-2
Symon 1592, Woodford-on-Nene, m. Dorothy, 48, 50
Sir Thomas, Temp. K. H. 2, Walton, 2, 7-8
Sir Thomas 1296, Kirkby Mallory, 3, 96
Sir Thomas 1412, Bramcote, 5, 11, 14, 17, 29-31, 59

Thomas, ca. 1450, Holcot (Le Morte d'Arthur), 57
(Sir) Thomas d. 1469, Papworth St Agnes (Le Morte d'Arthur), 56, 58, 60-65, 73, 82
Thomas ca. 1470, Canterbury (Le Morte d'Arthur), 81
Sir Thomas d. 1471, Newbold Revel, etc., (Le Morte d'Arthur), 22, 25-7, 29, 31, 63, 65
Sir Thomas of Studley Royal, see Studley Royal index
Sir William 1216, Kirkby Mallory, etc., 2, 3, 9

Sir William 1280, Lichborough, 39, 44
Sir William, 1293, Walton, Tachebrook Mallory, etc., 2-3, 8, 21
Sir William d. 1445, Papworth St Agnes, 48, 56, 60
Sir William d. 1585, Papworth St Agnes (built house), 66, 69, 71, 72
William d. 1614, Papworth St Agnes, 69, 72
William d. 1820, Warwick (Australian Mallorys), 130

INDEX OF PLACES

GENERAL INDEX

LIST OF SUBSCRIBERS

Dorothy Mallory Allen
Nellie A. Andrews
Cynthia Ashton (nee Mallory)
Miss C. R. Ayre
Peter & Barbara Ayre
J. W. Bailie
Muriel Mallory Baldwin
Dr. Mae Guild Barrett
James Mallory Bentham
Kerry June Mallory Biddle
Mrs. Arnold Blachford (Mary G. Rous)
Vernon H. Brophy
Bruce Mallory Burnham
Dr. C. J. D. Catto
Jean Christie
Delma Clanfield (nee Mallory)
Ruth Clapham
C. Merle Mallery Clare
Dawn Lorraine (Keene) Cooke
Mrs. J. A. D. Craig (Elizabeth H. Rous)
Mallory John Craig
Michael Davey
Sandra (McQuay) Davey
Steven Davey
Grace Dawes
Leith Adele Doherty (nee Mallory)
Wanda Mallory Eisenhut
Alice Marion Ramsay Mallory Emmerson
Ralph Carroll Evans, Jr.
P. J. C. Field
Thomas Mallory Forsyth
William M. Foster
George Francis Garbutt, M.P.S.
George Mallory Garbutt
John Mallory Garbutt
Marjorie Mallory Garrett, U.E.
Nora Mallory Goforth
Marion L. Goulet
Mavis Lura Mallory Grieve
Joseph Guild
Joyce E. Guthrie
Christine Kay (Ward) Harmsworth
Phyllis Mallory Hatton
Mary Edith Mallory Heaton
Mrs. Doris Herman
Bruce Mallory Herring
C. Gordon Mallory Herring
G. Douglas Mallory Herring

K. G. Herring
Mary Hey
Jim Hingston
Prof. R. C. Honeybone
Yvonne Johnson
Grace Ellen Mallory Keene
Kenneth Roy Keene
Norma R. Lindberg
Alan Lindsay
Eliza Annie Anderson Gibbs Loughran
Leonora Mallory McMeans
Lola Knowles McNaught
Alan A. Mallery
Harold Claude Mallery
J. R. Mallery
Herbert Mallorie, M.M.
John Royston Mallorie
Judith Mary Mallorie
Air Vice Marshal P. R. Mallorie, C.B., A.F.C.
Paul Michael Mallorie
Peter Mallorie
Susan & Dennis Mallorie
Thomas Percy Mallorie
Adrian Mark Mallory
Alan Faux Mallory
Alan Percy Mallory
Albert Mallory
Alec L. Mallory
Alexander Mallory
Andrew Wodehouse Mallory
Anne Mallory
Arthur Mallory
Arthur Richard Mallory
Averill Mallory
Commander B. S. Mallory, R.N.
Lt. Col. B. W. Mallory, O.B.E.
Brian R. Mallory
C. K. Mallory
Cecil R. Mallory
Charles Shannon Mallory
Clifford D. Mallory III
Clive Mallory
Colin Mallory
David A. Mallory
David Glenn Mallory, M.D.
David S. Mallory
Donald Mallory
Douglas Thomas Gordon Mallory

E. H. Mallory·
Garry Robert Mallory
Geoffrey Robson Mallory
George Henry Mallory
Gordon Baden Mallory, Jr.
Gordon Charles Mallory
Greg Mallory
Gregory Leith Mallory
Harry Leslie Mallory
Henry Peter Mallory
Herbert Mallory
Hubert L. Mallory
Hugh & Annie Mallory
Hunter Mallory
Ian Wodehouse Mallory
James Patrick Mallory
Janet Mallory
Joan Mallory
Kenneth Dale Mallory
Kenneth Ian Mallory
Kenneth Lyall & Blanche Mallory
Kevin Leslie Mallory
Lawrence E. Mallory
Lawrence Jr. Mallory
Lester D. Mallory
Lester McAllister Mallory
Lloyd Richard Mallory
Malcolm James Mallory
Margaret L. Mallory
Mary Louise Mallory
Maxwell Robert Mallory
Michael Langton Mallory
Michael Lawrence Mallory
N. Burnham Mallory
Neville Graham Mallory
Patricia Margaret Mallory
Patrick Ralph Mallory
Patrick Shaun Mallory
Paul Colin Mallory
Perry A. Mallory
Richard Fetter Mallory
Richard William Edward Mallory
Robert Frederick Mallory
Robin D. Mallory
Robyn Annette Mallory
Rodney Eric Mallory
Ronald Bevan Mallory
Roy W. Mallory
Scott O. Mallory
Sheila Mallory
Spencer Morgan Mallory
Steven Mallory
Susan Mallory

Terence Mallory
Captain Thomas Mallory
Prof. V. Standish Mallory
William Mallory
William & Noel Mallory
Wilson Eldon Mallory
Daniel C. Massey
Audrey. May Mallory Melling
Edmund Miller
Susan Margaret (Mallory) Morrisson
Colleen Avril Mullock (nee Mallory)
Edith Newman
The Order of St John, Library & Museum
Mary Partington
Helen James Patrick
Raelene G. Keene Persal
Joan Mallory Reeves
Vivian Merle Reid (nee Mallory)
Wesley Howard Reynolds
Frances Catherine Richard
Karen Elizabeth Saunders
Narelle Ruth Ward Savage
Martha Mallory Sawyer
Frederick Mallory Schnader
Mr. & Mrs. Allen Seaman
Susan Mallory Shaw
Pearl Mavis Mallory Shimmin
Margaret N. Short
Sonia Wodehouse Mallory Skinner
Barry Smith
Sally Smith
Mrs. Kathleen Swales
Valerie Ann Sweeting, B.Sc
Margaret Townend (nee Mallorie)
Jean Lorraine Margaret Mallory Ursin
Henry Vyner
Barbara Mallorie Walker
Joyce Elizabeth Mallory Ward
Neil John Ward
Stephen Francis Ward
D. J. Watts, M.Phil
Peter D. Weaver
Judy Webb, C.G.R.S.
Edith Webster
Waynell Mallory Wiebener
Beryl Ada Mallory Wood
Angela Woodman
Elizabeth Woodman
Nita Woodman
Evelyn Worley
Donna Mallory Wright
Gail Ellen Mallory Wright
Lois Wright (nee Mallory)